PERCEPTION PSYCHOL

AND IT IS FLEXIBLE BECAUSE WE CONTROL FOR INPUT.

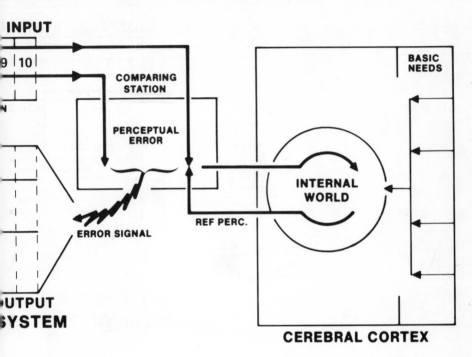

INPUT

9 | 10

COMPARING
STATION

PERCEPTUAL
ERROR

ERROR SIGNAL

REF PERC.

BASIC
NEEDS

INTERNAL
WORLD

OUTPUT
SYSTEM

CEREBRAL CORTEX

STATIONS OF THE MIND

STATIONS OF THE MIND

New Directions for Reality Therapy

WILLIAM GLASSER, M.D.

1817

HARPER & ROW, PUBLISHERS, New York
Cambridge, Hagerstown, Philadelphia, San Francisco,
London, Mexico City, São Paulo, Sydney

Grateful acknowledgment is made for permission to reprint lines from *After All* by Clarence Day, copyright 1936 and renewed 1964 by Katherine Briggs Day. Reprinted by permission of Alfred A. Knopf, Inc.

FIRST EDITION

Designer: Sidney Feinberg

LIBRARY OF CONGRESS CATALOG CARD NUMBER: 80-8205
ISBN: 0-06-011478-9

81 82 83 84 85 10 9 8 7 6 5 4 3 2 1

This book is dedicated to those who work to make schools a better place for students to learn, and especially to my staff at the Educator Training Center.

Douglas Naylor, Director
Barbara Naylor
Elizabeth Mahoney
Leslie Ann Butcher
Fred Sander
Tom McGuiness
Jeff Peltier
Carol Kennedy
Marya Barr
Lena McInerney
Dennis McLaughlin

Acknowledgments

I wish to acknowledge the contribution to my thinking made by W. C. Ellerbroek, M.D., whose ideas are expressed in the provocative paper "Language, Thought and Disease," published in the *Co-Evolution Quarterly,* Spring 1978, Box 4281, Sausalito, CA.

I would also like to thank Sam Buchholtz, whom I consider one of the most outstanding scholars in the behavioral sciences, for directing me to Bill Powers's book.

Contents

❧

Foreword

Bill Glasser has invented an unusual method for learning a new theory: write a book about it. Judging from the result, I think I can recommend this method for those with the intellectual honesty, the energy, and the persistence to carry it through.

The new theory is called control theory. It's about forty years old, which makes it an adolescent on the time-scale along which scientific revolutions develop. Control theory started its major growth in the 1930s, among engineers trying to design not *controllable* devices, but *controlling* devices.

Without being particularly interested in psychology or biology, these engineers succeeded in discovering a kind of organization which could have inner purposes and which, instead of reacting to external forces, could sense and act on the world around it and thus control aspects of that world. The result, the servomechanism, has caused a second Industrial Revolution already, but science is just starting to realize that the industrial side of the revolution may be far less important than the revolution in our understanding of living systems that grows from this new concept of organization.

Scientific theories of human nature have never made much sense to nonprofessionals. Scientific theories either have been so statistical that they don't say anything interesting about individuals, or have implied things about us that anyone with common sense can see aren't true (for example, the preposterous assertion that what we think can't have any effect on what we do). Psychology in particular has been a disappointment, promising much and producing essentially nothing with the power to change our lives that, say, the transistor has had. Unless we have to take a test to get a job or enter college, most of us aren't touched by psychological theories at all. When we do brush against them, the result is usually threatening or annoying.

Control theory, the theory of how living organisms control what happens to them, does make common sense. It makes so much common sense, in fact, that in this book you won't find anything that sounds like technology, unless you count one diagram and about four specialized terms. For example, you'll hardly encounter the term "feedback," even though feedback is what makes control systems work.

What you will find are the basic organizational concepts of control theory so cleverly worked into Glasser's exposition that most of the time you're likely to think, "Great—but doesn't everyone know that?" The answer is *no*, not by a long shot. Common sense can be trusted only so far; it lets us down nearly as often as it works. Scientific theories, when they get on the right track, can bolster our common sense, but also refine it and change it to fit more of the facts. Control theory doesn't just reaffirm common sense. But one strong hint that control theory *is* on the right track is that you won't have to know any control theory in the mathematical or engineering sense in order to grasp its meaning correctly. There's nothing that can be said about control theory that can't be said another way in plain language, still correctly.

Glasser has been scrupulously careful to check his understanding of control theory with me every step of the way. If there are any differences between his concepts and mine as the book now reaches its final stages, they are unimportant, and tend to be in areas where the theory itself needs work.

As far as the main concepts in this book are concerned, you can be sure that Bill has checked his translation against my understanding, and that in the background there is a solid scientific foundation for what he asserts about systems that can control their own inputs.

Bill Glasser didn't ask me for a book review or a testimonial; he just asked if I'd write a little about the origins of control theory as we use it. Having exercised my freedom of speech, I suppose I'd better do as he asked. My path to understanding has been devious, and I've worked alone for the most part, so this is a personal story even though others have influenced and taught me in degrees from a little to a lot.

Warren McCullouch first influenced me when I was in high school. His daughter Taffy joined my class, and I became aware of her father, a tall figure with a long straggly beard and fiery eyes that scared the hell out of me. McCullouch lived in a house that Charles Addams could have drawn, and I was certain that I would never be like that mysterious and crazy-looking man. A neurosurgeon, I heard—brrr! A theoretician—yuck!

He was in fact a famous neurologist who was already a leading figure in cybernetics, of which I had never heard. Some of his friends and colleagues were named Pitts, Ashby, Von Foerster, and Wiener—Norbert Wiener, who while I was fresh out of high school and immersed in learning electronics for the sake of World War II, was starting cybernetics and launching this scientific revolution that is still developing. None of these people knew me, but five years later, in 1950, I came to know of them. I read most of what they wrote, and was hooked.

In 1953 I became convinced that the phenomenon of feedback and especially automatic control based on feedback held the key to a new understanding of human nature. With only a BS in physics and no funds for graduate school, I resolved to work on this new theory in my spare time, earning a living in the fields of technology that I knew. That approach became a habit; I'm still working at honest labor and being a theoretician on the side, although my family might disagree with that order of priorities. In retrospect I can see that there was no other choice. My path diverged enough from the paths followed by others that there was no way to pursue my work in more conventional surroundings. Scientific revolutions are not popular among their victims. There are good reasons why theoreticians often work alone.

You've never heard of R. K. Clark (until now), but I owe this to him. From 1953 to 1960 he headed a department of medical physics in which I worked, and provided the means and the intellectual support needed for my first concentrated work on my version of control theory. Many parts of this theory were probably contributed by Bob Clark, and I've never properly acknowledged this in print. My first scientific paper on this theory was published in 1960 with Clark and MacFarland (who provided some official blessing as a psychologist).

From 1960 to 1973 I worked on electronic systems at Northwestern University's department of astronomy, finally producing a book called *Behavior: The Control of Perception.* That book earned me some recognition, and circulated about for a few years until it eventually reached Bill Glasser, who seems to have been waiting for it. He'll tell you what happened next, as soon as I'm through here.

You'll probably want to know how control theory stands today in the world of competing scientific theories. I'd say it's just getting to its feet. During the past seven years I've been invited to speak at universities all over the country, to linguists, philosophers, anthropologists, sociologists, and even psychologists. Scientific journals seem quite willing to publish what I write on the subject. Especially among the younger people, students and faculty, there is a positive enthusiasm for control theory once the basic ideas are understood. All told I'd guess that there are now two or three hundred full-fledged life scientists who have accepted my approach and are at least rolling up their sleeves getting ready to start trying it out seriously.

In Philip Latham's wry words, the "grizzled veterans of a thousand seminars" still sit in the back rows and frown. I can't see any easy way to win them over. A lifetime of dedication to one point of view makes it hard to grasp a different one, much less accept it. I don't hold their reluctance or apprehension against them, because basically I agree that science shouldn't latch onto new ideas without a great deal of skepticism. Those of us who see the promise of control theory can be confident that its day is coming, but still a little more patience yet is needed.

One last word. I've found that most people take about two years to reach the point where they suddenly realize that they understand the basic concepts of control theory. It takes about a week for them to *think* they understand it. After the initial understanding, don't be dismayed if a host of questions and confusions arise; they always arise, because of beliefs that are in conflict with the principles of control theory, but which don't turn up until you encounter appropriate situations. Most of these confusions and questions will clear themselves up as you continue to think. The right answer always turns out to be the simplest one. Just keep returning to one basic principle: *we control what we perceive, not what actually exists, and not what we do.* The meaning of that principle will grow deeper the longer you think of it, and the more situations you encounter in which it clearly holds true.

I'm beginning to lecture, and that's my signal to turn the floor over to the author. Tell them, Bill.

William T. Powers
May 13, 1980
Northbrook, Illinois

Introduction

It is a pleasure to introduce this excellent volume on the brain and how it works as an input control system. Since the book presents its data in a clinical way, describing the behavioral implications of the theory, I feel it would be instructive to present a brief discussion of the code of behavior I have worked out on the basis of more than four decades of stress research.

In 1936, I observed that the human body responds in a stereotyped manner to such diverse factors as fatigue, nervous tension, trauma, infections, intoxications, etc. No matter what the demand made upon the adaptive mechanism of man, the result is a patterned response called the "General Adaptation Syndrome."

Stress is now defined as *"the nonspecific response of the body to any demand."* This means that pleasant and unpleasant, useful and harmful stimuli—irrespective of any superimposed specific effects—produce a stress reaction. These, depending upon special predispositions (genetics, diet, life habits), can cause severe stress diseases (gastric ulcer, nervous breakdown, high blood pressure, cardiac infarcts) or remain without detrimental consequences.

The great laws of Nature that regulate defense of living beings against stressors of any kind are essentially the same at all levels of life, from individual cells to entire complex human organisms and even societies of men. It helps a great deal to understand the fundamental advantages and disadvantages of "catatoxic" and "syntoxic" attitudes by studying the biologic basis of self-preservation as reflected in syntoxic and catatoxic chemical mechanisms. When applied to everyday problems, this understanding should lead to choices most likely to provide us with the pleasant stress of fulfillment and victory, thereby avoiding the self-destructive distress of failure and frustration.

Each person must find a way to relieve his pent-up energy without creating conflicts with his fellowmen. Such an approach not only ensures peace of mind but also earns the goodwill, respect and even love of our fellowmen, the highest degree of security, the most noble "status symbol" to which man can aspire.

Any moral code must begin by considering that we are living organisms with certain built-in tendencies, among them the propensity selfishly to expand the range of our power and activity, and to accumulate goods both as an aid to development and as a means of preserving what we have attained. To quote *The Stress of Life:* "Organs that are not used . . . undergo inactivity atrophy. Every living being looks out for itself first of all. There is no example in Nature of a creature guided exclusively by altruism and the desire to protect others. In fact, a code of universal altruism would be highly immoral, since it would expect others to look out for us more than for themselves.

And yet the common denominator of all man's noble or vulgar efforts—whether it be to please God, to find self-expression in a great work of art or science, to obtain happiness, love, money, or power, or even to commit serious crimes—seems to be a striving, consciously or subconsciously, to earn goodwill and gratitude from one source or another. But is this not, in fact, one of the most valuable commodities we could ever seek, for maintaining our personal safety and homeostasis? In addition, it also satisfies the requirement for self-expression, since we can only be certain of gaining benevolence through creating things which actually are beautiful, enjoyable, or useful.

Thus, it turns out that there is no real conflict between practical egoism, and altruism. *The philosophy of gratitude or altruistic egoism* is best suited to our ideals as well as to our physical nature. But we must add a further element to this guideline, one that takes cognizance of individual differences and shows each of us how to apply the above principle in all the varied circumstances of life. It is imperative that we decide on the amount and kind of work we consider worth doing to assure our homeostasis and security; this takes much soul-searching, because it depends on our most fundamental personal motives.

Here are the basic tenets of the code I have put forth:

1. Find your own natural stress level, the level at which you can comfortably advance towards your own selected port of destination.

2. Be an altruistic egoist. Do not try to suppress the natural instinct of all living beings to look after themselves first. Yet the wish to be of some use, to do some good to others, is also natural. We are social beings, and everybody wants somehow to earn respect and gratitude. You must be useful to others. This gives you the greatest degree of safety, because no one wishes to destroy a person who is useful.

3. **Earn** thy neighbor's love. This is a contemporary modification of the maxim "Love thy neighbor as thyself." It recognizes that all neighbors are not lovable and that it is impossible to love on command.

Put another way, what it comes down to is:

Fight for your highest attainable aim/But never put up resistance in vain.

To my mind, the views described in *Stations of the Mind: New Directions for Reality Therapy* are in perfect harmony with my own concepts as outlined above.

Hans Selye
President, International Institute of Stress
Montreal, Quebec

Preface

In my book *Positive Addiction,** I set forth the idea that certain regular physical behaviors, like running, or mental behaviors, like meditating, could become addicting in a positive way. That is, they could help us to grow stronger and to function better in every aspect of our life. If we pursued the behavior long enough, and on an almost daily basis, we could become addicted. Then, if we attempted to stop abruptly, we would suffer the pain and misery of withdrawal similar to withdrawing from a negative addiction like alcoholism. For the behavior to become addicting, we had to experience during the activity an altered state of consciousness that I called the positive-addiction state of mind.

My interest in this meditative state led me into several years of intensive study of the human brain to try to find out not only what happens in our brain when we experience this state of mind, but also how our brain works generally. As I read books and articles I learned a great deal, but what I seemed not to be able to find was a theory that related the functioning of our brain to our daily experience—in a sense, to almost all we do, think, or feel.

Then a friend suggested that I read *Behavior: The Control of Perception* by William Powers,† and after going through it

---

* William Glasser, *Positive Addiction* (New York: Harper & Row, 1976).
† William T. Powers, *Behavior: The Control of Perception* (Chicago: Aldine Publishing Co., 1973).

several times, I became convinced that this book had the key to much of what I was looking for. In it Powers describes the brain as an input control system which attempts to help to fulfill our needs. It is, however, a very human system, one that, as we read this book and learn how the brain works, can explain much more than I ever thought possible. Powers's book, which was inspired by Norbert Wiener's cybernetics, had received praise from the highest echelons of the behavioral sciences, yet no one had taken his theoretical ideas and attempted to translate them into usable psychological theory and practice.

After reading his book four times and thinking about it almost constantly for six months, I contacted Powers and asked him if he would work with me and help me to write this book, which should be usable by the layman. He read my earlier books, felt we had much in common, and agreed to act as consultant to the project.

Stations of the Mind is the result of this collaboration. In it, at times on my own and often with his help, Powers and I have moved the ideas in his book beyond the basic concepts of his more theoretical volume. If, as you read, you notice that I use the term *we* on most occasions, I do this because the thinking was mostly a collaborative effort. The writing I must take responsibility for alone.

It is our hope that what we have worked out together here will be a major step forward in helping everyone to understand both how each of us functions and how we might, with this knowledge, function better.

1

The Forces That Drive Us

Several years ago two highly agitated and obviously distraught parents came to my office dragging with them their reluctant seventeen-year-old son. He had become totally involved with a religious cult whose beliefs they could not tolerate. What especially galled them was his insistence that, not only should they stop trying to change him, but indeed they should give up their present lives and join him in the cult. Their idea of psychiatry was for me to talk to him and "bring him to his senses." And also to tell them what they should do that would help. The son was polite in the condescending manner that many true believers assume with those who have yet to find the way, but it was also clear that he still very much cared for his mother and father.

After listening to everyone for quite a while I disappointed the parents by telling them that there was nothing specific that I, or they, could do to change their son. I strongly suggested that they stop their barrage of criticism against his religious beliefs and instead try to ignore the fact that he had joined the cult. I urged that they at least keep a warm, accepting attitude toward him and warned them that the more they tried to do things to change him the more they risked losing him for good. By pointing out that it was unlikely he would succeed, I was also able to persuade him that it would reduce the tension if he would stop trying to convert them.

They had banked a great deal on my expertise to *solve* their problem, and my attempt at compromise and negotiation was hardly what they wanted to hear. Like almost all those who seek help for someone they love, they wanted me to begin to change their son there and then and also to lay out a definite program they could follow to complete the change. I could not offer them the program they wanted because no such program exists. *It does not exist because the human brain does not function in such a way that it can exist. The purpose of this book, beginning in this chapter, is to attempt to explain how our brain does work, an explanation that will make clear why these typically frustrated parents cannot get what they want from me or any outside agent.* Nevertheless, almost everyone, including most social scientists, thinks such programs do exist, for example, that people can be brainwashed, conditioned, or raised to do willingly what others want them to do. It is our premise that this and many other wrong beliefs *persist because almost no one has an accurate understanding of the way our brain works.*

I started this book with the cult example to show that the leading misconception concerning our brain is the common belief that our behavior is stimulated by what happens to us from the outside. The parents firmly believed that their "naive" son had been coerced into joining the cult and that I, as an expert on the mind, could coerce him away. Throughout this book, as we explain how our brain works, *we will make clear that because we are living creatures we are moved by inside forces. While outside forces affect what we may choose to do, they do not cause us to behave in any particular or consistent way.* Any attempt to explain how we behave on the basis of outside forces denies the fact that we are alive, since only nonliving things are driven from the outside. For example, as difficult as it may be to accept at this point, we do not even answer a phone merely because it rings. The young man was not coerced into joining the cult by the "ringing of the proper bells." He joined because it fulfilled his needs.

Powers and I don't, however, deny that outside forces affect us and that people may find that a specific behavior, like answering the phone, satisfies the forces within them and use it over and over. But however much we may seem to be, we are never locked into any specific behavior. We will not always choose to answer the phone, no matter how long it rings. If more of us understood how our complex brain functions we would not, to cite just one example, spend so much of our lives in futility and frustration trying to do things to other people so they will do what we want them to do.

It makes good sense here to begin by attempting to come to grips with the internal forces that drive human beings, the highest living creatures on the evolutionary scale. While many other creatures are driven by similar forces, ours are the most complex and varied. For example, only people join cults. To begin this explanation I must tell what drives me because, no matter how much I study and talk to others, as will be explained later, all I will ever really know is what drives me. But because we are all members of the same species it is likely that the same or similar forces drive us all. Certainly, after spending as much time as I have in helping others to try to get what they want, it seems to me we are all very much alike in this respect. If you read my description of what I believe I need and find your needs are not the same, this shows that among us there are individual differences. It is not important, however, that we agree completely. What is important is for us to face the fact that as living creatures we constantly find ourselves wanting something and that because as human beings we want so much, we are never, for more than a short time, satisfied with what we have.

When I review what I need I am tempted to start with the standard answer that I want to be safe, secure, warm, well fed, and healthy—to be personally comfortable. But truthfully, as I sit here thinking about these "basic" needs, I *am* comfortable, so perhaps I should say that unless I'm uncomfortable, I really don't pay much attention to comfort.

What I am almost always strongly aware of is that I want to belong. I want to be part of a group, maybe of many groups. There are times when I want to be alone, but I never want to be lonely. Even when I am all by myself and temporarily satisfied, I want to know that if I reach out, someone is there. I need my family, my friends, my professional associates. I feel a sense of belonging to my country, my state, my city, my basketball team and very much a part of the neighborhood where I have lived twenty-five years. It's what I guess the anthropologists call being a part of a culture. There may be those who say our culture is fragmented, but I don't see it that way. It is larger, more varied, less close than we might like, perhaps because we get around so much, but still very much a culture. And I feel very strongly the need to be a part of it. But besides being a part, I also want to be separate.

I want to be somebody. I don't have to be Winston Churchill, Mohammad Ali, Albert Einstein, Neil Simon, or the Maharishi Mahesh Yogi, but I don't want to be a nonentity. And if I were able to be rich, famous, a genius, or all three, I wouldn't mind giving it a try. If I can't get to the top in my field, I want to get as far as I can. I'm willing to work hard, but if it takes some luck to get there, I would accept a little luck. If it takes looks, I would like to have good looks. If it takes talent, brains, or physical strength, I would like to have at least what seems to me enough. Unlike Sam Walter Foss, I will not settle for living in a house by the side of the road and being a friend to man. And regardless of John Milton, I don't want to be one of those of whom he says "They also serve who only stand and wait." In my head, I guess in my brain, I want to be someone both for myself and for my wife, children, mother, father, teacher, boss, neighbor, and friends to think of as important.

I want to be important for what I choose to do and maybe also a little because I am the unique person I believe myself to be.

It's not easy to reach importance, but I've done it at times. I know I was briefly there when I won the spelldown in the second grade. That was the only time that I ever won anything in school. I even feel a little important now, recalling that great afternoon forty-seven years ago. I felt I was someone seventeen years later when I got into medical school. Though my first book didn't sweep the country, the day it was accepted by the publisher I felt as if I were standing in the middle of a spotlight. I fell in love several times, but it wasn't until I fell deeply in love and got married that I got the solid feeling I was someone and I belonged. I never had that feeling much before that time. Together my wife and I built a life, had children, created a home, and much of the time when all of this was going on I had what I wanted very much. Just the small act of picking an orange from my own tree makes me feel like someone, and when I share the orange with someone I care for, it is even better.

I am always aware that I want to love. I can't seem to get too much love, to give it, to share it, to try to spread it to others. I am often close to tears when I work in a classroom with a group of children whom I've just met, and I feel them reach out to me as I struggle to reach them. And I guess as I write books and lecture I would like to get love to people I don't even know. As I think about what I have just written it seems a little grandiose, but it really isn't, because as hard as I try I'm hardly able to get what I want, give what I want, or share what I want. I really don't believe any of us can, but that doesn't stop me from wanting always to do more. I guess I can't give, get, or help spread as much love as I would like to because I haven't learned how. And partly I haven't learned because I am always afraid of hurting and being hurt. It is so easy to be rejected, frightened, tongue-tied, ashamed and to become unsure of myself when I try to love. I'm sure I have loved less because of fear that I would be rejected, but that hasn't stopped me from doing my share of rejecting either. Regardless, I would like all the love I can get and give; I have never had too much.

Fun is also terribly important to me. I am miserable when I go too long without fun. Fun is hard to define. Mark Twain once said, "Fun is what you do when you don't have to do it," and that seems to me a good definition. There is no one activity that I can point to and say is fun; it comes from many things and I never know in advance exactly what will work. I do a lot of things that I don't have to do just because I enjoy them, just for the heck of it, just because they make me laugh. I like to relax and let my mind wander, my body wander, play games, see places, entertain new ideas and new thoughts. I want to meet new people and try new things, all because they might be fun. I rarely want something new because I desperately need it, because there is money in it or some big social payoff. Rather, because it seems to me that it might be a lot of fun to have it. When I feel down and I don't have a good idea why I am semidepressed, I say to myself, "When did you last have a little fun? When did you last relax and really enjoy yourself?" And then it becomes apparent that it has been a while, maybe only a couple of hours, but still too long. I really have no idea how much fun I need or how long I can go between laughs. All I know is that, like love and, I guess to some extent, like feeling important, I can never have too much fun, too much relaxation, and too much enjoyment. People say there can be too much of a good thing, and I suppose there can be, but I have yet to experience too much of many good things.

Something else that I have noticed is that, in what I want, age doesn't seem to make much difference. Maybe feeling like somebody develops a little bit of age and "dignity", but as for fun, I like it as much now as I did when I was four or five. I can remember having a lot of fun when I was younger. In fact things that were fun remain pretty clear in my memory. It is misery that seems to die away, thank goodness. I even remember some fun in the army. It wasn't all miserable; there were lots of pranks and jokes. I remember a glass fight in college in a hot attic chem lab. Suddenly we started throwing glass at each other and went crazy. Before we could stop, the floor was ankle deep with broken glass. It was destructive. It was senseless. But it was fun. Even cleaning it up was kind of fun. Paying for it I suppose wasn't that much fun, but fun is temporary anyway. And if you have to pay, you pay. If you think ahead to the consequences of everything you do, it is pretty hard to relax and have what most of us would call fun.

Beyond all of these or perhaps before all of them is the fact that I want to be free. I want, at least, to have the feeling, the belief, that I am free. This doesn't mean no relationships, no responsibilities, but it does mean that no one can put me in a cage and keep me there. I don't want to be pushed around by anybody. I want to be able to control my own contingencies and most of all my own thoughts. I don't want somebody to have the water supply and me to be outside begging for a drink. I want free access to what most of us believe there should be free access to. I don't want to have to ask if I can do what I want to do or say what I want to say every time something comes into my head. I want to believe that if I really want to do something within reason there is a way. Since I'm fortunate enough to live in a free, lawful society, I will accept reasonable control of my body but none of my mind. Still, I'll try to live by the rules and the customs, but I also want to believe that I can choose not to accept them all the time without horrifying consequences. I might have to suffer moderate consequences, but I can at least make the choice not to accept this or that rule without living in abject fear. That is my limited definition of freedom. It is what I want.

Finally, when I think about what I want, I have at times

noticed something that doesn't seem right. What I mean is, I want at the same time two or more things that seem to be opposites. For example, I want the freedom to come and go and do what I want, yet I also want to belong. But to belong limits my freedom and to be free reduces my sense of belonging. At other times I want to work hard and succeed, but I also want to stop, say the hell with it, and play tennis. I dream of retiring and never going to the office again, but when I look at some friends who have retired I don't want that kind of freedom. It seems that whatever drives me can be out of sync, as if I am a car with two engines front and rear and with a gear box that can drive them in opposite directions. No sane engineer would build a car that way, but I truly feel, at times, that I am in that peculiar forward-reverse gear. It doesn't happen often, but it happens enough so that I wonder about the soundness of my basic design. It's just a thought, and maybe I overstate the case, but truly sometimes I want so much so strongly, in so many different directions, that I feel as if I'm being torn apart.

When at times I can't get what I want or I'm in conflict, I feel quick anger and lose my temper. Sometimes I try to go on a power trip, something that normally I don't care that much about. From long experience I know I am capable of feeling depressed, anxious, tense, guilty, upset, miserable, and of having crazy thoughts. I can get sick, break out, become frightened and immobilized; the forces that drive me don't take frustration lying down, they always let me know that something is wrong.

What puzzles me is *what makes it happen?* What makes my mind do these things to me or to itself or to my body? Or perhaps *with* me is the best way of describing all that happens. I also wonder about how I got this way. How did I get to want all these things? This desire to be somebody. This intense, constant, almost burning need to be loved and cared for and to love and care for someone else. This continuing urge to have some fun, relax, and enjoy myself. The idea that I should be free to do what I want to do, even, at times, when I may hurt someone else.

These are questions that have been on my mind a long time, and in this book I will make an attempt to answer them. To do so I will call extensively upon William Powers's sensible theory of how our brain works, but first we must take a look at how our brain grew and how our needs came into existence.

2

The Old Brain and the New Brain

≈§⧽≈

When I was thirteen years old, I woke up one early afternoon on the floor of a carpeted room with my junior high school principal bending over me. My pants were off, he was wiping me with a towel; evidently I had wet myself. The only thing I could remember was that I had been in school, but I had never before seen a carpeted room in any school, so it didn't seem to me that I could be in school now. But where I was or what had happened was a complete mystery.

The principal seemed very relieved that I was awake; he told me I had fallen, hit my head, and been knocked out. He said that I had wet my pants but that my mother was on the way to school and she was bringing dry clothes. There were no further ill effects, my mind was clear, I had no headache, but I still have no memory of the accident itself.

I relate this incident because from it I can explain the fact that our brain is divided into two major parts, each with its own functions and each able to act, to a remarkable extent, independently of the other. The largest part is called the new brain or cerebral cortex. It is the bulging, convoluted mass of nervous tissue that we see whenever the brain is pictured. The old brain is made up of all the complex structures lying below the new brain and above the spinal cord. From the outside it is mostly invisible because it is much smaller than the new brain and because the new brain tends to hang down around it like a curtain. When I was knocked out it was only my new brain that was temporarily put out of commission; my old brain continued to function well, hardly affected by the trauma.

In this chapter I would like to explain the functions and the relationship of what might, for the sake of understanding, be called our "two" brains. Of course, they are intimately related but they function quite differently, and, as we will learn later, the new brain is even capable of interfering with the functioning of the old brain so that we can become seriously ill with what is commonly called a psychosomatic illness.

It makes sense to describe the functioning of the old brain first because this part of our brain came into existence first. In fact, from an evolutionary standpoint, it probably preceded the new brain by at least 100 million years. What the old brain does is very simple. Its whole purpose is to keep all of the machinery of the body functioning well. It also is concerned with reproduction, at least to the extent that it keeps our bodies as sexually ready as possible during our reproductive years, but its continual and ongoing concern is to keep us alive.

When I had my accident and lost the functioning of my new brain, my old brain continued to function flawlessly, even possibly causing me to urinate to protect my bladder and my kidneys. *But it has nothing to do with consciousness or with all the things that I talked about wanting in Chapter 1. These desires are all functions intimately associated with my new brain, with awareness of how I as a person relate to the world around me.*

To insure my survival as an individual, the old brain, even in times of sickness, trauma, or environmental hardship, acts as a master control to keep all the complicated physiology of the body coordinated and working properly. It regulates my breathing, my heart rate, and my body temperature. It controls my swallowing, my digestion, and has backup control on my elimination. It regulates my hormones, sexual functioning, and probably is in charge of my immune system, the system that protects me from infections and poisons. *Under most conditions it is capable of keeping all my bodily processes, or internal environment, at a homeostatic or stable level, that is, working smoothly, evenly, and well within the upper and lower limits of what my body is capable of doing.* It works when I am awake, asleep, unconscious, or sick, always striving to keep me as healthy and sexually ready as possible.

Something equivalent to the old brain has been in existence for more than 700 million years for almost all living multicelled animals. In mammals its structure has changed very little for the past 50 million years because mammalian physiology has been stable for that period of time. The human old brain has probably not changed for the past 12 million years, when our earliest ancestor appeared, because even though the structure of our body has changed, and our new brain is vastly different, our physiology, that is, how our body functions, is probably identical to the first creature that could be called human.

In contrast, the new brain has had a remarkably different history. Some form of the new brain came into existence about 600 million years ago when animals became not only multicelled, but also started to move around actively and develop awareness of their environment. If the animal was to survive under these conditions, in a world that was constantly changing, it needed more than a brain that only regulated its internal environment. To find food, shelter, and to make contact with a sexually receptive animal of the opposite sex, it needed a brain that dealt actively with the external or outside world. Since none of these functions can be performed by the old brain (its functions relate only to the body or physiologic world), we must conclude that as the need to deal with the outside world arose, a new brain that could do this evolved.

As it deals with the outside world the new brain acts as an executive, that is, it gives orders, but it is the old brain that provides the voluntary and involuntary muscular activity the body needs to carry them out. For example, when we wish to eat, it is the old brain that starts us salivating, regulates our swallowing, and provides the physical and chemical processes to digest the food. Without the old brain the new brain would be a general without an army. We can become aware of this dual process easily any morning when we try to spring out of bed as soon as we hear the alarm. We may issue the new brain order, leap up, but it takes a moment for the old brain to get all the leaping machinery ready to move. It is a tiny interval but it is easily detected if we look for it. If the old brain does not do its part, for example, when its actions are drugged with curare, we cannot move.

Here we can easily get into a chicken and egg argument because there is no way of knowing whether the evolution which produced our new brain or cerebral cortex allowed animals to separate from plants and move actively through the world or whether some plants broke loose and developed concomitantly a tiny cortex that could deal with this changing environment and allow them to survive as animals. What *is* important is that it *did* occur and after eons of evolution, about 15 million years ago when the first human beings appeared, they had the beginning of our present new brain and an essentially finished old brain. Therefore, while our cerebral cortex has probably grown to be five times what it was 12 million years ago, our old brain has hardly grown at all.

Since the old brain regulates physiology, and since the physiology of all vertebrate creatures is extremely similar, all vertebrates have an old brain whose structure and function is about the same. It has also been shown that the size of the old brain is proportioned to the size of the body whose physiology it controls. For example, a 160-pound fish will have about the same size old brain as a 160-pound person. *It is the new brain that has no relationship to body size; its size is determined by how complex its dealings are with the outside world.* A fish, even a big fish, because it deals in a very limited way with the world around it, has a new brain that is at most one ten-thousandth the size of ours. And what new brain it has is so different and so simple that its function is only remotely analogous to ours. In fact, the only strong similarity is that both our new brain and a fish's new brain look for food and try to avoid danger; we are both concerned with staying alive.

For example, when we or a fish need food, something is monitored in the old brain control panel, as perhaps a lowering of blood sugar in certain cells of the hypothalamus, and this information is transmitted to the new brain, where it is perceived as hunger, causing both us and the fish consciously and actively to seek food. But the old brain has no knowledge, no awareness of the hunger or the food seeking. It can only monitor the decrease in body sugar and then transmit the information that to stay alive we need something that will raise the body sugar. How it transmits this information to the new brain is not known, but somehow it occurs. If the new brain of a fish or a human being cannot interpret and act upon this "information" through successful food seeking, neither the fish nor the human being can stay alive.

This is what would have happened to me when I was knocked out. If I had remained unconscious for more than a week I would have run out of water, and without enough fluid I would have died. Someone or some machinery, commonly called a life-support system, by performing among other functions the food and water gathering operation, would have been needed to keep me alive. And as long as this was done, my old brain would keep me alive indefinitely. The moral question as to whether or not I would have been humanly alive without a cortex comes to mind but is not pertinent here. The point here is that the new brain came into existence because the old brain could not keep us alive when we began to move around. Unlike a clam, a sponge, or a coral, simple old-brain animals which can live quite successfully with essentially no new brain at all because their food comes to them, we and our mobile ancestors had to have this additional mental capacity.

As important as these life-support new-brain functions are, however, they require very little cortex to be handled successfully. A fish certainly hasn't much of a new brain, but it has enough cerebral cortex to get along well in the world it inhabits. Fish seem to be, to some extent, aware of their surroundings. They certainly avoid fishermen, get themselves up over sizable rapids, and swim around and reproduce in the company of fish they recognize to be just like themselves. They find food, escape from danger, and considering the fish-eat-fish-and-people-eat-fish world they live in, they do pretty well with the tiny cerebral cortex they have. Some fish, like carp, live to be several hundred years old, and other fish, like the salmon, live very complex lives. *Therefore, just to deal with the physical environment enough to keep alive, a little cortex goes a long way.*

Moving up the scale from fish to dog, again the difference is in the cortex. The new brain of a dog has been fairly stable for 40 million years; it continued to evolve for at least 30 million more years than that of the fish, but then it stopped. During this additional evolutionary period, during which it became able to cope with a much more changeable world, the new brain of a dog grew to be many hundred times larger than that of a fish of similar body weight. Their old brains, of course, are proportionally about the same size. By the time the dog's new brain stopped growing it had reached a point where it dealt with the outside world in many ways that we recognize as similar to ours. For example, Madge, our Labrador, has a strong sense of belonging, seems to have a sense of love, obviously likes to have fun, and enjoys the freedom that she sometimes gets to ramble around without restraint. She accepts the fact that she is part of a family and can't always do what she wants. But unlike us she almost never has conflicting needs. This is because she has no need for status, for worthwhileness, for doing something important. She, indeed, is more than satisfied to "live in her house by the side of the road and be a friend to man." And even where she is similar, her brain, which has not changed for 40 million years, has little capacity to get what she wants if it is not easily obtainable. She has absolutely no ability to do anything complicated to satisfy the needs that are similar to ours, and most of the time her mind is on the old brain needs of food and of sex as she sniffs for other dogs. Because she seems to have the capacity to love, she is infinitely more new-brain motivated than a fish but probably much less so than an ape. None of these creatures, however, even comes close to experiencing the needs and the conflicts that dominate our lives. And no other creatures enjoy the huge brain and complex cortical functioning that we take for granted.

Why have we, among all creatures, developed the complex, often conflicting needs that we constantly experience? Why do we, for example, have needs that seem to bear little relationship to what the old brain requires to keep us alive and healthy? For example, why do we overeat, overexert, or commit suicide, all activities that conflict directly with health or life?

There are no accepted answers to these questions, but there is some evidence that may point the way to reasonable speculation. Two events took place millions of years ago that seem to bear directly upon why we need so much and also why our brain has grown so large. First, perhaps what made us human and distinguished us from apes, was that we learned to walk upright. This must have happened about 12 million years ago.* and when it happened our hands were free for carrying. Once we could carry things comfortably we could set up a home base and live there safely in stable groups for months at a time. We did not have to be constantly on the move for food and shelter; our old-brain needs for nourishment

* See Richard Leakey and Roger Lewin, *Origins* (London: McDonald and Janes, 1977) for the anthropological evidence to back up much material in this chapter.

and comfort could be better met. When this happened we had a great survival advantage over most lower creatures, who are, in a sense, "slaves" of their old brain. This left our new brain with time, and much of this time was used to engage in social activity. To get even more time to socialize, we developed technology, for example, tools and fire that made our life more secure. We chose to socialize because in the beginning it had obvious survival advantages, and we see socialization as a need in almost all primate and even many subprimate cultures, like that of the wolf.* But we did it better and enjoyed it more because we had the technology and the time. From this grew our need *to belong* and maybe even the beginnings of our need *to love.* And as we now lived in small societies, also our needs for *fun and freedom.* Because it was to our advantage to learn how to socialize when we were young, we engaged in a lot of seemingly random social play that gradually we came to know as fun. Fun helps us to learn how to get along in ways that others can accept and also to learn in a safe, nonpressured way, a lot of the physical and technical skills that we use all of our lives. Freedom, obviously, became important once we had time and could make choices. Creatures who are constantly being driven by old-brain needs to search for food are not really free. Freedom only exists in the sense that we can use it to choose what we want when choices are available. We are not free if we are restricted by hunger in everything we do.

Also at this time, probably starting with dominance, which is a new-brain refinement of an old-brain sexual need common to many creatures, we began to want a little more for ourselves and to concern ourselves less with belonging and the needs of the group. We began not only to want the best mate but also the best food, the best place by the fire, and the driest cave as we searched for comfort beyond survival. Therefore,

---

* And to some extent in all living creatures. See Edward O. Wilson, *Sociobiology* (Cambridge: Harvard University Press, Belknap Press, 1980).

I'm sure that early we developed what we all experience now as a need to compete, to get the best or the most, while still trying somehow to belong, to love, and to share. As this occurred we began to experience conflict. Now it was much harder to fulfill our needs but always we tried. And it is this struggle to resolve conflicts that may cause us to overeat, overexert, or even attempt suicide.

But in the beginning this conflict was minimal. The need to cooperate took precedence for most early groups over the need to compete and get the most for oneself. Life was so chancy and belonging continued to have such a strong survival advantage over the separateness of competition that this individual need must have developed slowly. It probably was not until we experienced the second and most significant of all human accomplishments, learning to talk, that the whole process accelerated. Now for the first time we could easily give another person "a piece of our mind." And we had a tool to socialize and to create in a way that no other creature can. It is likely this occurred about 3 million years ago because at that time our brain began a rapid and explosive growth that is probably still going on, a growth that is not matched in any other creature. As our needs, especially our individual or competitive needs, started to expand, we grew more technically competent and we experienced more and more conflict. This in turn took more brain power to resolve, and I believe it was then that conflict started, and it continues unabated today, especially the conflict between the desire to *belong and share* and the desire to *compete and keep*. This has complicated our social nature and caused our brain to grow so fast.

Perhaps another and remarkably perceptive way of expressing this same idea is summed up in a short article by the philosopher N. K. Humphrey entitled "The Origins of Human Intelligence."* Humphrey's thesis is that the great intellectual

---

* Humphrey, N. K., "The Origins of Human Intelligence," *Human Nature* (December 1978).

capacity that human beings possess has little to do with what could be called practical invention, or gaining the intelligence to deal with a difficult or changing external physical environment. We didn't get as smart as we have become, and our brain didn't grow as large as it has grown, in response to our struggle to satisfy the direct or indirect pressures of the old brain, the pressures based on survival that moved us to become better at gaining food and shelter, and at reproduction. Even to invent tools and weapons, tame fire, and, I would suspect, learn what it took to walk on the moon, we don't need as big a cortex as we have. We may use it now for high technology, but it didn't grow this big in response to any particular need for mid-sized or even big inventions. Humphrey also denies that the rigors of our natural environment or our desire to explore caused us to become so smart. *He claims that it was the pressure of our inherent social nature, expanding rapidly with speech, that caused the explosive growth of our new brain. Driven by the need to belong, we must choose to live close to one another, but because we also need to compete we have never found this to be an easy choice. As much as it may seem to be a contradiction in terms, we are a social-competitive animal.* Using the graphic example of Robinson Crusoe, Humphrey doesn't see the hostile island enviroment as Crusoe's main problem. Rather, to quote Humphrey, "it was the arrival of the man Friday on the scene that was the real challenge for Crusoe. If Monday, Tuesday, Wednesday and Thursday had turned up as well, Crusoe would have had even greater need to keep his wits about him." As long as they would subordinate their needs to Crusoe's, there was no problem, but because we are competitive and we want to be free to choose, we do not subordinate easily. Conflict is built into our structure.

Therefore, long after we learned to walk upright, it was the continuing growth of our new brain coupled with some fortuitous change in the anatomy of our throat, that sparked our progress. With the ability to talk to each other, to express complex ideas, and suddenly to have a past and future, we had countless more ways than before to learn to belong and to succeed in competing. None of the complexities of the needs discussed in Chapter 1 makes much sense if you can't talk, and to expand upon Humphrey's point, the first thing Crusoe did was to teach Friday to talk his language. So much can be explained by this occurrence, so little would be possible without it. Try to conceive of thinking without language. While it may be possible, it is terribly difficult. We think mostly through logical language, and grammar is claimed by one of the world's great linguists, Noam Chomsky, to be built into our brain. Pictures of the living brain in action published in *Scientific American**, show that huge amounts of our brain are involved when we talk, more, it seems, than during any other activity. While all this is no proof that language per se was the evolutionary force, there is no doubt that it was related to this sudden growth and there is good reason to infer that it was much more the cause than the result.

Until people could talk to one another, there was no good way to give or to gain recognition, from which came the desire to excel as an individual. Once we could talk, we could also plan, scheme, fool, joke—in short, begin to learn the social skills that we have developed to such a fine art today. At this point it's not necessary to study anthropology to begin to understand Humphrey's thesis that social pressure led to intelligence; just examine your own life. Think about what I said I wanted in the first chapter. It takes a lot of sense and creativity to get along with those around us. Think of the conflicts you encounter as you struggle for individual fulfillment, but at the same time try to get along even with those close to you, much less others. Think of the times you have to mesh your life with the lives of your child, spouse, friend, and still get what you want while trying not to take anything away from them. See

* Niels A. Lassen et al. "Brain Function and Blood Flow," *Scientific American* (October 1978), pp. 62–71.

how difficult it is to get along with those around you for a day; if you mesh perfectly for a week it's like a miracle. Compare this to the mundane task of painting a picture, planting a garden, or "inventing your wheel." When any task depends only on you, or you can do it successfully without others or their approval, it becomes much easier, no matter how complex it may be technically or artistically. Van Gogh's trouble was not with his art, it was his inability both to paint and to fulfill himself as a social creature.

Suppose you find yourself lonely with nothing to do, and you want to find someone to spend an enjoyable few hours with you. It takes a creative mind to start from scratch and end up with a pleasant social afternoon. Think of all the upsets, miseries, and disappointments you've had in the past six months, and ask yourself if they are not almost all caused by your new brain's inability to control, predict, cooperate, negotiate, or compromise with other people and still get what you want. Fulfilling old-brain needs occupies only a fragment of our time and effort.

In this remarkable shift where the new brain now predominates there are more and more situations where the old brain fails us badly. In its attempt to keep pace with the increasing demands of the new brain we can become sick with psychosomatic diseases like heart disease, ulcers, and arthritis. Driven by the need to excel, we may in a competitive effort struggle day and night to get money and power. This struggle is not physical; our work is often in an office where the most effort we exert is to talk on the telephone. Even though we are not expending much effort we are still caught up in a fiercely competitive struggle just the same as if we were leading the hunt 50,000 years ago to be the first of our tribe to kill a mastodon. Our old brain has no knowledge of our struggles in the outside world, it only tries to make our body functional under all demands. It can't distinguish between the need to provide muscle power and blood flow for combat with a mastodon or combat with the stock market. It can only sense that the new brain is in some sort of a fierce struggle and its job is to alter the inner environment of our body to provide the body with all it needs to succeed in that struggle. It will do so if the struggle lasts six hours, as in hunting the mastodon, or six years, as in trying to beat the market. In each instance it responds in the only way it "knows" how, in this instance, by raising the blood pressure, heart rate, and muscle tone. It will also increase the sugar and fat in our blood and put out more clotting elements so we won't bleed to death if the mastodon rips us open. For the hunt this is "sensible" old-brain behavior; we need to function at a higher than normal physical level because of the rigor of the chase. To beat the stock market we don't need this fight-or-flight body preparation, but the old brain "misreading" our situation provides it anyway. When this goes on too long, our vascular system can become overtaxed, blood clots obstruct our coronary arteries, and our old brain has inadvertently caused us to suffer a heart attack. Later, in Chapter 11, when we discuss psychosomatic illness we will examine this complicated process in much more detail.

With psychosomatic illness we have now (inadvertently) traveled the full circle. The function of the old brain is to keep us healthy and alive. To help it do this we evolved the new brain which makes it possible for us to find food and shelter in the outside world. Then with the advent of walking upright and speech the new brain became so efficient that we had a lot of time on our hands. With this time we pushed our initial survival needs far beyond their original purpose as we became social and competitive beyond any other living creature. But as we did so, we put demands upon our old brain that frequently cost us our health—in the case of coronary artery disease, too often our life. But ironically, it was to stay alive in a changing world that caused the new brain to appear in the first place.

As frequent and disabling as psychosomatic illness is, how-

ever, most of the misery we suffer, for example, when we are depressed, alcoholic, or psychotic does not involve our old brain. In these situations, miserable as we may be, our body functions well. Our suffering is psychological, which is another way of saying that it originates in our new brain, occurring when this brain is unable to satisfy the complex needs that drive it.

Therefore, if both our happiness and our physical health depend upon how well our new brain functions, it seems only sensible that we learn as much as possible about how this complicated organ actually works. In the next six chapters, following Powers, I will attempt to explain this process in such a way that we can apply it usefully to our lives.

3

An Introduction to the Way the Brain Works

⋞§ ⋟

When my father, who hated to shovel coal, installed a gas furnace in 1932, all the neighbors predicted disaster. They said the fumes would be dangerous, gas would never heat the house, and it would be so expensive we would go broke. What they were most dubious of was the tiny control that hung on our dining-room wall and could be set for any comfortable temperature. No one around us had ever seen a thermostat before, and it was laughable to them that this small unit could control the temperature of a whole house. I was told never to touch it. My father adjusted it carefully each day, but I couldn't resist the temptation to set it higher to see if it really worked. I would show my friends how the house could be made warmer, and I was surprised that when I set it back down, the house didn't cool off immediately. For a long time I didn't understand how a thermostat worked. All I knew was that it did seem to control the temperature of the house.

I use this illustration for two reasons. First, this is analogous to the position that most of us are in today when we puzzle about how our brain works. We know it works but we don't know how, much as I didn't know why the house didn't cool down as quickly as it warmed up. The second and perhaps more important reason that I relate this particular story is that our brain works very much like a thermostat, a very complex wonderful thermostat, but basically in the same way. Today we all know that a thermostat works by turning the furnace on and off to maintain the temperature set on the dial. If it isn't hooked to a cooling unit, as most are not, it can only heat the house, or stop heating the house; cooling takes place through the cold outside air getting in while the furnace is off.

In this example the thermostat is analogous to the new brain. It gives the order on or off to the furnace, which is analogous to the body. Both thermostat and furnace are needed to heat the house properly, but the thermostat is the brain of the system. Together they could be called a *control system* because when they are working properly, they control the temperature in the house. Like the new brain, which has many built-in needs, the simple thermostat "brain" also has a built-in need, which is to maintain the house at the set temperature, for example, at 68 degrees. If it could talk, it might say, "What I want most of all is to control the temperature of the air around me to stay at the right temperature," just as the young man in Chapter 1 might say, "I want to control the people in the world around me so that everyone joins my cult."

In order to do its job (or fulfill its need) the thermostat must be able to sense the temperature of the room, just as the young cultist must be able to sense who around him is or is not a member of his cult. The thermostat, therefore, has a sensing device built into it so that at all times it knows the temperature of the room. It must also have a way to compare that temperature with the temperature it wants. If the room is at 62 degrees, the thermostat must be able to detect this difference. It isn't important that it know the exact difference, what is important is that it knows that a difference exists.

But even when it "knows" that the temperature of the room is below what it wants, it alone cannot heat the room anymore than the cultist's realization that people are not cult members can get them to join. The thermostat brain must be connected to an action or behavioral system, in its case the furnace. When the thermostat detects a lower temperature than is desired, it starts the furnace. If the furnace is working properly, it will put heat into the room; the thermostat will sense the rising temperature and turn the furnace off when the room reaches 68 degrees. In the same way the young man will stop his converting activity if he senses that all those around him are now members of his cult.

The next important fact about our new brain is that it controls for *input* or for what it senses. To do this it always starts with a mental picture (or idea or perception) of the way we want some part of the world to be or, in other words, a picture of some part of the world that will fulfill our needs. In the case of the young cultist, he starts with the idea already in his head, based perhaps on his need to belong, that he would like to see everyone around him a member of his cult. This is a very specific idea; he does not want *any* cult or even a similar cult, he wants his *exact* cult. He then looks around to see if those around him are members. In other words he checks his present input: does it correspond to what he has built into his head that he wants? In the case of the thermostat brain it has built in the exact idea 68°, not 71° or 69°. It then senses the air around it to see what the input is, and if it is not 68°, it will turn on the furnace or output system to raise the room temperature until it gets the input—the room at 68°. When it gets this input, it is satisfied and turns off the output or the furnace. If the young man gets the input that those around him are not members of his cult, he will start trying to convert them (output) until they join. He doesn't concern himself with how hard he has to work or, in control-system terms, he doesn't control for the effort or the output needed to do the job. *What he controls for is the input,* that is, he tries to get the sense that those around him correspond as closely as possible to the idea of what he wants. In the same way the thermostat does not care how long or how hard the furnace has to run (output) to get the room up to 68°, the *input* it desires.

All new brain control systems, like a thermostat, must have an accurate sensing capability. In our case, to sense the world around us, we have the ability to sense light, sound, odors, flavors, touch, heat, cold, and pain. We also have a whole array of other more subtle senses like proprioception, or the sense of where all parts of our body are in relationship to each other and to the world. What these sensors do is provide a huge amount of information that goes into our new brain, information that all together is our *input*. Where the thermostat brain can only sense temperature input, we can sense to an unbelievable degree all shades of the world around us. For example, it is likely that the young man could easily sense the distinction between a true cultist and a pretender, even though you and I might be fooled completely.

Even though the new brains of all creatures work the same way—that is, they control for input—there is with one exception a marked difference between the output of people and that of lower animals. In fact, the lower the animal the more its output resembles that of a machine like a thermostat and the less it is like that of a human being. The exception or the way all output systems are alike, both living and nonliving, is that all of them generate some sort of signal to get the output going. This means that when the young man senses that those around him are not cult members, a signal is generated that starts his converting behavior. In other words, when there is a difference between what we want to sense and what we do sense, that difference generates a signal that activates our behavior. This occurs in people, it occurs in earthworms, and it occurs in thermostats. It is common to all input control systems.

There is, however, a huge difference between human output or behavior systems and lower animal or mechanical behavioral systems, both of which are activated by a similar signal. All the thermostat can do is start and stop the furnace. It has no choice of outputs; there is only one, and if the furnace does not work there is no other way it can get heat into the room. On the other hand, the young cultist is not restricted to one way. He has available maybe fifty different ways to try to get others, even his parents, to join the cult. In fact, the reason he agreed to see me was to get me to pronounce him sane so that his parents could not call him crazy and pay no attention to his efforts. We, more than any other creature, have a wide variety, in fact almost an infinite number, of outputs or behaviors. When one doesn't get us the input we are controlling for, we try another and then another. This flexibility gives us a tremendous advantage over all lower creatures whose behavioral systems are much more restricted. Most lower animals have built-in behaviors which work well in the animal world, but when animals run up against people who have so many more behaviors, these built-in behaviors can put them at a disadvantage. For example, when salmon get the idea in their head that it is time to spawn they must try to swim up to the brook where they were born to do it. If they can't get there they die trying, because this is the only place they will spawn. Obviously, nature has made it this way because, if it was safe for them, it should be safe for their offspring. Salmon evolution did not contemplate that men would build dams or pollute the streams. Human beings on the other hand can and will spawn eagerly almost anywhere. When we get the idea in our head that we'd like to spawn, we have no restrictions on our spawning behavior; all we want is to gain the input that we are spawning. How or where makes little difference to many of us. This is one reason human population is rapidly rising, and the salmon's is falling precipitously. Therefore, an input control system will use all the outputs it has available; and the more it has, the more efficient it will be at successfully controlling for what it wants. And because we have more outputs than any other creature, we are the most successful of all mammals. *Output is both the signal from the new brain to do something and any behavior generated by that signal.* In human beings it includes all of our physical activity, voluntary, like running or speaking, and involuntary, like sweating and shivering; all of our mental activity, like thinking or imagining; and *almost* all of our feeling activity, like joyful socializing or miserable depressing. While we ordinarily don't think of feelings as behaviors, when we discuss them in detail in Chapters 5 and 6 we will point out that most of what we now call feelings, such as depression, are more accurately feeling behaviors. Because they are, after a more detailed explanation which will come later, we will, for example, call what we generally speak of as depression, *depressing.*

Therefore, except for one exception which will be explained later, when we discuss feelings in detail, all that we experience can be divided into two parts—what we sense or what goes into our brain, which for the rest of this book we will call our *perceptions* or *input,* and what our brain generates as it attempts to control some part of the world, which we will call our *behavior* or *output.* It is interesting that output can, under unusual circumstances, be mistaken for input, as in hallucinations. Here the hallucinator thinks the voices he hears are coming in through his sensory system. He does perceive them through this system but they originate as an output or a mental behavior generated by his own brain as it tries desperately to control for something the hallucinator needs.

While we believe that our explanation of our new brain functioning as an input control system is clear and sensible, we are aware that what we claim is not generally accepted. Neither experts on human behavior nor lay people in any significant number believe that this is how our brain works. What they believe or act as if they believe—because many people probably don't think much about how the brain works—is that we control for output not input. This means they believe our behavior is motivated from the outside and that we try to behave in specific ways to cope with what happens to us or is done to us by the world. While most people understand that the thermostat brain is not activated by cold air alone, but that the air has to be colder than the thermostat "desires" before it will turn on the furnace, they don't understand why I or other psychiatrists can't do something to the young man, *regardless of his desires,* to get him to quit the cult. This "common sense" psychology that we can do things to people to get them to behave differently, also known as stimulus-response psychology or S-R, ignores or tries to ignore the fact that we are internally motivated. What most people believe is that our behavior is an attempt to reduce the pain or increase the pleasure of an outside event. They also believe that we are concerned that what we do be as specific as possible to get this to happen.

Because this S-R way of thinking is so widely held and because so much harm is done to people by those who try to force people to behave "their" way, it is worthwhile to spend a little time explaining why this common belief is not correct. The difficulty seems to be that most of us, including experts, will accept the fact that we are human with internal needs, but then, when we deal with people to try to get them to change their behavior, *we ignore what we know.* Over and over we see those around us treated as if what happens to them sporadically from the outside, from us or their teacher, mother, father, wife, husband, boss, or minister, is more important than what happens inside their brain all the time, *the constant pressure of their needs.* For example, we have to learn that the more than a million children who don't read, despite much good instruction, don't because reading right now does not fulfill their needs. Just because we think reading is good for everyone, or because we think that those who don't read really want to read (many "say" they do), does not change the fact that right now they don't read, mostly because they don't want to. And as long as they don't want to, no one, no matter how expert, will teach them. Despite what most of us believe, we cannot coerce people either with vinegar or honey to get them willingly to do what goes against what they believe they need. The old adage "you can lead a horse to water, but you can't make him drink" is completely true.

Perhaps a good way to see the flaws in "common sense" S-R psychology is to imagine that an observer has been sent from Mars to Earth to investigate how the brains of people on Earth function when they behave. She chooses to do so by observing how we handle the telephone. She sits quietly, invisible because she lives in a nonvisible spectrum, observing a man working in a busy office. The telephone on his desk rings, he picks it up and talks into it. He does this again and again in "response" to its ring. Because she is careful, she doesn't observe just one man. She observes a hundred people all over the world as they "react" to the ring of a telephone, and all except one seem to do the same thing. When she goes back to Mars, she reports that people on Earth respond to the stimulus of bells, buzzes, or lights on their phones very specifically by picking them up and talking. And as soon as they pick up the receiver the stimulus stops. There seems to be nothing wrong with this S-R observation, and most of us on Earth would agree that the telephone ring is a signal stimulus. It causes us to "respond," to pick up the phone. At headquarters on Mars she is questioned; is she sure? She defends her belief that stimulus-response is the way we function by showing her chief some strong additional evidence that she picked up, material that describes the S-R work of a very prominent psychologist, B. F. Skinner.

Skinner has devoted much of his life to experiments that "prove" that S-R is the way our brains work to cause us to behave. He has "proved" it with rats and pigeons, putting them in many different situations and showing again and again how they respond specifically to "reinforcing" stimuli.

The key word here is reinforcing, which means to stimulate

animals with something they want which will reinforce their efforts to get it. What S-R psychologists or operant conditioners are good at is figuring out what animals want, and since most animals want food much of the time this is not too hard to do. Once an animal figures out an efficient way to get the food, he will stick to that way and then he is conditioned. People with their complex, often conflicting needs are much harder to figure out and are therefore much harder to condition.

Following S-R reasoning, psychologists have put rats in mazes, where in one instance the rat has a choice of running down several different paths from the starting point. At the end of one path is a lever which, if pressed, delivers food. Another path has a lever but no food, and a third path has a lever which when pressed delivers an electric shock to the paw. What the observers have noted is that most of the rats spend most of their time pressing the lever that delivers food. They spend very little time at the end of the other two paths. With food available as a "stimulus" hungry rats would rather eat than not eat. They would much rather eat than be shocked. Behaviorists claim that since most animals behave this way and human beings are animals, they also choose appropriate behavior in response to stimuli. Before Skinner, Pavlov concluded that when he presented food to a dog and simultaneously rang a bell, a dog tethered in a harness would eventually salivate to the bell alone, even though no food followed. He also called this conditioning, claimed that it was a kind of simple cerebral learning, and got much recognition for "proving" that the well-accepted, common-sense psychology of stimulus-response is the way our brains work.

Basically what Pavlov and Skinner did prove is not that we behave in the S-R mode, but that when something gets our attention we will consistently do something about it *if what gets our attention is in some way important to us.* Doctors tell many patients whom they can find nothing wrong with that if they take a certain medicine they will get better. Often people *do* get better because what they wanted was a *good* medicine. Their sickness was the way they dealt with frustrations, and the good medicine relieved their frustration. Parents tell little children, "Look both ways when you cross the street or you will get run over," and the children who have on their mind that they don't want to get hurt look both ways. There is certainly nothing wrong with trying to get people to respond to what we say in the way we want them to, but they "respond" not because of what we say but because it fulfills what they believe they need right now. We don't stop at a red light because it is red, we stop because we don't want to get killed or we don't want a ticket. The S-R way of thinking about how our brain functions *seems* to make sense as we live our lives, but it is not really how our brain works. If we are in a hurry to get somewhere important—like to the hospital—we will crash the red light. The hospital is more important this time.

Our brain "obviously" seems to work in an S-R manner to an observer from Mars, a Pavlov, a Skinner, or even to most of us because as observers we never can see what the people we are observing need. And because we can't, our observation may be faulty. Suppose that the chief on Mars was still skeptical and sent her observer back to continue to observe. Sure enough, in that one office, when the telephone rang again, the man didn't pick it up. Her immediate conclusion was that the man must be deaf, but the intercom on his desk buzzed and he answered. Well, if stimulus-response is correct, he should have picked up the phone. How could he ignore the powerful stimulus? The answer to this riddle is that she doesn't know why the man didn't pick up the phone because she cannot see inside his head. All she knows is that he heard it but didn't respond. Since she wants to give an accurate report to her skeptical superior, she faithfully records that she observed 100 people and 99 picked up their phone when it rang. Because Martians, like Earth people, are trained in statistics and correlations, she also decides to report this discrepancy by saying that there is a very high probability (99%) that when a phone rings, someone on Earth will answer it. Just as Dr. Skinner is forced to say that because not every single rat, if he uses hundreds and hundreds of rats, will run the food path, there is a high probability that food will cause a rat to run the food pathway because about 95 out of 100 do. Even Pavlov might have noticed that not every dog salivated when he rang the bell, but most of them did, maybe 99 out of 100. So here we have a basic flaw in S-R psychology that the S-R psychologists correct by saying that because most animals, and therefore most people, seem to respond to stimuli, this is a typical human response. And if the S-R people can't explain why the mavericks don't, what's the difference—most do. Many behavioral scientists are satisfied that our behavior is caused by outside stimulation if 95 out of 100 of us "seem" to respond this way.

But there is a big flaw in this kind of mechanistic statistical reasoning based on external observation. It is our contention that we cannot ignore the internal needs that cause the man not to answer the ringing phone, the rat to run away from food, or the occasional dog not to salivate. We insist that any theory that explains how the brain works must explain how it works all of the time and not just almost all of the time. We also refuse to go along with the S-R approach that attempts to guess what a complex human being with a myriad of internal needs and desires and an infinite number of behaviors will do to satisfy those needs and then concludes from these lucky guesses that S-R is a psychological law as the law of gravity is a physical law. We know that if we hold a coin in our hand and then release it, it will fall to the floor and that the law of gravity holds that we can release the coin once a second for a hundred thousand years and the coin will always fall to the floor. It will never fall sideways. It will never fall up because there is nothing in the coin to make it do anything but fall down. Therefore, if there is such a thing as a psychological law for vertebrate organisms, it ought to work 100% of the time for human beings as well as for lower vertebrates. So, in the case of the man who didn't answer the phone or the rat who didn't press the lever for food, if nothing prevented them from perceiving the stimuli, why didn't they act as the others did? Why didn't their brains work the way many psychologists say their brains should work and most brains "seem" to work? We refuse to accept this discrepancy by saying, "Most brains work that way, and don't worry about the ones that don't." We worry about the ones that don't. We worry just as much as we would worry if, when we were dropping coins from our hand, suddenly one coin flew up in the air and stuck on the ceiling. This would be of tremendous concern to us, and I am sure you and I would question the law of gravity immediately.

What we are going to do here is to try to explain in more detail why these deviant creatures did what they did. We refuse to explain these discrepancies away with statistics. Suppose you like lemonade. You are lucky—a good friend makes you some fresh lemonade, hands it to you, and says "Sweeten it to your own taste." You take a teaspoon of sugar and put it in the lemonade, stir it, and take a sip. If it is still too sour, you take another teaspoon of sugar, stir it, and sip again. It now tastes pretty good, but you add half a teaspoon more and say, "Perfect." This would be puzzling to an observer from Mars. Why did you stop? If one teaspoon makes it better and two teaspoons make it even better and half a teaspoon makes it better yet, why not put in another 15 teaspoons and make it better than ever? Certainly if sugar makes lemonade better, the only reason to stop is that you have run out of sugar. The sweet stimulus of sugar, which we like, should trigger our response to keep putting in sugar, but you and I know and probably the woman from Mars will find out very shortly that it isn't that way at all. We all know that we have something in our head that says we like lemonade about "this" sweet. And when around

2½ teaspoons have reached that point in our head, we stop because more sugar will spoil the lemonade.

The flaw in S-R psychology is now so obvious that to correct it people who believe that our behavior is caused by outside stimuli have to introduce an in-the-head term, satiation. They say we stop adding sugar because we are satiated, but this is just another way of saying that we stop because to continue to add sugar would spoil the lemonade for us. What we believe is that this is not just an isolated instance of in-the-head behavior but that all of our behavior is initiated inside us. What happens in the outside world is important only as it relates to what is already in our head. As we said earlier, based upon our needs, we develop an idea or a picture or a perception of what we want. These pictures or perceptions may change as our needs change in importance, but they are always there. If they are not there, then we will pay little or no attention to what goes on in the outside world. If we have no set idea about a ringing phone it can ring forever and we will pay no attention. Or if we pay attention it may be to leave the room because we have an idea in our head that we like peace and quiet. We believe that the reason the man did not answer the phone was not that he did not have a phone-answering idea but that he had another idea that was even stronger, that said ignore the phone when it rings. Perhaps he owed a lot of money and was afraid that he was going to be dunned that afternoon by phone. Since he didn't want to talk to his creditors, he let the phone ring. The ringing, to him, was a signal to do nothing, a stimulus but with hardly the predictable S-R response.

If we were to hear a loud noise outside, we might or might not investigate. It would depend on whether or not we had some internal idea related to that noise. If we had none, the chances are we would ignore it. The reason most people pick up a ringing phone or most rats run to food or most trained dogs salivate to a bell or most children learn to read is that in some way they have built into their brains the internal perception that these behaviors are *desirable perceptions,* or perceptions that will fulfill their needs. Locked in the maze, ninety-five mice out of a hundred shrug their mouse shoulders and say, "What the hell, food isn't everything, but right now it is just about the only thing." So having food in mind, they press the lever, they get the food, and that food-getting perception then corresponds to food-wanting perception in their heads. Five mice, however, have another idea. They say, "I don't want to be in this cage; what is important to me right now is that I want to be out." Probably every creature from a paramecium up continually has the idea or the perception "I want to be free." So five mice, possibly related to Papillon, have said to themselves, "I don't care about eating, I don't care about electric shocks, all I care about is getting out of here." They will constantly explore the cage. They will take the shocks. They will work a lever that delivers no food. They will check the door, the gate, the latch, every possibility in the cage in an attempt to get out, caring no more about food than you and I would care if we were locked in a cage and it occurred to us that there might be a chance to get out. As we said earlier, these mice control for input. Their endless, exploring behavior is an attempt to gain the idea or the perception in the outside world that they are free, a perception that will satisfy the in-the-head freedom perception that they desire.

If Pavlov's dog hadn't been strapped into position so he could hardly move a muscle, he wouldn't have spent his time salivating when a bell rang. He salivated when the bell rang because he was totally immobilized. To have wanted freedom under these barbaric conditions would have been to torture himself with a desire that he could not fulfill. In his prison he began to think about food, then he was given food, and his old brain caused him to salivate or he couldn't swallow. He soon learned to salivate to the sound of the bell because the bell told him food was on the way. But if he hadn't wanted to eat, that is, if he hadn't had the perception of wanting food already in his head, the bell would have meant nothing to him. Take the dog off the restraints, open the lab door, and that dog will be three miles down the road before you can say Ivan Petrovitch Pavlov. He will be pursuing the freedom that dogs cherish continually in their head, and Pavlov could ring a bell till hell froze over, and it wouldn't affect the dog at all.

We can even go a step farther and say that if we are forced into a specific behavior that does not fulfill our needs, the experience is very painful. Since we control for input, we want very much to keep our behavioral options open, and we resent bitterly being locked into anyone's behavior. For example, most of us take many objective tests, like true-false or multiple choice, tests that, especially in the case of multiple choice, are very painful because they force our brain to work in a way it was not designed to work. This doesn't mean the brain can't be used this way; we can also use our hands for shovels and open beer bottles with our teeth, but when we force our brain to accept the single answer demanded by an objective test, we feel the pain of this unnatural demand. The mandatory answer is often an input we don't want because in our head is a better answer. Our whole being cries out for us to modify or to explain even the best answer, but we are not given this choice. It would take a genius to construct a test that could satisfy us all. The "genius" seems to be in constructing tests that satisfy no one.

Let's take a final example to make sure that we understand what has been explained so far. In Chapter 1 I talked about how strongly I felt the need to belong. Here we would say that whenever I feel this need is unsatisfied, I concentrate upon controlling for or gaining the perception, or the input, that right now I do belong. Perhaps I want to gain the specific input that I belong with my wife because right now that idea is in my head. To gain that specific *input* I will contact the world through all of my senses. Through them I will try to perceive or gain the input that my wife cares for me now.

Does she, for example, talk to me, write to me, look at me, hug me, kiss me, cook for me, or work for me? Somehow or other does she provide me with perceptions that with her I belong? These perceptions, one or more, are an example of the input that my control system may desire right now.

To gain that input, or one or more of those desirable perceptions, my control system starts to generate some output which may be any combination of doing, thinking, or feeling that my output system can conjure up. I may, for example, cry, scream, threaten, hug, kiss, write, phone, send money, become despondent, threaten suicide, or create an imaginary wife. The more I feel I don't belong the more I push my behavioral system to try to get my wife to attend to me. If I can find a behavior that corresponds to what she wants, then I will get the attention I desire. If I knew that my wife's brain was an input control system I might stop my desperate, almost random behavior and try to figure out what she wants from me. Not knowing this, too often I try to force her into doing what she doesn't want to do, but it doesn't work. And it never will. She is not a stimulus-response creature; none of us is.

4

The New Brain as an Input Control System

❧ ❦ ❧

It is never easy to buy an expensive gift for someone that we care for very much. Constantly the thought passes through our mind *will she like it?* We ask the salesperson, consult a good friend of hers, but still it's a tense moment when she opens the gift. Will a look of exhilaration flood her face, or will there be a more controlled, almost forced expression of thanks that tells us the gift missed by half a mile? Here, even when you know a person well, it's possible to miss badly. Think how much harder it is when you know little or nothing about the other person. That's why people advise you, when you don't know a person well, to get a gift in a department store where it can be exchanged. In terms of this book, what we are talking about are the specific desires that right now are important to us and how hard it is to guess what these may be in someone else. In Chapter 1, I spent a lot of time talking in general terms about the kinds of things I and probably most people want, for example, love. But in the real world, when we try to express love, gifts are only one of the many ways we can do it. Today we hope it may mean the gold chain that we think she has had her heart set on for so long. Our guess was a thin, finely wrought chain that can be worn in one loop or two. We were right, it's exactly what she wanted and she is ecstatic. And we are ecstatic. But how did love get to become a gold chain today, a trip to Hawaii tomorrow, a walk through the hills on Sunday, or listening to problems she is having at work on Monday night? All of these and thousands more are love, or, to malaprop the old movie, love is a many specific(ed) thing.

Derived from the general needs which were probably built in during the past 3 million years and which we all share are a world of specific desires or needs which are not genetic at all. They are learned. We begin to learn them almost at birth, when love may be a dry diaper, a soft nipple, or a toss in the air followed by a hug and a kiss. Even as a tiny infant, we quickly learn what to want, and we spend our whole lives building into our new brain an almost infinite number of specific desires that are important to us but may or may not be important to anyone else.

In practice, like a thermostat which controls for an exact temperature, we always control for specific needs. We are usually aware of the general needs, that is, we can easily relate the gift of the gold chain to love, but in our day-to-day existence it is the specific needs that concern us. When you forget an important birthday or anniversary, try to get away with saying "What's the difference as long as I love you?" and see how poorly this washes. She knows you love her, but every once in a while a tangible expression still seems to be needed. It is as if the general needs discussed in Chapter 1 serve as a large background. They activate the system, but they themselves need to be satisfied or controlled for in many specific ways.

When I want to have fun I must find a way to have it. I can't just fun. I can swim, sail, watch a ball game, or read a good book, but to have fun I must do something specific. Most of the time when we talk about fulfilling a general need, we are just talking, or perhaps hoping someone will suggest something specific. It's only when we're stuck for something specific to do that we find ourselves referring to a lack of general need. For example, in psychiatric practice many clients lament how they aren't loved, or appreciated, or they never do anything that's fun. This can be a trap for therapists who fail to focus, who keep the conversation general, when the problem can only be solved with specific plans.

Although this is not a technical book, it seems worthwhile here to mention that research, especially from the study of people with serious brain damage, tends to show that the general needs like love, worth, fun, and freedom appear to reside within the frontal lobe, the large bulging frontal part of the new brain, the part that was the last to develop fully. Most of our frontal lobe developed in the past 3 million years, another bit of evidence that it was during this recent time of our 12-million-year history that our needs became so intense. The size of the frontal lobe, much smaller than ours in the higher primates, is one of the obvious differences between our brain and theirs. If our huge, recently developed frontal lobe is the seat of the general needs, that is, the strong needs such as love and worth discussed in Chapter 1, it would follow that severe injury to the frontal lobe would produce a person who needs very little. In practice this is exactly what happens. In fact, surgical lobotomy stemmed from the discovery that when very disturbed people suffered frontal-lobe damage they became more tranquil. While this is true, it is now well recognized that this calmness is at the expense of the desires. After all, if you don't want much of anything except to keep alive, an old brain function, and you have food and shelter, what is there to get upset about? If there is a part of our brain that makes us uniquely human it is the frontal lobe. This does not mean that beside the general needs there are no specific learned needs within the frontal lobe; probably there are. Specific needs can be any place and every place in the new brain. Maybe many of them are a product of interconnections all over the cortex, but the general needs do seem to be localized in the very large frontal lobe. Without it we become lesser beings whose cortex is pretty much in the service of their old brain, much more like a fish than a human being. Our drive, our life force, our humanity, what keeps us vital and seeking to satisfy the hundreds of specific desires that move us day by day, these are almost all in the frontal lobe of the new brain.

What happens is that everything we want is learned and then stored in our new brain as memory, but actually what is stored or remembered *is the perception of exactly what we want.* As we explained in the last chapter our brain works by controlling for input, or to gain the perception of what we want from the world around us that coincides as much as possible to a perception we had already built into our head. It turns out that our loved one had a perception in her head of a fine gold chain, and when she opened her present and there it was, what she saw, felt, and hung around her neck was exactly what had been in her head. When this happened, or when in this instance her new brain control system worked perfectly, she exclaimed with joy, experiencing a small ecstatic moment that makes life worth living.

You might ask how that perception got into her head; the answer is no one exactly knows, but out of the sum total of her real and imaginary experiences it gradually formed and became more and more tangible. I'm sure you have heard the expression "I want it so bad I can taste it." This is a colloquial way of saying I have something in my head that is so real to me that the best way I can describe it is with one of the oldest of the new-brain perceptions, taste. It is also a way of saying I am controlling for whatever it is very strongly right now. I don't think it's so important to try to find out exactly why any specific desire gets into our head. The point is we all have in our new brain a huge storehouse filled with exact memories of the perceptions we desire. And we are constantly adding perceptions we want and occasionally deleting those we no longer want. It is likely that my loved one will continue to keep the perception of a gold chain in the storehouse of things she wants and now, perhaps, add an opal pendant because it would look so nice hanging from the chain. When I was young I loved to drive fast, but now I have deleted speeding from my storehouse because it no longer fills any need for me.

This constantly changing storehouse of all that we want could be called our *internal world,* or the world in our head that we build from our general needs. This is a very personal world. In it we have the perception of all the things we want, for example, our loved ones, our hopes for success in our work, our aspirations for our children, the games we wish to play, and our desire to be free and unfettered in our thoughts. This world is so important to the way our brain functions that we will devote all of Chapters 5, 7, and 8 to describing how this world is built and how it affects us as we live our lives. Here let us assume it exists and from it come all the specific perceptions that we want or, in terms of this book, that we control for daily. It was from this world in my love's head that I hoped she was presently controlling for the perception of a gold chain. Had she not wanted that chain, my gift would have fallen flat. And as I said, there is no way that I can know exactly what she or anyone is controlling for. I can guess and, the more I know a person, guess correctly, but that's the best I can do. Even if I ask and she tells me this is what she wants or if she tells me without my asking, I still can't be sure because she may love me and think that it is important to me that she have a chain. It's all very complicated and there is no total explanation for why we want what we want, because usually what we want is an attempt to satisfy more than one need. My loved one may have wanted the gold chain because its beauty pleased her and made her feel more worthwhile, and she also may have wanted it because she loves me and knew I wanted her to have it. Perhaps the best we can say here is that some perceptions are more important than others and that we always want something.

We believe it is easier to understand the relationship between our basic or general needs and our internal world if it
is pictured:

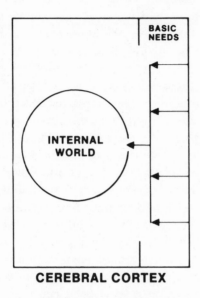

CEREBRAL CORTEX

In this diagram of the new brain or cerebral cortex we see
the basic needs on the right. There is also a partial division
on the right that suggests these needs are in the frontal lobe.
From the confluence of these needs we build the world in
our head or our internal world. I show four arrows, not because
there are exactly four basic needs—there are maybe more or
less—I do so only to indicate that there are at least several. I
also don't label them, I invite my readers to search their minds
and call them as they see fit. What *I* believe is in Chapter 1.

In the last chapter when we discussed the thermostat as
analogous to the new brain we mentioned that inside the thermostat there must be a place where the temperature it wants
or controls for can be compared with the temperature it per-

ceives the room to be. Since the thermostat has only one simple need, it needs only one such place. What we believe is that our new brain functions in a similar way, that is, it also has a place where we compare what we want, or what we are controlling for at the time, with what we perceive in the outside or external world. But because in our internal world we may have hundreds, perhaps thousands, of specific needs, we probably have not one but many places where we can make this comparison. There is in theory at least one place for each of the countless specific desires, like a gold chain, that comprise our internal or personal world.

In practice, however, since we don't want everything at once—for example, while she opens the box containing the gold chain, little else may be on her mind—there are probably far fewer of these comparing places than there are desires. Since in a sense we can open and close these places (for example, when we stop actively wanting a gold chain, we close down the gold-chain comparing place), I would like to call these places *comparing stations* because we usually think of stations as places that open and close. Stations can also be very active, barely active, inactive, and totally shut down. For example, if we are controlling for food we can actively want to eat or barely want to eat, perhaps because we are engrossed in a good book which is far more important than making dinner. As we get hungrier we will control more and more actively for food, and our food comparing station will become predominant, our book reading station less important. *Therefore, when we want anything or, in these terms, when our new-brain control system is controlling for anything, it does so by sending that perception to an active comparing station.* In these stations the perception of what we want from our internal world is compared with whatever perceptions are coming in through our senses, or input systems, from the external world. The perceptions that we actively want right now we could sensibly call *reference perceptions* because they set the reference level

Carol—

Please order
me a 1982 pocket
planner.

Thanks

Vickie

---

reprimand pulled

	Before/After	Team Leader
nt		
	Before/After	Team Leader
	After	
/	Before/After	Team Leader
	After	
ion	During	Community Worker Volunteers	Team Leader
on	During	Peer Counselor Volunteers
on	During	Community Worker Volunteers	Team Leader

or the standard for what we want. It is against these that we compare what we sense from the world. Before my loved one received her gift, she had sent a reference perception of approximately the chain she wanted to an active comparing station where, when the time came, she could compare the gift with that reference perception. With this in mind let us expand the control-system diagram to include the comparing station and the sensory or perceptual system.

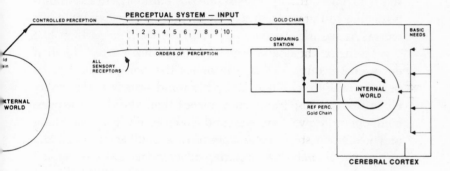

In this diagram, the perceptual system and the comparing station which are actually inside the new brain have been depicted to make their functions easier to understand. The diagram shows a person who right now is controlling for a gold chain. She has sent the gold-chain reference perception to the active comparing station, and she has just opened the gift box. The gift exactly fits what she had in mind, a situation which is shown on the diagram as the arrow, which is her perception of the chain, going through her perceptual system to the open gold-chain comparing station. Because her control system has provided her with exactly the *input* she wants, this is a *controlled perception*. The fact that it is controlled is shown on the diagram as the two arrows meeting in the comparing station, that is, she now sees in the external world exactly what she wants.

The perception system contains all of our sensory receptors, but it does much more than sense. It also interprets what we sense, doing so from simple to complex, through at least ten orders which we will explain in detail in Chapter 7. Here it is sufficient to know that all we perceive, or all of our input, passes through this system and what we want goes directly to one or more active comparing stations. If we are not controlling for what we perceive, we pay little attention.

It is also important to note on the diagram the arrow coming out of the comparing station, starting at the intersection of the controlled perception and the reference perception and returning to the internal world. This shows how we build our world. As we have explained, when we want something like a gold chain, an idea of it is already in our world. We then get a chain, but now, as we see it, it is not just an idea; it becomes the exact chain that we wanted. And it is that exact chain that we build back into our internal world as a precise component. Now, if we should lose the chain, it is that chain and no other that we will want to replace it. What was originally an idea of a chain has become, in our head, an exact chain.

To take another example, when we were a tiny baby we wanted comfort. Someone comforted us. As we got the comfort we also noted who did the comforting, and we learned it was mother. Then along with comfort we built the idea of a comforting mother into our world, and soon when we wanted comfort we wouldn't be satisfied unless we got it from mother. No one else would do. If we didn't have a mother we would build in anyone who did it for us.

In contrast, the thermostat is always satisfied with what it gets; it neither wants nor takes note of anything more than the feedback that the room is 68 degrees. We are like a special thermostat that could decide that it would accept heated air only from an Acme furnace. If the Acme broke down it would not accept heat from an Ajax replacement. *This ability to add to and enhance our world when we, more than successfully, control our perceptions is one of the living qualities that separates us from machines.* It is based upon the fact that unlike machines (and most lower animals) we have multiple and often conflicting needs. We constantly struggle to build a huge internal world to try to satisfy these complex forces that drive us, and if we don't like the people that run the Ajax Co. we'll freeze before we use their product. Look again at the diagram to make sure that you see this arrow which runs back from the controlled perception into the internal world.

To explain further how this works let us say that right now, as I write this chapter by hand on a yellow pad, and see the words forming in front of my eyes, sentence by sentence, *I am controlling for this book,* and in doing so I have at least two comparing stations operating actively. Besides the overall book station I also have a Chapter 4 comparing station open, and to this station I have already sent the internal reference perception that today I want to make progress on the chapter. Therefore, as I write and read what I write, I am now sending the words to the Chapter 4 station where these actual words are being compared with reference ideas that I already have in the station. As I read I stop; it doesn't seem correct. What I see is not precisely what I want. I think, I write a little more, I scratch it out, I proceed laboriously through a difficult paragraph. Then I get it. I write rapidly and smoothly, and a few good sentences appear on the paper. These sentences are now a *controlled perception,* often better than I anticipated, and I build them into my internal world.

What happened, and this is what is happening all the time, is that in this comparing station I am constantly comparing what is coming in (my words and sentences) with some built-in set of ideas for the chapter. For a while what was coming in didn't compare very well. I felt I was close but I wasn't there. What was then coming to this comparing station was an *uncontrolled perception,* a perception that was not what I wanted. And what I was experiencing in my Chapter 4 comparing station was a *perceptual error,* which is the difference between my reference perception (or reference level) and what

I had written. This is exactly the same as when the thermostat wanted 68 degrees and experienced 62 degrees. The difference between these two temperatures is the perceptual error. This perceptual error activates the output system; in this case it turns on the furnace. In my case this error caused me to change my behavior, to slow down, to cast about for different words, all in the attempt to send better words to the comparing station, words that would satisfy the reference levels in the Chapter 4 station. If I finish this draft of the chapter satisfactorily there will be no error; I will close down the Chapter 4 comparing station, and for a while there will be no more work on this chapter. I will continue to control for the book; that goes on all the time until the book is finished. In that whole book station I will have an error until it is accepted by my publisher, but tomorrow I will open a Chapter 5 comparing station as part of my whole book control system. If I get stuck on 5, as I probably will, I may have to go back and open up Chapters 1, 2, 3, and 4 comparing stations until I finish the book.

Let us now show the diagram with an uncontrolled perception and a perceptual error.

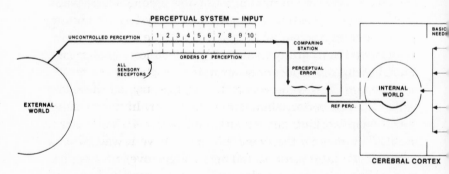

Here we see me having difficulty with Chapter 4. I have an idea of what I want to say, but I just can't seem to say it. All the words on the yellow pad (which is in the outside world) are coming through my sensors and perceptual system, but they are not what I want. Therefore instead of meeting the reference perception arrow (as did the gold chain) they are coming in some distance away *as an uncontrolled perception.* My Chapter 4 control system is desperately trying to find the right words, but it hasn't been able to so far. The separation between the arrows in the comparing station is the difference between the perception I want from my internal world and the uncontrolled perception I have right now. As stated *this difference we will call the perceptual error.* It could also be called the perceptual discrepancy or the perceptual gap, but we will call it the *perceptual error* (or mostly just *error*) because this is the control-system term which is commonly used. Some people have objected to the term error because it connotes a failing, even a moral failing. We do not use it in that sense, only in the sense that it is not what we want, and like all errors we will work to correct it.

This leads us to the next important concept. When I suffer a perceptual error, as I do frequently as I write this book, I have the strong urge to correct it. Like the thermostat which starts the furnace when it detects a temperature difference (or error), the error in my open Chapter 4 comparing station will activate my output or my behavioral system. It does so by generating a signal which we will call the error signal. In my brain this is probably an electrical or chemical signal, maybe both, but this signal does only one thing—it activates my behavioral system. This is the system I will use to try to reduce the error or, even better, eliminate it altogether. In this example I will keep working and reworking Chapter 4 until I get it right. (This may be the twentieth time I have reworked it.) I still detect a little error, so tomorrow I'll go over it again, but it does seem it's getting closer to what I know it should be in my Chapter 4 comparing station. How I actually behave is so complex that we will devote Chapter 6 to explain it, but here it is important to understand that for all practical purposes *all my behavior is initiated by the error signal caused by the detection of an error in an open comparing station. When there is perceptual error there is always an error signal, and I must do something. It is a neurological fact of life; it cannot be disregarded.* The only way that I can avoid dealing with this error is to close down the station and thus cut off the error. This is not easy to do, as in this example it would mean closing down at the same time the whole book comparing station, something I am hardly ready to do. I think I have at least twenty more reworkings in me before I contemplate giving up.

Here is a more complete control system where I have now added the error signal and the behavioral or output system.

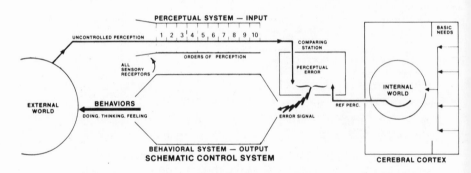

What we now have is almost the whole system. We see the error signal that is generated by the perceptual error which in turn activated our behavioral system or our output. Now we try with all of the behaviors at our disposal to do something to some part of the world—including ourselves, since we are part of the world—to gain the perception that we want. As you can see by the large arrow that comes out of this system at the left, our behavior is made up of all we do, think, and much of what we feel. We will discuss feelings in detail in Chapter 5. Here it is sufficient to say that when we reduce an error it feels good, when we increase an error it feels bad.

This leads us to the final diagram, shown below, which depicts two states of this control system. Here we see both the uncontrolled state, as when I am struggling with this chapter, and the controlled state, as when I successfully finish it. The information source and the components of the behavioral system, shown here for completeness, will be explained in Chapter 6.

BEHAVIOR: THE CONTROL OF PERCEPTION PSYCHOLOGY (BCP)

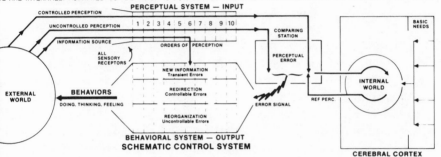

WE ARE INTERNALLY MOTIVATED OUR BEHAVIOR IS PURPOSEFUL AND IT IS FLEXIBLE BECAUSE WE CONTROL FOR INPUT

Remember, all except the external or outside world is actually within the new brain or cerebral cortex. I have pulled out the perceptual system, the comparing station, and the behavioral system so that their relationship to each other can be better seen. This diagram is reproduced inside the front cover for easy reference because from here on we will refer to it frequently.

Also following Powers's lead, for shorthand purposes we will call this input-control-system functioning of our new brain BCP, where B stands for behavior, C for control, and P for perceptions. Our Behavior is our constant attempt to Control our Perceptions, or BCP. From here on we will call what we discuss in this book *BCP psychology* or just *BCP*, in contrast to the usual Stimulus-Response or S-R, or "common sense" psychology, which we hope BCP will supersede.

To make this contrast clear, now that we know more about BCP psychology, let us again take a look at Pavlov's dog in its restraints and ask ourselves what comparing stations the dog had open. Considering his predicament he must have kept his comparing station for freedom wide open for quite a while, but if he was harnessed too long, eventually he would reduce it almost to inactivity. This is because it would be too painful to keep an active station open for a perception that never seemed to come. When he finally accepted his predicament and became "conditioned," only his eating comparing station remained active, because this was the only station in which his control system worked. Pavlov would not allow him to control successfully for anything but food. Therefore to condition people or to get people to do consistently what you desire them to do, you must either have enough power over them so you can dictate what stations it makes sense to keep active. Or as we described in the last chapter, you must be able to guess what stations they ordinarily keep open. To do this well they must be much subordinate to you not only in power and intelligence but also in the complexity of their needs. Dogs are easier to "condition" than people because they need less and it's easier to guess what they want. People, who need more, are much more stubborn about closing down stations. But even a dog, as soon as it is released, will at least temporarily reactivate its freedom station. It may even open up an antibell station and be hard to catch around bells and buzzers in the future. Therefore, the part of S-R psychology that is called conditioning is just an exercise in power over weaker, less intelligent, less needful creatures who have little or no sense of the future and who are making the best of a bad situation. People are not that way at all. We need a lot, and it is very important to us which stations we keep open. Because we constantly have a sense of the future, we are in many cases prepared to fight and even die to keep them open.

At this point I would like to use a few common situations to explain further the difference between BCP and S-R when dealing with people. For example, Frank is a manager and wants more production out of Bill, one of his salesmen. Since Frank "instinctively" believes that Bill will respond to a stimulus that he, as manager, can generate, he calls him into the office and tells him that he is dissatisfied with his work. Frank threatens that if Bill doesn't improve next month, when he is due to get a raise, he is not going to get it. Frank believes, as bosses have believed for thousands of years, that Bill will respond to his threat (stimulus) by working harder. In practice, many employees do. That is why S-R psychology is so widely accepted. But it is also known that not every employee will respond to threats by working harder. Let's say that Bill begins to work even more erratically. He starts reporting late, becomes hard to get along with, and once in a while comes to work under the influence of alcohol. To Frank this is a puzzling response, and even though he threatens to fire him, Bill continues his poor performance and ultimately Frank lets him go. In this not too uncommon example, the manager didn't understand the way the salesman's brain worked. He treated him as if he would respond to a painful threat by working harder. In practice, Bill did change, but from Frank's standpoint he got worse, not better. Frank wrongly assumed that Bill had the same comparing stations open that he himself had. But this assumption is often wrong. In this case Bill wasn't controlling for money, and the punishment didn't work. Or if he was controlling for money, perhaps it was by painting not by selling the company's product. The control system is the same, money, but the comparing stations are different. Therefore, while rewards or punishments do frequently change behavior they only do so in the direction desired by the rewarder or punisher if in this case both the boss and subordinate have the same comparing stations open, a situation much less common than most "bosses" believe.

Now let's look at the same example in terms of BCP. First of all, no one, not your boss, your husband, your wife, your child, your mother, your father, or your best friend, can actually know what goes on inside your head. They never know your present internal reference levels or what you are controlling for. All they can do is attempt to guess what those levels may be. Since Bill worked less, not more, under threat, we can assume that Frank guessed wrong. Perhaps Bill was controlling for a desire to leave the job and paint full time because, like Gauguin, he saw himself as a frustrated artist. His comparing station to paint pictures was wide open, his comparing station to sell vacuum cleaners was almost shut down. It was open only enough to earn a little money, but his job performance was poor. He didn't perceive much error because when it came to selling vacuum cleaners, he was satisfied with his small effort. The threat to deny him a raise was happily perceived as an excuse to shut down the selling-vacuum-cleaners comparing station altogether. Why work at all if there is to be no raise? As long as he was paid a little for doing almost no work he had little error and no excuse to quit, but when he was denied the raise, he used this as an excuse to stop working almost completely. He could now open up his painting station wider, because with no raise he saw even less reason to continue to make a selling effort. When his boss threatened him it reduced his error; he didn't want to sell anyway, so he slacked off in random ways and got fired, which left him completely free to paint.

It is also possible that he couldn't explain to his wife, who needed money to run the house, that he really wanted to quit and paint, because her upset would cause a perceptual error in the I-care-for-my-wife station. But when he was "unjustly" denied a raise she could accept his slacking off (who would want to put out for a boss like Frank?) and this also helped. It gets complicated: even in this simple example there are quite a few stations open, and some may even be in conflict with each other, but regardless, Bill did perceive the threat as beneficial and error reducing, a perception far different from Frank's. S-R psychology would find it difficult to explain this and much other behavior which seems to fail to respond to the proper stimulus.

Therefore, if you want to change a person's behavior, you must first try to find out what he is controlling for and which of his comparing stations for that need are now open. Modern operant S-R psychologists try to do this, but when they do they are using BCP. But even if they do find out what someone is controlling for, that's only the first part; to get the desired behavior they have somehow or other to help him to get the need-fulfilling perception and also to do what they want. In this case it may be impossible; I'm sure that having Bill paint vacuum cleaners would not have done the trick. Getting fired might, of course, produce other complications in Bill's life, but the point is if we want to motivate a person we have a better chance if, following BCP instead of guessing, we sit down and talk with him to try to find out what it is he is controlling for and if it is at all compatible with the work assignment.

Let's take one more example and follow it through a step further. A tenth-grade teacher in a tough, inner-city school has a pupil, Jim, who ordinarily sits quietly in his classroom but does little or no schoolwork. The teacher, in an attempt to get Jim to work, asks him to read in front of the class. The student, a poor reader, stumbles, falters, and finally slams the book down on the teacher's desk, calls the teacher a son-of-a-bitch, and walks out of the class. Jim is then suspended from school for gross insubordination. When the suspension is over, he comes back to class, but where before he sat quietly, he now becomes a constant irritant. Eventually the teacher sends him to the office, where he is again disciplined with a suspension. When Jim returns to class, he starts singing in a loud voice. The frustrated teacher tells him to get down to the office. Words ensue, and the student physically assaults the teacher and is expelled from school. Using S-R psychology, the teacher tried to force the boy to participate, following the ancient S-R reasoning of "I can *make* you behave," and when that failed, the student was expelled. The ironic part is he was expelled for a behavior that he didn't have in the first place; he had been quiet when the episode started.

Let's look at this from BCP psychology. The teacher is controlling to teach everyone in his class something. He has a comparing station open in which he has the reasonable reference level "I want to perceive that everybody in this class is learning something." When he perceives Jim paying absolutely no attention, this high error perception generates an error signal which causes him to choose the not-too-smart behavior of asking the boy to read aloud when he probably knows he can hardly read. The teacher, still controlling overall for teaching, is now specifically comparing for reading, and it is from his student-must-read comparing station that he asks the boy to read. Then when Jim responds with a disturbance, the teacher experiences a large error, throws him out in an attempt to correct the error, and the vicious circle starts. This is an illustration of the fact that when a large error signal drives behavior, it doesn't necessarily or even usually drive it in a better direction. This ineffective behavior caused less effective teaching, and a small Greek tragedy ensued. After Jim was expelled, the teacher could say he was no good, he didn't want to learn, he had no right to assault me. As the expulsion perception floods into the teacher's comparing station for classroom management, a station that for most teachers is always open, the usual behavior is to rationalize, to attempt to avoid perceiving his part in the unhappy result.

Now let's look at it from the student's standpoint. Jim has long since given up the idea that he can learn in school. He is, in BCP terms, controlling only a tiny bit if at all for learning, and all of his comparing stations related to learning are shut down. This shutdown has nothing to do with this particular teacher. He had given up before he even went into that class. What Jim is primarily controlling for is status, and status is to be cool. In one of his status comparing stations the reference perception for school is that as long as I am treated with respect by the teachers and the students of this building, I am satisfied. I am not interested right now in learning, but I do want and even demand respect. As long as the teacher respects me enough to leave me alone, I will sit quietly. Jim has no error relating to academics as he is not controlling for learning, and therefore he has no academic behavior. What the teacher did was to cause the boy to have a massive perception of looking stupid in front of the class. To deal with a huge status error, he behaved as he did and the first suspension resulted. His behavior was his desperate, although not too successful, attempt to regain status. At that point the student is not thinking rationally or reasonably about rules, teachers, principals, suspensions, school boards, or paddles. All he is thinking about is that I have this tremendous pain, because suddenly he is not perceiving himself the way he would like to perceive himself, as cool. When he slams the book down, he gets the whole class's attention; when he calls the teacher a son-of-a-bitch, the students silently applaud, because there are few students anywhere who don't keep a comparing station open for the perception of teacher discomfort. That behavior reduces a lot of errors besides his and by it he regains some status.

The problem was that the student and teacher were controlling different quantities. The teacher was controlling for his belief "I have to teach everybody." The student was controlling for the fact "I will stay cool as long as they treat me with some respect, and leaving me alone is satisfactory." As soon as Jim was asked to read, the problem became unsolvable by the use of S-R psychology.

Could the problem be handled better using BCP psychology? Let's say the teacher understands BCP and perceives the same student not doing anything in class. He takes a reasonable guess that Jim has no currently active comparing station for learning in this particular class, probably not in any class. He is not certain what the student has in his mind, but if he has been around a while, he may suspect that this quiet student is controlling for status based upon the general need to feel worthwhile. Now understanding BCP, instead of asking Jim to stand up and read, something which the teacher can easily predict will cause him to stumble and make a fool of himself, the teacher asks him, when he enters the class, if he would stay a moment after and chat. He does this in a respectful, interested, friendly way. Since we usually control for respect, for care, and to be treated as a person, the teacher guesses correctly that Jim will respond favorably, and they talk.

During this chat the teacher says, "I'm upset because you are not learning as much as I would like you to. Is there anything I can do to help?" The teacher says this quietly and confidentially. Now they are both controlling for care and concern. The young man perceives that his usually large care-concern error is being reduced by the teacher's interest and the time the teacher is spending with him. When we are controlling for the same quantity, we tend to listen to each other because what each of us says comes into an active station. Jim, sensing the teacher's concern and interest, starts to control a tiny bit for learning and says he would like to learn but he can't read the text. The teacher suggests that maybe he could get Jim a tutor, perhaps someone who has a high status in the school so that the student wouldn't feel that he was losing face. If the tutoring works, the student would then open a comparing station for reading and begin to do some schoolwork. As Jim responds positively to the tutoring, he opens up more school comparing stations and he begins to control more for learning. He now begins to have a reference level for learning which is similar enough to the teacher's so that learning in class becomes a possibility. BCP has given the teacher a chance. The "I'll stimulate him and he'll learn the way I want him to," of S-R was totally destructive. Although we will take this up in more detail later, we see in this example a practical application of BCP to good counseling.

5

Pure Feelings and Feeling Behaviors

~§~

Several years ago I was watching the final day of the U.S. Open golf tournament with one of my sons. To the surprise of everyone a young unknown had the lead, but in the last few holes he began to slip. In a finish filled with drama he had to make a fifteen-foot putt or go into a playoff with the favorite. The golf gods were with him; he calmly stroked it in and then exploded with joy. At that point I nudged my son and said, "Take a good look; what you are seeing is very likely the happiest moment he will ever experience."

My guess may have been wrong, but it was a time of such pure euphoria for the golfer that what I said seemed possible. In any case, it was a peak moment, one that all of us wish for, and most of us experience a few times in our life. And that capacity to generate directly the perception of pure joy, we believe, is built into our comparing stations. We experience it whenever we or good fortune suddenly eliminate a large perceptual error. To understand what we mean, try to imagine that you are sitting inside a large active comparing station. Place your hands far apart but in a position so that you can bring them together easily with a fast, loud clap. Think of your right hand as the reference perception, in this case, the overwhelming desire to sink the winning putt. Imagine your left hand as your perception of the tense situation of the eighteenth green. The ball looks to be about a half a mile from the tiny hole. Now bring your hands together as quickly as you can with a loud clap. This is how I think of a large error being suddenly eliminated or closed in a very active comparing station. It closes with a bang and that closure is euphoric. Suddenly there is no perceptual error at all, our behavior becomes a random stumbling, jumping, hugging, laughing, crying expression of joy as we experience a short time with everything we want, a moment with no error at all.

Suppose, however, that fortune had not smiled that day, that the young golfer three-putted the eighteenth green and lost the tournament after leading all afternoon. Now, where there had been substantial error before he putted, there would be a huge error; our arms are not long enough to illustrate the miserable situation in the active comparing station. Think of it as if our left hand flew off and landed five miles down the road; this is analogous to the pain and misery associated with this sudden increase in error.

Even though we have not yet discussed feelings in any depth, we did say in Chapter 3 that most of what we feel consists of feeling behaviors. Here we would like to explain this concept in detail and also explain the other source of what we feel, how we experience at the comparing station the pure joy or misery we have just described. These quick intense feelings are built into the comparing stations because through the perception of sudden pain or pleasure we get an almost instant evaluation of the state of our control system in a way that we cannot deny. Millions of years ago when our ancestors were walking down the trail, satisfied and in good control, suddenly they may have come face to face with a sabre-tooth tiger. At that moment they needed a quick evaluation of their present behavior, and most likely we are descended from those who got it. The sudden pain that they experienced gave them that evaluation, they didn't have to stop to think. They knew instantly through the sudden appearance of this pain that they should mobilize their behavioral system and start running. And on the other side of the coin, if we did not experience a sudden burst of pure sensual pleasure when we culminate the sexual act, would we be as interested in reproducing as we obviously have been? Pain tells us to change what we are doing, pleasure says stand pat. These strong feelings are always conscious, always short in duration, and we always can tell them apart. We do not mistake pain for pleasure. And each of us probably feels these strong comparing-station feelings in her or his own unique way. For example, when I experience a crushing disappointment, unexpected upset, or sudden danger, I get a sharp, tearing pain in my chest, something similar to what I imagine a heart attack may feel like. The pain is so severe that I sometimes worry for a moment, am I having a heart attack? Others I know describe it in their stomach, back, or head; some say it's just pain all over. We all have our own way of experiencing it. On the other hand, when I hit the jackpot in something I have wanted for a long time, I get an all-over feeling of total exhilaration. I don't want to do or say anything, I just want to sit and savor the moment for as long as it will last.

In either case, however, neither the pure pain nor the total euphoria lasts very long. An hour would be unusual, fifteen minutes more likely. After the euphoria fades, I may continue to feel good, but not great, for weeks or even months if I recall the triumph. The acute pure pain of disappointment also dissipates quickly. After minutes the chest pain stops, but I still feel a dull, heavy ache that extends into my head and acts like a strait jacket on my movements. This also slowly fades, and in about ten or twenty minutes, if I don't get going and do something active to reduce the error, it usually blends into what was briefly mentioned in Chapter 3 as a *feeling behavior* that may last for days. In my case what I usually choose is depression, or, as we will explain next, I choose to depress. In people that I know or have worked with the depressing may last for years. Lasting for life is not unheard of.

Painful feeling behaviors like depressing, which until BCP I called depression, do not come from a comparing station. They arise from my behavioral system, that is, they are the feeling part of how I perceive the behaviors I choose when I attempt to reduce an error. Because it is generated by my perception of a behavior or behaviors, depression has a *doing component* of lethargy and inactivity, usually coupled with tension, a *thinking component* in which I may think I'm worthless and hopeless, and a *feeling component* which is the depression. Ordinarily, we tend to call any behavior by the part that we perceive as dominant, for example, we call what we do when we move quickly running, or when we try to solve a problem we say we are thinking. So it makes sense that when we try to reduce an error through a behavior where the perception of depression predominates we call this a *feeling behavior* or *depressing*. This is, for most readers, a new concept and one which is further explained in the next chapter when we take a look at our whole behavioral system. Here it is only necessary that the reader understand that it is possible for what we ordinarily think of as a feeling to be generated by a behavior or our perception of an output of our control system. In the sabretooth tiger example, when I suddenly see the tiger I experience the pure pain of the error, but as I run I experience the fear. Here, however, we would say that as I run I am mostly aware of *fearing*. The running is, in terms of how I feel, the lesser component of my behavior.

Thus we have two major sources of our feelings. The first is the intense, but short-lived, pure feeling generated by a substantial increase or decrease of an error in an active comparing station which quickly tells us the state of our control system. The second is the less acute, but longer lasting perception of a behavior or output which, miserable as it may be, is our current attempt to reduce the error. Most of the time when we complain of feeling badly we are not talking about the short-term, pure, comparing-station feelings, we are talking about long-term, miserable behaviors. This is because when we are upset (or euphoric) our *pure* feelings are so obvious and so painful that to talk about them is superfluous, and few people of any sensitivity would ask. Personally I cringe when a crass TV reporter asks a family whose house has just been washed away how they feel. No one had to ask the young man who won the golf tournament how he felt, and when several reporters did, he was not too articulate. Without error in the only control system operating right then, he had no need to talk, and his few remarks were obviously inadequate to describe how good he felt.

Unlike pure feelings, feeling behaviors are not always obvious. At times we even tend to try to hide them both from ourselves and others, saying we feel fine or composed when we are terribly upset or angry. We do this because we believe that if we express how we feel right now we may increase our error. For example, if I tell the whole world how much I am angering right now because my car won't start, I may lose friends I know I need.

Feeling behaviors, which are initiated by substantial errors and large error signals, are always miserable, unhappy behaviors like depressing, anxietying, guilting, headaching, fearing, angering, hating, or lying. When we are pushed by a large error usually caused by a conflict, which we will discuss in detail in Chapter 9, and we have no good behavior to reduce it, the urgency to rid ourselves of it makes us rigid. We easily get locked into a painful behavior as if this were all we could do. Try to stop depressing the next time you choose this painful behavior and you will see what I mean. It's like trying to change horses in midstream. To change we usually need a temporary respite from the error that is driving us. In part this is what good counseling should provide. A warm, interested counselor, just being there and helping us to focus on alternate behaviors, causes enough error reduction so that with less error we gain the flexibility to figure out a better behavior than depressing. Keep in mind that good counseling is changing verbs not nouns.

When we are upset we also tend to forget that most of us have a vast array of long-term behaviors which feel very good and which we call upon every day of our life. Probably in the case of the young man who won the golf tournament, golfing will always be a happy behavior even if he never again wins a major event. There are many more happy behaviors than miserable ones—behaviors like golfing, playing tennis, socializing, eating, loving, working, painting, reading, and writing, to mention a very few. Unlike painful behaviors we choose these not when we suffer a large perceptual error but when we want to do something that we know feels good. They are part of our inner world, and we are usually able to control for them successfully. They may help us to reduce an error— for example, we can substitute socializing for depressing, but this is not easy to do; mostly the error that starts these behaviors is small and easy to control. With the exception of euphoric sexual intercourse, where we always reduce a large error, only a tiny part of the joy of these behaviors is error reduction; the pleasure is in satisfying what we have built into our inner world that we enjoy. For example, I enjoy working on this book, even though it is also very frustrating, because I like to write. I like the activity and I guess it is gradually closing a large error, but I don't feel that closure very much. The good feeling, I believe, is much more in the writing behavior itself. Maybe it is a pleasurable behavior because it once closed a substantial error, but now I do it because I like the activity itself.

Naturally I would like to experience pure euphoria every once in a while, but as a steady diet I can't expect it. But I can *do* lots that I enjoy, and when writing becomes a drag, as it may when I keep at it too long or I get completely stuck, I can take time off and play tennis. It's hard to reduce my total error if I sit at my desk and stew; it's easy if I go out and hit the tennis ball with a friend. Unfortunately, if we do not have access to some enjoyable behaviors, then when we experience a large error we will more likely choose a miserable behavior and stick grimly to it. How often have you stayed too long at a frustrating task, knowing full well you would be better off doing something else? But you have to have the something else.

Therefore, it is important to learn that much of what we feel when we are upset is the major component of an unsatisfactory behavior through which we are trying to reduce an error. And these feeling behaviors do to some extent reduce the error or we would not choose them, a process that we will explain in the next chapter. If we can learn this we may be able to force ourselves to look for a better behavior. There is no sense in sitting around depressing, for example, if we can do something better.

If, however we believe we are the S-R victims of an unfortunate outside event over which we have no control, we tend not to make the effort. We may not, for example, be able to stop someone we love from rejecting us, but we can, if we understand BCP, make the effort to remove that person from our personal world and look for someone else. To keep him in our world and control for him and then choose to depress because he doesn't love us hardly makes good sense. Unfortunately the effort that many of us do make is not to look for someone else but to try to blot out the depressing with a drug. Alcoholics blot out their misery, and "feeling no pain" they allow their lives to disintegrate. In a sense they have jumped from the frying pan into the fire. We'll discuss in depth in Chapter 12 the part drugs play in how we feel and what we do.

There is also a final, somewhat uncommon situation which is worth looking at for a moment. Suppose we set a reference level for staying where we are on the job for the next six months, and suddenly, before that time, the boss calls us in and gives us an unexpected promotion and raise. What happened happens to all of us once in a while; our perception of the world suddenly exceeds the reference level in an open comparing station. When we overshoot our expectation, that is euphoria time. In a sense we have created a positive or reverse error, and if we could do this all the time life might be unbelievably joyful. But of course what we do, although many of us try not to, is raise our reference level at least to where we now are and usually higher. It's hard to keep your expectations below reality for more than a short time, but it's a good strategy not to expect too much. It makes getting there that much better and prevents a lot of disappointment. On the other hand, if we set our sights too low we may never get there at all, so we are always juggling for the best reference levels to send to our active comparing station. It's an interesting game that most of us continually play with ourselves, and if we have a behavioral system filled with adequate behaviors it's a game we can mostly win.

We now move on to examine our behavioral system, to find out why it is that we choose to do what we do. And especially to find out why, when we suffer large errors, so many of us choose painful feeling behaviors.

6

Behavior: Reorganization, Redirection, and New Information

❦

A discussion with a colleague who is an expert on suicide confirmed the unhappy fact that too often high-school students, usually boys, kill themselves. In a typical case, the parents of a seventeen-year-old boy thought, in retrospect, he spent more time by himself than seemed normal. In school, where his work was satisfactory, what was noticeable was that he was not noticed; he tended to blend into the background. He did have a few close friends, and he did not complain that anything major was wrong. Obviously, he must have been suffering from a huge and growing perceptual error; the life he wanted was not at all working out. Even though he appeared outwardly calm, we believe that disturbing ideas that had never been there before were racing through his mind. More and more the idea that life was overwhelmingly painful crowded out other thoughts. To relieve the pain, he threw a rope over a garage rafter, fixed it around his neck, and stepped off the chair. He had, as we will explain, reorganized his life away.

Unlike this desperate young man, most of the time we know what to do. Our behavior is usually smooth and well organized because we are not suffering a large perceptual error. As we live from day to day, we are able to fulfill our needs with behavior that is fairly routine. Mostly we use behavior that we have used before, behavior learned a long time ago. With day-to-day adjustments it works pretty well. Nevertheless, there are times for all of us when we don't know what to do. For example, what do you do when you find yourself snowbound on a lonely country road, certain that no one knows that you went in this direction? What do you do when your wife or husband without warning announces he or she is moving out and filing for divorce? You have spent the last four years immersed in study to get into medical school, and every application has come back rejected. Your job is a nightmare, your boss never stops riding you, but you need money too badly to quit. Your teenage son quits school and refuses to leave his room, where all he does is listen to records and smoke pot. You have been trying for ten years to discover why a certain virus causes cancer, and you seem no closer to the solution than when you started. The list is endless. We all experience situations like these where we don't have the vaguest idea of what to do. Yet we feel a tremendous urge to do something. We find it almost impossible just to sit quietly, to bear the pain without complaining and do nothing.

What we commonly do when we don't know what to do is to choose the pain or discomfort of a feeling behavior; for example, we depress. From the standpoint of BCP, our control system is working poorly, but it is still working. Bad as it may be, a feeling behavior is still better than many other behaviors. If the young man who hanged himself could have depressed enough to get the attention of someone who could have helped him, he might not have ended his life. Most feeling behaviors work to reduce the error enough so that destructive behaviors like suicide do not occur. Often, however, to get rid of the pain of a miserable feeling behavior we stop controlling for what we want. This is because, as long as we control for something we *cannot* get, we will almost always do something painful or even self-destructive in a vain hope that it will reduce our error. But whether we are controlling for something possible or impossible, *we must behave, that is, do, think, and feel as long as we experience an error.*

For example, if we are rejected this year for medical school, we can try again, go to a foreign school, get a doctorate in a related field, sit around depressing and do little, or give up the idea all together and do something else. If we close down all our medical-school comparing stations, we eliminate our error, but this is not easy to do. If we can't find another way to gain worth, it may be impossible because *we must keep at least one comparing station open for each of our general needs.* Therefore, most of us struggle for quite a while to get what we want when a viable alternative is not apparent. We may succeed or fail, but *it is this struggle to find the behavior or the output that works that we will discuss in this chapter.*

Animals need less than we do, and have many built-in behaviors that satisfy their needs. Our needs are complex, and we have almost no built-in behaviors to satisfy them. In fact, except for a few early behaviors like blinking, coughing, or kicking, everything we do is learned. To learn to behave, that is, to act, think, and feel, Powers and I believe that we have a three-component behavioral system to provide us with the behaviors we use to satisfy our needs. The total system—which contains the major subsystems—*reorganization* and *redirection,* and the minor subsystem *new information*—is shown on the diagram on page 72. This is a portion of the total control system which for easy reference is on the inside cover.

Of these three systems we will devote the most time to explaining reorganization, because this system is both the most interesting and the most complex. It is also the system that completely separates us from machines. Computers can redirect and use new information, but only living creatures can reorganize. Early in life it is essentially the only system we have, but by the time we are two or three years old we will

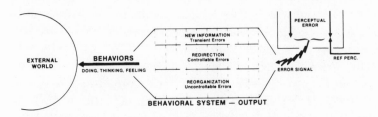

rarely, except in unusual circumstances, reorganize in any substantial way. As we grow very old, we may again begin to use reorganization, especially if we become senile, but most of our life we will generally use the redirection and new-information components of the total system. Nevertheless, whenever we suffer a substantial error we may through reorganization add tiny bits of behavior that are valuable and reduce our error. But we are generally unaware that this important system is active.

To explain how reorganization, our fundamental system, works try to imagine yourself a newborn child. At birth you have a few simple behaviors mostly associated with eating and sleeping. You are born knowing at least how to swallow, breathe, eliminate, kick, grasp, grimace, sleep, suck, cough, sneeze, and randomly vocalize in a minimal way. You may have a few additional innate behaviors, but for the purpose of understanding reorganization these are enough. You are also born with all the parts of your control systems described in Chapter 4 intact, except for the subject of this chapter, the behavioral system. This means that you have when you are born all of the general needs that you are ever going to have. Some needs like worthwhileness and competitiveness will take time to become known to you, but from the old-brain demands for food and water to freedom and the other new-brain needs, they are all there. And from them you have already built a very simple personal or internal world where staying alive is foremost. Intact at birth, although it will develop much more as we grow, is our perceptual apparatus, and also our ability to compare for what we want through comparing stations. Already we can experience a perceptual error and we are capable of generating an error signal.

As we have explained, the purpose of the error signal is to drive our behavior to reduce the error, but at birth it can only drive the limited behavior that is available. Since we have not learned anything yet beyond what works in our mother's uterus, we haven't the slightest idea which behavior will reduce any error we feel. Therefore, the error signal *randomly* drives all the behaviors we have available in an attempt to find one or more that will reduce any error we feel. When this occurs, that error has activated our earliest and later our most important behavior system, reorganization. For several months before birth (assuming a healthy mother and child), we lived an organized, comfortable existence in our mother's womb. That we could move around is obvious, and recent prenatal research reveals that before birth the infant probably has the ability to cough, eliminate wastes, and maybe even suck his thumb. Chances are that inside our mother we are probably as comfortable, as physically well cared for, and, in BCP terms, as organized as we are ever going to be. At birth, thrust out into the cold, cruel world, we must experience a huge error in one of our first comparing stations, comfort. It is this discomfort error which initially activates our reorganization system, and when this system is active it reorganizes behavior without stopping until the error is reduced, which means our behavior is again organized, or we are exhausted or dead.

To begin with, the first important characteristic of the reorganization system is that it is not a smart system. It causes us to behave in random ways, but it does not know and never will know what to do specifically to reduce the error. As we grow and develop a redirection system, that sensible system by rejecting foolish behaviors will limit what we will accept from our reorganization system, but the reorganization system itself never has any inkling whether one behavior is better than another. *It is a random system.* If, however, our basic behavior system, the one we use when we don't know what to do, were not a random system we would suffer a biologic disadvantage. If there were any bias in the system, that is, if it were "smart" in any way, then possible survival pathways would be closed to us. Whenever we get into a very difficult survival situation we must keep all our options open, and only a random system does this. For example, if we did not know how to swim we would be afraid of the water and might starve if we were cut off by a flood. The bias would kill us. Under these severe circumstances our reorganization system would force *some of us* into the water, where *some of us* would randomly learn to swim (more reorganization) and *some of us* would survive. Without such a "dumb" random system we would never learn anything new. Reorganization is a property of all living creatures; inability to reorganize in time is one of the reasons that so many species have become extinct.

This leads us to the second characteristic of this system, which is that all it knows is to do, that is, as we will see, to keep offering behavior after behavior to our redirection system until our perceptual error is reduced. To do this it will fragment and recombine the behaviors we have to produce new variations, or if this does not work it will also initiate totally new behaviors in an attempt to reduce our perceptual error. If none of these behaviors works singly or in combination it will keep driving and come up with new possibilities until one works well enough to reduce the error which will turn the system off. It is therefore a random, illogical, nonlearning, but highly energetic system that produces behavior after behavior, new or some combination of old and new, until the error is sufficiently reduced so that reorganization is no longer needed or we stop controlling for what is causing the error. *It is strictly activated by an error signal; it senses nothing else.*

At birth, when we experience an error, the reorganization system goes into action. We can no more turn it off than we can stop the earth from turning, because when we are born it is the only system that we have. Without it we would learn much more slowly, we would never learn anything unique, and, unless we were taught by others much of what we learn through this system, most of us would remain babies forever. Since it is a random creative system, as we reorganize we find that a wide variety of behavior satisfies our needs. This is what causes people to be so different that even identical twins usually turn out to be vastly different as they mature. Reorganization provides the variation in behaviors that allows some of us to adapt and even prosper under highly adverse circumstances. Animals who have small brains have less reorganizing capacity. They tend to be much more alike and, therefore, less adaptable to changes in their environments.

Even the old brain, as we will discover in Chapter 11, is capable of this process. Since we have the largest and most advanced brain, we are, by far, the creature most benefited, but also, since only human beings commit suicide, the most capable of being harmed by this system. It is likely that it was this system, through fortuitous reorganizations like learning to walk upright and learning to speak, that made it possible for our brain to grow as much as it has.

As soon as we are born and our error-free, organized prenatal life is abruptly shattered, we very quickly start to reorganize in the attempt to reduce the sudden error we now experience. We begin by running through, at random, fragments and combinations of the limited behaviors that we have available. We have no idea which one will work, but almost instantaneously we put together the fragments that lead to crying, and they work. When we cry, someone makes us comfortable, a situation that we perceive favorably because our discomfort error disappears. As soon as this happens the reorganization system turns off, and usually we go to sleep, a behavior learned prenatally.

What happened was that a nurse, or someone else who controlled for comforting crying infants, responded to our crying and made us comfortable. At this point we know nothing about mothers, nurses, or even people. All we know is that when we quickly found the combination of fragmentary innate vocal behaviors that led to crying, we got the comfort that we wanted. Kicking, swallowing, grimacing, urinating, coughing, grasping didn't, but crying did. Through reorganization we have learned something from essentially nothing. We had no idea which behavior would work, but we had an open comfort comparing station, and as the perceptions caused by each behavior came in, crying got us the comfort we desired. We have now learned a complaining vocal behavior that many of us will use for the rest of our life whenever we are uncomfortable.

In the beginning, reorganization is the only system we have. From it, however, the other systems soon develop, and while at any time for the rest of our life when we suffer large errors we may still use reorganization, as we said, most of our behavior is generated by two other systems, redirection and new information. Simply stated, reorganization means to attempt to go from one organized low-error state to another but because learning is not a part of the reorganization system it is often misdirected. Because it uses a lot of energy and its results are always chancy, very quickly after birth we develop the ability to behave much more precisely through the use of our second major system *redirection*. Reorganizing, however, develops the ability to redirect, and the better the ability to redirect becomes, the less often we have to reorganize.

Unlike reorganization, redirection is a smart learning system. For example, when crying got our error reduced, crying very quickly became a learned behavior or in this case also a logical strategy, because we had no reason to believe that it would not work again. So the next time we experienced an error, perhaps hunger, we cried and presto, we were fed. Later we soiled our diaper, it was uncomfortable, we cried again and got a fresh diaper. To the newborn it seems as if a miraculous behavior has been discovered. Anytime we feel discomfort we cry and we are soon comfortable. Now, when we are uncomfortable, we need no random reorganization. We know exactly what to do—change direction. When we wake up hungry we go from sleeping directly to crying and our problem is quickly solved. Thus our redirection system, unlike our reorganization system, soon becomes a storehouse of learned behaviors and logical strategies that will reduce error. We may try one and then another, but we start much closer to the solution when we try behavior that has either worked in the past or is very close to one that has worked. Only when redirection doesn't work will we return to the reorganization system which in its random and, compared to redirection, stumbling way *is still the only system capable of producing new behaviors to reduce our error.*

Early in life, in an attempt to perceive love, we may right now want to be held, kissed, hugged, tossed about, stroked, and caressed. In a loving family we have experienced a lot of this enjoyable attention, but we haven't yet figured out exactly how to turn it on. When we want loving we turn to our "magic" redirection system, but all that it has stored within it so far is crying. When we cry we are made comfortable, perhaps fed, but not always loved. Loving is what we want now, and we sense that our magic system isn't working. But we don't quit easily, and we keep crying. A continuously crying baby, however, is hardly lovable, so in many cases we are ignored, which increases our error. We scream, but still we don't get the loving we desire. Our love error is now substantial and crying has done nothing to reduce it.

Soon our large, unresolved error activates our reorganization system, and it again runs through the whole gamut of available behaviors, but none of these works. Undaunted, however, because this random senseless system cannot be daunted, it offers the redirection system to try a whole group of new behaviors, and, in the case of most babies, somewhere around three months old it offers the new behavior of chortling and smiling. As soon as we chortle and smile, immediately we get a lot of loving attention. Certainly it took us a while and goodness knows how many behaviors, but again we have successfully reorganized. Error is reduced as we bask in the loving attention, and we lead an organized life for a while, enjoying being loved when we chortle as well as being made comfortable when we cry. Now we quickly add smiling and chortling to our redirection system, and when we want loving we redirect, using these behaviors. This is how the redirection system, which is our sensible learning system, grows. More and more successful behaviors, including some new ones initiated by reorganization and many more learned from others around us as we look about and see what works, are added until by adulthood we have thousands of successful behaviors stored in this system and instantly ready to use.

Before it adds a behavior offered by our reorganization system or from any other source, like observing or being taught, the redirection system is capable of mentally running the new behavior through the open comparing station or stations to see if it might work. If, on the trial run, the behavior seems as if it would increase the error, it is rejected. It also might decrease the error in one station but increase it in another, as when we think how much fun it would be to go swimming but also we learn how terribly cold the water is. We might reject swimming, but then we further redirect by thinking of a rubber wetsuit. When we put one on we are able to go swimming comfortably in cold water. Our redirection system is learning all the time; in fact, almost all learning that takes any effort is redirection. What it can't do is come up with a totally new behavior. It cannot for example invent a wetsuit if none exists. For that kind of novel behavior, in all our life from infancy on, we must turn to our reorganization system. But it doesn't invent a wetsuit either. It has no logical or sensible ability, but it can keep giving us the idea that maybe some-how we could keep warm in cold water. As it bombards the redirection system with this concept, the redirection system may eventually try something like a shirt, and under the contin-ual bombardment of the random idea *warm in the water is possible,* it may come up with a wetsuit. The reorganization system doesn't do anything. It just provides a sensible concept that is seized upon and used successfully by the redirection system. Eventually, if we can last long enough, it will almost always work. But it can also drive us to suicide as in the example that began the chapter.

In contrast to inefficient reorganization which requires a lot of energy, our redirection system develops gradually into an efficient, ingenious system which we almost always use. It knows all we know and will always try to come up with a behavior or strategy to reduce error. Even when the reorgani-zation system throws out the random thought that life is too painful, leading the redirection system to consider suicide, this system, because it is intelligent, moral, judgmental, and able to take into account past, present, and future, will usually reject suicide as not desirable or a bad error-reducing behavior. Un-like the reorganization system, which has no memory and cares nothing about the future—present error is its only motivator—the redirection system has access to all of our memory, and constantly tries to predict the future course of its behaviors. It will run suicide through the system mentally, and as it does so it detects a huge potential error in a whole series of compar-ing stations that have to do with life, especially with our future. Therefore, suicide is rejected and not stored in our redirection system as desirable behavior. Only when we are exhausted by chronic error may we close down our life comparing stations and then accept suicide into our redirection system as a "sensi-ble" possibility. This is why we must never let tired, despondent people be alone for too long. They may suffer so much pain that they reorganize (and then redirect) by killing themselves.

While at times it may be dangerous to reorganize, it is also important to understand that without the continuing bits and pieces of reorganization that our redirection system continually accepts, our life would slow to a walk at the point reorganization quit. We would have whatever redirection were present, but we could not cope with any error beyond its capacity. This is often tragically illustrated after a stroke or other serious brain damage, when both systems are damaged and the victim temporarily can learn nothing new. But the reorganization system is a basic survival system, and in whatever brain we have left it will again begin to function and may eventually cope with some or all of the damage by coming up with new functions in the remaining brain to replace the damage. It is through reorganization that a stroke victim may learn to speak again, but therapy is needed to keep the victim controlling for speaking. Otherwise the aphasic may give up, and without error there will be no reorganization. But there is no guarantee reorganization will work. It can also produce ideas that are worthless or crazy, and this too is apparent in brain-damaged or senile people.

Reorganization is like a slot machine being fed coin after coin by a person desperate to win. It may hit a jackpot that the desperate redirection system can use, but it also may never pay off. We may exhaust ourselves and put all our mental money into the machine, with no results. But even worse it is a slot machine without bias. Gambling machines are biased in our favor, that is, they take the money we put in, but that's all— they never take any out of our pocket. The reorganization system is like an unbiased slot machine, that is, one with a negative as well as positive jackpot. It is capable of coming up with a totally destructive idea like suicide or murder, much like a slot machine that can reach into your pocket or spit out a promissory note that you must pay off.

To summarize, the reorganization system may become active

anytime we have a large error, but all it can do is suggest at random that we do something to reduce the error. Usually the sensible redirection system evaluates these suggested behaviors and tends to reject the negatives and accept the positives. In this way a delicate symbiosis is maintained between sensible redirection and random, erratic, but potentially creative reorganization. Only when our redirection system is desperate, when, for example, we suffer a huge error, will it entertain destructive or bizarre suggestions and even try them out because nothing better is available.

Finally, we have another system, a new-information system that we use to deal with small errors. While this is best classfied as *a very simple subsystem under redirection,* it is worth looking at for a moment, because in practice, if we don't want too much or suffer misfortune, this is the system that we mostly use. When our lives are well organized we still have many things to do, and we do most of them by the simple application of new information. For example, we knock on a friend's door and wait. The friend calls out, "Come in, the door is open," and we go in. We acted upon the new information that the door was open and entered. This is all new information is. There was in this case almost no redirection and certainly no reorganization. This is why on the control-system diagram we show the new information perception as going right into the behavioral system, where it helps us to know what to do.

Much of what we do all day long is to eliminate transient errors with new information. Sometimes the new information is complex, like following a maintenance manual to tune a car. Still, unless you lose a part, break something, or run into a situation not in the manual, you can use its new information alone. If any of these complications occur you may have to redirect, but it is unlikely that you will ever reorganize. Perhaps if you just can't get the car tuned, you will, as Rudolph Diesel did, invent a new engine that doesn't need tuning. But even that was probably an extreme form of redirection; it was still an internal-combustion engine. Maybe if you invent a chlorophyll engine or an atomic engine, that would be reorganization. But it is much more likely if you couldn't get your car in tune you would drive it into the lake. That would also be reorganization, although not what anyone except the salvage people would call successful. Remember our redirection system is constantly on the lookout for new information. It deals with reality, and it struggles to learn as much as it can to keep abreast of all possible behaviors. Our formal education is a combination of new information and redirection, but whether we are aware of it or not, we are always learning through the bits and flashes that our reorganization system constantly suggests to our redirection system when we are struggling with an error.

From these three sources of behavior come all that we do, think, and much of what we feel. *First we try to do or to think,* as doing and thinking are ordinarily our two most effective error-reducing behaviors. But, as we said, when we don't know what to do or think we usually redirect, or on rare occasions reorganize, by using the feeling behaviors described in Chapter 5. What we promised then, and can explain now, is the purpose of *feeling* behavior. Let's say that you have your heart set on going to a concert tonight, but you fail to get tickets in advance. You stand in a long line, and just when you get to the counter the ticket seller closes, sold out. Suddenly you have a huge error. You feel the quick pain as the error takes over your comparing station, but there is nothing you can do—there are no tickets. Driven by the sudden large-error signal, your reorganization system becomes active and may suggest violence like breaking the box-office window or screaming in anguish or walking in without a ticket. Your redirection system entertains these ridiculous suggestions only for a moment before it takes over. It may cause you to depress, because depressing, miserable as it is, can reduce your error.

As we discussed in Chapter 5, there are two kinds of feelings. One is exemplified by the rather pure feeling of pain, associated with the sudden error caused in this case by the closing of the ticket window. That pain is about the same for any of us and lasts only a short time because we may immediately start to reduce this painful error by redirecting with a miserable behavior like depressing. Depressing, like most of our high-error feeling behaviors, was initially a product of reorganization. Perhaps early in our life, when we were frustrated and when crying, screaming, and throwing tantrums (all earlier angry reorganizations) did not work, depressing was suggested to our redirection system. Our hard-pressed redirection system gave it a try and it worked reasonably well for the following four reasons. *First,* when we depress we feel sorry for ourself and therefore can ask for help more easily. Other people are sensitive to our depressing and tend to offer help. *Second,* we can partially justify the failure to get tickets in advance by showing how upset we are, and depressing is an easily communicated upset. We can rationalize all kinds of failure because we are depressed. *Third,* it replaces and protects us from the more violent redirection of angering, which might cause us to start a fight or make a scene. We are sensible enough to realize this would cause us more error. *Fourth,* if we seem very upset, others will allow us to do or say things that ordinarily they wouldn't put up with. Therefore, a powerful error-reducing aspect of depressing and other feeling behaviors is that when we use them we can control others. How many of us tiptoe in fear around a depressing relative in an attempt not to invoke further upset? Together all four of these functions of depressing help us to deal with the error better than any behavior we can think of right away. The price we pay for this "better" behavior, however, is to suffer the depression. And it is a price most of us are willing to pay. In almost all instances it is a lot better than angering—if we angered too much we could get into serious trouble with other people whom we need to fulfill our needs. In this simple example our depressing probably won't last long. We will get over it quickly when we find something else we enjoy. Often, however, when we suffer more substantial error, like losing a good job, this kind of feeling behavior can last a long time, because until we find another job it may be the best redirection we have. Remember, for the four important reasons cited, depressing and many other feeling-behavior redirections reduce the error enough so we will use them again and again until we find a better behavior. Bad as they are, they give us a sense that we are still in control, and all of them help us avoid reorganization, which may be worse. But we don't choose them to prevent reorganization—we are never that rational—we choose them because we recognize that without these behaviors we will be out of control. And no control system "likes" to lose control, because when it does it must cope with huge, painful errors. We will explain more why we choose and use these feeling behaviors in Chapter 10, which is devoted entirely to this subject, but it was necessary here to begin the explanation.

Finally, let's look at several other examples of the all-important reorganization system in order to understand it clearly. Remember it is a random system activated by an error signal. It works by suggesting behaviors to our redirection system, which accepts or rejects what it offers. It is the redirection system that takes the randomness out of what the reorganization system suggests, so ordinarily we won't sing or dance when we are in the desert starving, but if we have enough error so that the redirection system is helpless, we may. In the desert our reorganization system also may suggest we try a wide variety of things to eat that we never thought of trying, and a desperate, out-of-control redirection system with nothing better to offer may accept one of these "foods" even though it might be dangerous. Unlike redirection, which has judgment, morality, logic, learning, much information, and the sense of the past and future, the reorganization system acts only in the immediate present, *right now*. And since its only motivation is to reduce error it does not care whether the behavior is good, bad, appropriate, moral, immoral, dangerous, illegal, disloyal, stupid, or anything else. If it can possibly reduce error, a desperate redirection system may try what it offers. If it works, the error-reducing behavior will immediately be put into the redirection system as learned behavior, where it can be used again. If eating grasshoppers kept us alive, the next time we are lost we'll eat them quickly as redirection; we won't have to reorganize. Remember, the reorganization system can't be turned off except by error reduction or closing down the comparing station in which there is the error. It never sleeps. As we will explain later, we experience it nightly in many of our "crazy" dreams. For our survival it is ready, in its random, illogical way, to act anytime it senses there is an error that redirection cannot reduce.

For example, you are locked in a room with no food or water. Very quickly your need for survival and freedom becomes strong because other needs temporarily turn off. You control only for these quantities and as the error increases you begin to redirect, but what can you do? You notice that there is a tiny slot in the window and you see people below, but how can you get them the message? There is in the room a funny machine with several hundred keys that looks like a typewriter. There is also paper. You put some in the machine, press the keys, but all you get is gibberish. You are desperate, your redirection system is stymied. Nevertheless you keep hammering away and in desperation press three keys together, whistle Dixie, and stomp the floor nine times. Now you are reorganizing, trying every possible combination, sensible as well as nonsensical, and as you do so suddenly a letter appears. In fact it is the letter H. This means that you might be able to type the message help, so you redouble your efforts. It appears again and again and you focus on how you produced it. Your redirection system has grasped a product of that random reorganization, but you contine to reorganize. Anything you do that might work is seized by the redirection system, and if you keep going and successfully learn to produce enough letters to type the message help, you now have a possible redirection that can save you. If no one responds when you drop the message out the window you will go back to reorganizing, but now you have a chance. Without the message for help things were hopeless. As you continue to reorganize, your redirection system may even learn how this crazy typewriter works. If you have to use it again you can do so with little error.

We have said reorganization can be lifesaving. After all it is the only way we have to develop new behaviors. But, as in our example of the suicide, it can also be disastrous. Some years ago there was a motorcycle race across Baja California. One cyclist got lost, and when he didn't appear at the next checkpoint a rescue team went out to look for him. He was found dead several days later a few miles from his shiny motorcycle, which, incidentally, was found almost immediately. It was evident from his tracks what had happened. He had stayed near it for a while, then as his error grew he began to panic. He disregarded the information *don't leave your bike, stay where you are if you get lost,* and he started to redirect. He tried to find the trail to the checkpoint, but gradually as his panic grew he began to reorganize. He ran in large circles, exhausting himself until he died of exposure, lack of water, and eventually from noninterrupted reorganization. Maybe if he could have kept alive longer he might have reorganized successfully and found someone in his random trek through the desert. In panic we always reorganize, but what may happen is that the error is so large and the redirection system so ineffective that the results of our reorganization are wiped out by continuing reorganization before our redirection system can test whether they might be beneficial. With the motorcyclist we see this occur. He just kept going until he died. Pushed by a huge error, he never stopped to evaluate that his random trek was hopeless. It is important to develop a good redirection system which will slow you down in moments of panic and at least let you test what your reorganization system has provided. Reorganization is invaluable in these situations, but since it *is* random, it must be filtered through a strong redirection system or the lifesaving idea that it may come up with is liable to be overlooked.

We should learn to recognize when our redirection system is failing and develop some general redirection strategies to avoid the kind of panic and despondency that may fragment this system so much that we reorganize to our own destruction. The main strategy when panic "demands" action is to *slow down, count to ten, sit on your hands, don't be in a hurry, and if that doesn't work, ask for help.* If you recognize someone else in this critical condition, offer help. If the young man who hanged himself could have redirected himself toward a friendly counselor, he might have found a much better solution to his problem. Evidently failure to take other people into his confidence, even though he seemed to have some friendly people around, was a fatal flaw in his redirection system.

On the other hand, if we are in a safe situation where we are looking for new ideas or principles, as in science or art, we should not be afraid to take on a huge challenge, to run a large error and still refuse to do anything sensible to reduce the error. What we are doing, which is a redirection, is trying voluntarily to overwhelm our sensible redirection system enough to tempt our reorganization system into action. It may take us on a wild-goose chase, but without it we would not have calculus or the wheel. It is too bad that schools can't push students intellectually to reorganize and be patient while they do. That sort of pushing is something that teachers could learn to do, but as long as schools maintain the standard that students be quickly penalized for poor or slow results, few teachers (or students) want to have too much to do with this sometimes slow, random, often stupid, but potentially brilliant system.

Scientific breakthroughs, like the discovery of the theory of

relativity or the invention of radio, which are products of reorganization, rarely occur in a formal school setting. In those cases
great minds, struggling with huge perceptual errors and un-
hampered by academic restrictions, were given a series of hints
by their reorganization systems, sometimes even a dramatic
jackpot, as when Newton observed the apple or Einstein at
age four wondered at a magnet. These perceptions which initiated large intellectual errors were later acted on by their reorganization systems, and their errors were reduced with brilliant
scientific insights. With these insights others may redirect to
explain and explore the breakthrough. But the initial breakthrough, often seemingly illogical at the time, is reorganization.
Scientists also have the ability to tolerate huge intellectual errors, that is, to keep comparing stations open for problems
that most of us would find too painful and shut down. They
are tolerant of their stumbling reorganization systems, almost
like a patient gambler or fisherman. They believe the wait is
worth it, as there eventually may be a lucky jackpot or bite
on their line. Therefore, the true scientist reorganizes and then
may redirect. The engineer redirects and then on occasion
may reorganize. When the engineer reorganizes, he or she
becomes a scientist.

With the explanation of how we learn to behave, the basic
model of our brain functioning is almost complete. Our behavior is an attempt to control our preceptions so that they are
as close as possible to our built-in perception derived from
genetic needs, or, in short, BCP. With this much in mind we
must now return to where we started, to perception, because
how we perceive the world is much more complex than we
have explained so far.

7

The Orders of Perception

❦

In the ancient Japanese play *Rashomon* a wealthy nobleman
and his wife are set upon by a bandit as they travel through
the forest. The bandit is caught and brought to trial, during
which each tells the story of what he or she says happened.
The husband tells how, after a fierce struggle, the bandit over-
powered him, tied him up, raped his wife, and took his money.
The wife claims that her husband was so cowardly that he
offered both her and his money to the bandit to spare his life.
The bandit relates that when he came upon the couple, the
wife became so enamored of him that she threw herself upon
him, helped him to tie up her husband so that he could not
interfere, and then for his loving attention rewarded him with
her husband's money. Certainly they were all there, and they
all agree as to the physical events, but how are we to establish
the truth? In the play a sorcerer is used to get at the facts,
but in real life sorcerers are hard to find. And even if we could
find one, all we would learn is how the world appears to him.

It is our contention that all of us, including sorcerers, perceive
the world in terms of our own needs; none of us is capable
of perceiving the world as it actually is. It will appear different
to each of us because even though our basic needs are about
the same, *our specific needs from which all of us create our
internal world are never the same.* For example, you and I,
both like music, a general need, but as a Bach devotee it is

hard for me to understand why you like Mozart so much. Most of the time, however, when we talk about the real world we tend to agree with those around us, because we find it comfortable to associate with people, music lovers perhaps, whose internal worlds are similar to ours. We don't like people, even our husband or wife, if they dispute our view of the "world," because to us it is the real world and how dare they see it differently! In *Rashomon* the husband and wife disagreed as violently with each other as they did with the bandit because their specific needs, and therefore their internal worlds, were so much different. As we will explain in this and the following chapter, *all we ever know of the real or external or outside world is the energy that comes from the world and strikes the sensory receptors of our perceptual system. Everything else that we claim is the real world is in fact our own perceptions of that world, perceptions which we constantly try to change so that they coincide with the world in our head.*

As we have said, we begin to build this world the moment we are born. Suddenly the energy that strikes us from the external, or real world is much different from the energy of our mother's uterus, from which we have built the tiny but comfortable world that has been in our head for several months. Quickly we cry to try to reduce the difference. If the outside world were as comfortable as the world in our head we would not cry at all. Recent work by a French obstetrician, Leboyer, who creates a comfortable, secure childbirth where all is love and gentleness, has shown that many babies born this way do not cry. Crying is not a response to the stimulus of birth; crying is the baby's behavior (BCP) to move the energy it senses and interprets as miserable, closer to the satisfactory uterine world that exists within its head. *Starting with our first cry and continuing for the rest of our life, we care about what is going on out there only as long as we are unable to change it to be more like the world in our head.* If what is out there is what we want, if the real world is comfortable, then in a sense we don't care at all. We'll explain this more as we go along, but *here it's important to try to get the idea that it is only our world, or the world in our head, that counts for us.*

Therefore, based upon our needs, we transform the energy from the real or external world, which so far we have talked about as a single entity, input, into the complex, multi-ordered input which is the way we perceive the world. For example, the baby transforms the "cold" temperature of the delivery room into the idea of discomfort which is its in-the-head interpretation of that temperature. Starting with this first interpretation, we learn to experience the world around us through an orderly hierarchy of perceptions, low to high or simple to complex. Without this hierarchy or, as we will call it in this chapter, *the orders of perception,* we would lead random, disorganized lives struggling to gain order out of a haphazard world that would make little sense. For example, to read this sentence you have taken the black and white energy of this page coming from the curlicues printed here and transformed it into words and sentences. To do this you have followed the hierarchy which we will explain in this chapter, an ancient hierarchy that my colleague Bill Powers has spent much of his adult life trying to figure out. He cautions that what he has done so far may not be complete, but there is no doubt that it explains a great deal about how, from the energy that strikes our sensory receptors, we actually build our personal world. Turn briefly to the inside cover and look at the diagram of the perceptual system. Everything that we perceive from the external world, and from our own body because it is part of the external world, passes through this system, *beginning always with our sensory receptors* but then going through possibly as many as ten orders as we continually attempt to make sense out of the real world.

It is necessary to know that our input or awareness of the world is not always conscious. Consciousness can best be defined as any perception that right now we sense is going on. For practical purposes we will generally be aware of uncontrolled perceptions, or the perceptions associated with any control system that contains a substantial error. A simple example is that we are aware of hunger several times a day, but we are never aware of breathing unless we run short of air. Also, in this chapter, as we explain the hierarchy of how we perceive the world, it will become obvious that we *behave* to control our perceptions according to the hierarchy. When we are controlling for morality, a high, eighth-order perception, we both perceive and behave morally. This is shown on the diagram inside the cover as the dotted lines which define the orders of our perceptual system extending down through the behavioral system.

The Perceptual System

Any impingement on any internal or external sensory ending in the body—touch, smell, vision, hearing, taste, proprioception, kinesthesis,—anytime a receptor detects an increase or decrease in energy, this input is dealt with by our perceptual system. To see how this works look at the following diagram, which shows the perceptual system in some detail.

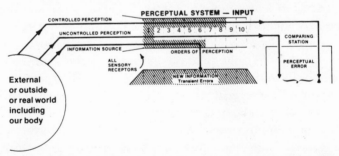

As you see, there are three perceptions coming into the perceptual system, a *controlled,* an *uncontrolled,* and a *new-information* perception. I show the new-information perception leaving the perceptual system at the sixth order relationship and going directly to the behavioral system, where it provides the simple relationship information needed for the behavioral system to act. It could enter at any order. I use the sixth order, which will be explained shortly in detail, because new information is often at this order. In this example I may be controlling for sweet coffee, and I ask you where the sugar is. You tell me, and with this information I now put sugar in my coffee, a simple sixth-order behavior that is initiated by my sixth order perception of the common relationship between sugar and coffee. I show the other perceptions going though the whole system, but that doesn't mean that they include all ten orders. All incoming perceptions can be interpreted by our brain at any order, one through ten. To explain this I will arbitrarily shade along each arrow and stop the shading at the *first order* for the uncontrolled perception and the *eighth* for the controlled perception. Note that the higher order must include the lower orders, as all perceptions, whatever their order, include all the orders below. As we explain how we perceive the world, order by order, this hierarchy should become clear.

First-Order Perceptions—Intensity

At the first-order intensity all we perceive is that something is there, or something is there that is different from what had been there. This and only this is a first-order perception. We call it intensity because this term is a good way to summarize all the simple and complex energy signals that come in through our sensory receptors. Mostly we are not conscious of first-order perceptions. For example, unless I call your attention to it you are not aware of the perceptions associated with sitting while you read this book. You don't attend to the pressure or the intensity of the chair on your bottom, to the room getting a little warmer or a bit colder, to the noise of the cars going by in the street. *Nevertheless, these simple energy signals are not only our direct contact with the outside world, they are in fact our only contact with the outside world.* Everything else we perceive, even high-order perceptions like right or wrong or a system of religious beliefs, is created out of these first-order, simple-intensity perceptions, although most of the time we are not even aware of their existence. It is also important to understand that it isn't necessary for these perceptions to arise from any particular or discrete stimuli. Nothing has to happen for us to experience a first-order perception. All we have to do is look around the room. This is perception, it is always there. If it weren't, there would be no reason for you to believe that anything out there exists.

To explain the confusing concept that our only contact with the world is through first order perceptions, again take the simple example of the pressure of the chair upon your buttocks. This pressure, the intensity of that feeling and nothing more, is a first-order perception of which you are now aware because I mention it. From the pressure receptors in your skin, you send that perception of intensity to your sensory cortex, but it doesn't mean anything, because unless you sit too long and become uncomfortable, you have no error associated with that control system. In other words, if you are satisfied with where you are sitting you will just stay put. If you sit too long you will become aware of the real world through your discomfort (error) and redirect by getting up and moving around. If all you had was intensity, however, the real world would make little sense, because you would have no idea why you moved. Very early, even the most primitive of creatures, through their reorganization system, learned to add to their perception of intensity some additional qualities which make the world more sensible and easier to live in. *But these qualities, or higher orders or perceptions, are all in our head.* They are part of our perceptual system, our in-the-head representation of the way we perceive the world, but not part of the outside world. At the next order up, sensation, they might best be described as the way we uniquely choose to interpret our simple-intensity perception. For example, if our bottom gets tired from sitting too long, we discover that a *soft* chair is much more comfortable. The intensity signals that come to our brain from the soft chair are, for longer periods of time, reasonably close to our reference level for comfort. What we have done now is to change intensity into a new, in-our-own-head, second-order perception that we call soft. The reason that other people often call it soft is that we are very much like other people, especially at these low orders of perceptions. But unlike intensity, which is much the same among all creatures of the same species, *softness, a second-order perception, is purely subjective.* It is based upon intensity signals, but it is not intensity. It is the first example of the many higher orders of our world that we build upon low-order intensity in our attempt to make sense out of the outside world.

Think of living in a world where all we have is the perception of intensity. We could, for example, feel pressure, sense shades of darkness, detect some odor and taste differences, know that quiet was not the same as noise, but the world would be a mysterious place where it would be very difficult to fulfill our needs. What we then begin to do as tiny infants, through continuing reorganization and redirection, is to expand our world as described in Chapter 6. The baby in this chapter has no idea what cold or warm is, all he knows is that when his milk is too cold he is uncomfortable. As he cries to express his discomfort, his mother guesses the milk is too cold. She warms it up, and soon he learns what cold is because that is how he doesn't like it. By the age of two or three he has built the ideas of warm and cold into his world. The rest of our life when we feel discomfort we may choose a *warmer* room and remark how comfortable we are now, but *we must emphasize that this perception that we now call warm was not there in the first place. We learned it and now it is all in our head.* There is no actual entity *warm* in the real world. All that exists is the energy (or intensity) that can be measured as temperature on a thermometer.

What I may call warm, my wife might call cold, as we are different people with different needs and different body surfaces. Often as we sit in the same room, she complains it's too cold and I claim it's too hot. Sometimes we argue, but the argument is foolish. It can never be resolved, because we are not arguing about the real world. We are arguing about the world in our heads. We only think it is the real world because we have no neurological apparatus to tell us differently. All we have that detects the real world is our heat and cold receptors on our skin that measure intensity. But we are not arguing intensity; we agree that the thermometer on the wall says 72 degrees.

Therefore, our perception of the real world from which these intensity signals emanate almost immediately becomes completely subjective. It is, except for intensity, our world and our world alone. And it may or may not relate to your world or to someone else's world, but fortunately it does so often enough that we can usually find people that we can live with. But among strangers it is chancy, which is why we have so much trouble cashing a check no matter how "honest" our face is to us. Therefore, because all higher orders are subjective, we have no assurance that any perception that we may have beyond intensity has any significance outside of what it personally means to us. As we live with others who often interpret intensity differently this fact must be learned, relearned, and re-relearned and still we find it hard to believe. Why can't my wife understand the room is too hot? Or as Henry Higgins lamented in his wonderful song from *My Fair Lady*, "Why can't a woman be more like a man?"

To continue the soft example, if intensity causes us to move from the chair too often, *we will move up to the next perceptual order, sensation,* which is for every one of us our unique way of interpreting a pure intensity signal caused by simple pressure. Here we may say the seat is hard, soft, hot, cold, damp, lumpy, all of the various sensations associated with how the energy detected by our buttocks is interpreted by our brain. Remember the seat is the seat and nothing more; the sensation of hardness, lumpiness, or dampness is created in our head.

To summarize, Powers explains—and essentially I quote— "We live as if the perceptions in our head are perceptions of the real world, and we suspect that there is a real world out there which begins just a fraction of a millimeter outside any of our receptors. But almost all of our perceptions are not of that particular world. They depend upon it, but the form of that dependence, the way they occur and present themselves to our brain, depends much more upon what goes on inside our head than upon the intensity signal (energy) that started the process."

Everyone of you has probably participated in a simple experiment of having someone whisper a short but complex instruction to another person, and then of having that person whisper the same instruction to the next person and so on through fifteen or twenty people until the instruction comes back to the original person. When the instruction comes back it probably has little or no resemblance to the original. On the other hand, when I dictate into my tape recorder, except for the loss of fidelity, what I dictate is going to come back exactly as it went in. This is because my tape recorder has only one level of perception, intensity. It reproduces the sound exactly as it comes through the microphone. It has no concern at all with what I say. While the sentence that circulated through twenty people is composed of sound waves of varying intensity, the way we put these intensities together in our perceptual system is our attempt to make it understandable as language. When the instruction is repeated by the last person it is still language, but because each previous person added his or her own higher-order perceptions to the initial instruction, the message is usually garbled beyond recognition. If there had been twenty recorders in a row, the sentence would have come back exactly the same except for loss of fidelity, but we are not machines. We are people controlling for a variety of needs, and because we control differently, we tend to alter the sentence to suit whatever it is we are controlling for at that particular time. For example, some people will remove the profanity from the sentence because profanity causes them too much error to repeat. Only if each of us were controlling for exactly the same quantities, and the message caused no error, would we be able to pass it along accurately. This again shows that when we suffer error we perceive the world only a little as it is and a lot as we would like it to be.

Suppose ten witnesses to a crime testify in court. It would not be unheard of for them collectively to say that the criminal was tall, short, fat, black, white, red, bent over, straight, well dressed, and shabbily dressed. This happens over and over, which is why the Chinese have developed the adage that one (low-order) picture is worth a thousand (higher-order) words. But in court, if you have a good lawyer, a thousand high-order words may turn out to be considerably better than a low-order picture.

Therefore, keep in mind as we live our lives that we create most of the world inside ourselves. The little bit that we actually contact through sitting on a part of it, hearing a bit of it, seeing a glimpse of it, may be representative of the real world, but because we add higher-order perceptions so quickly and without awareness, there is no sure way of knowing. Nevertheless, we each live our life as if our world is the real world. But since it isn't, as we attempt to live with other people, who all perceive *their* world as real, life is difficult, because it is so hard to agree. People often have difficulty agreeing on what color their car is; small wonder then that a question like "What is art?" causes so much argument. This is why we need so much intelligence; it constantly takes all we have to figure out how to get along with others whom we need but who live in a different world, their own.

Second-Order Perceptions—Sensation

Intensity, the first-order perceptual signal, when it occurs from a receptor, does not reflect whether the cause of stimulation was an electric current, chemical poison, heavy pressure, or just simply looking around. All one perceives when dealing with a first-order signal is the energy of the disturbance, the distortion of the sound hitting the ear, the vibration felt by the hand placed on the hood of a car with the motor running. This is intensity, nothing more.

In contrast, the second-order-system sensation, already partially covered when we discussed the first order, is totally within our brain. It just seems as if it comes from the outside, because, in almost every instance, we quickly elevate all first-order perceptions to the second order to gain more information about the intensity perception which came into us from the outside. To me, because I am almost tone deaf, there is little meaning to the hum coming from the other room, but to a musician this hum might be the musical note A, which could then be used to tune an entire orchestra. In his musical brain first-order signals are transformed instantly into the meaningful sensations do-re-mi.

In our lemonade example in Chapter 3 the tart-sweet taste that we like, made up of a combination of sugar and citric acid, creates a sensation, the taste of lemonade, which is certainly second order. The chemical receptors of the tongue picked up the intensity of the sugar and the intensity of the acid as different first-order perceptions. Our brain put these perceptions together in the sensory cortex to create a specific tart-sweet taste that we know as lemonade. But even here, the lemonade that I like in my world may be much sweeter than that horrid, sour stuff that *you* call lemonade in your world.

Therefore, when first-order signals come in they are often disregarded, as we disregard the pressure on our seat or the traffic noise outside. Or, if we become aware of them, they are quickly transformed by our brain into a higher order in an attempt to make the world more meaningful to us, so we can more easily fulfill our needs. But, to repeat, this meaning is *our* meaning. It is personal. It is in our head. We may agree, as we often do at low orders, but even when we agree there is no reason to believe that we perceived exactly the same sensation. For example, color is a sensation. What we call red is hardly an exact or precise wavelength of light, but still we call it red. It makes more sense to call it red than to argue over every shade from orange to purple. People, however, argue heatedly because one sees rose while another sees plum and a third sees wine when they look at my wife's car—whatever color it is, it is not a common color. They argue because the color sensation is in their heads. Only intensity is lacquered on the car.

Another example to prove the subjectiveness of sensation is that there is no combination of intensities in the real physical world that can be put together reliably to duplicate the sensation of a complex taste. That is why wine tasters spend their lives attempting to guess whether or not a particular wine is going to be close to the good-wine reference levels of many people. Or perhaps, if the seller wants a high price, close to the reference levels for good wine of rich people. An expert wine taster is highly paid for her ability to guess consistently what rich people will like or in BCP terms the wines close to those the wealthy store in their internal world.

Our most common second-order perceptions are the very complex sensations which we call emotions. They are built from the many combinations of intensity signals which arise both from within our body and from the world outside. Here at the second order, as introduced in Chapter 5, we become aware of painful feeling behaviors like depressing or anxietying or pleasurable behaviors like socializing or lovemaking. Also at the second order we experience the pure pain or pleasure that is generated at our comparing stations, sensations that give us the instant evaluation of our control system that helps us to survive. While emotions are extremely complex, they are low order because they tend to be so variable in the subjective way we experience them. They almost never provide the more precise experiences that characterize the configuration of even the next order up. But because each order is built from orders below, no matter how high we go we also tend to experience feeling and emotions along with the higher perception. For example, it is hard to perceive a situation as moral or immoral (eighth order) without also experiencing rather strong accompanying second-order feelings or emotions.

Third-Order Perceptions—Configurations

When a mixture of intensities and sensations are put together by the cortex, they may appear to be something definite. For example, a series of black curlicues on white paper are recognized as letters. Put the letters together and we have words, sentences, paragraphs, chapters, a book. Put sounds together and we have language. Put them together another way and we have musical notes; in a third way and we have chords. Even if the sensation that makes up the word varies a great deal we still have no difficulty recognizing the word *dog*. We may hear it in a Southern accent, Northern accent, spoken rapidly, slowly, high pitched, or low pitched. The configuration *dog* remains fixed regardless of how it is presented to our ears. The same for a musical theme; we may hear it played in a thousand different ways, but we still recognize the configuration of the basic theme. A chair is a chair; whether it be a high chair, a low chair, a doll's chair, or a throne, there is no doubt in our perceptual apparatus that what we are looking at is a chair. Gertrude Stein said, "A rose is a rose is a rose" (as we've heard and heard and heard), perhaps meaning that the energy coming to our eyes from that form is that form regardless of the variety of configurations with which it may be presented. Simply stated, every form that we recognize or even, if we don't recognize it, see as unique is a third-order perception.

Mostly we agree on third-order perceptions, but we still argue a great deal about whether Jane looks more like her father or her mother. Adding the third order makes our world much easier to comprehend. Things have a name and a shape. They can be distinguished from each other, grouped, and classified. The advantages to this are obvious: if we had to name or define something everytime we referred to it we would be in a quagmire. To lose this ability, as often happens in certain injuries to the brain, is disastrous. Victims of strokes are often able to recognize words as words but can no longer recognize which word. Or in ordinary life, how uncomfortable it is when you are greeted by a woman you know but can't recall her name.

Fourth-Order Perceptions—
Control of Transitions

When a configuration is presented in slightly different positions in rapid sequence, we get both the perception of motion, and with the motion sometimes a change in shape. Something has changed or, in our terms, has undergone transition. It is still a configuration, but now it is in the process of becoming something else. For example, the old nickel turn-the-crank movies didn't move if you turned the crank slowly. You would just see a series of configurations, perhaps Tom Mix on his horse, one picture looking pretty much like the rest. But when you turned the crank rapidly the slight difference in each picture seemed to produce motion, a perception of change. This is a visual fourth-order perception. We can hear this when a fire truck passes with a siren blasting; the doppler effect is at the fourth order with a higher tone as the siren approaches, lower as it goes away. Without the fourth order there would be absolutely no possibility of hearing music; it is a transition that changes sound into melody. We enjoy the change of taste as we experience various foods. Therefore, as we move through the fourth order, time becomes a factor, and in our head, when configurations move, the perception may change from third to fourth order.

Most sports require that we control for fourth-order perceptions. A batter attempting to hit a ball is attempting to control at the fourth order. The bestselling tennis book *The Inner Game of Tennis* by Tim Gallwey is an attempt to teach you to play tennis without perceiving much beyond the fourth order. Gallwey says, "Set a place in your mind where you want the ball to go and then just watch the ball move until it hits your racquet." Then don't worry about your behavior, how you hit it; just stick to the perception of the ball. From that moment simply concentrate (fourth order) on the moving ball. If you can do this, then your stroke will take care of itself much better than you can take care of it at that crucial moment by trying to attend to it. You have enough to do right then if you'll just watch the ball.

But to help your stroke, which is of course important, watch a good player, and his or her good strokes will become your strokes to the extent it's physically possible. When you watch them, however, just watch what they do (fourth order), how they move and hit the ball. Don't say to yourself how good they are, or how hard they hit; just watch (we explain this shortly) without a higher order of value judgment. This is not easy, but recent coaching advances utilize these concepts.

Also remember that the tennis ball is just a ball. It has no motivation, so don't ascribe motivation to it. Don't say it's coming at me murderously hard or wickedly spinning. These higher-order perceptions will increase your error and make it harder for you to hit the ball well. In athletics, as in any endeavor, the greater the error the poorer the performance, but it's more pronounced and more quickly seen in athletics than in many other places. Keep in mind that our brain works as a control system; the finer the control the better the performance. Introducing error from any source increases the work of the control system and we lose precision. A slow ball is easier to hit than a fast ball because it causes less error.

Also, in sports it would follow that getting opponents to concentrate on anything but the ball (fourth order) destroys performance by opening up other comparing stations. The more stations that are open the less precise will be the control. In athletics concentration means keeping as few comparing stations open as possible. Psyching your opponent out, or causing him to open more comparing stations, is gamesmanship that some highly competitive athletes employ. Even the simple psychout of saying to an opponent "my, you're playing well today" immediately both raises his perception to a high order and opens a competency station. He loses concentration and plays less effectively.

These ideas apply also to golf. Here watch the ball, don't bemoan where it is, for example, if it is in a sandtrap. Make up your mind where you want it to go and hit it. Improve your swing by watching others or by practicing (tennis too), but in practicing concentrate on simple, easy shots that you can keep at the fourth level. If you try too hard, you will swing badly, criticize yourself, a high-order destructive practice, increase your error, and play erratically.

Fifth-Order Perceptions—Control of Sequence

If all we had were the first four orders we would be simple-minded creatures, but still ones who could do a great deal. Movement and rate of change could be detected. There are objects, arrangements, and static patterns that could be recognized. Each configuration breaks down into a variety of sensations, and each sensation is associated with some degree of intensity. We still would have, however, a very elementary organism. It couldn't, for example, walk, a series of sequential third and fourth-order perceptions. It couldn't talk, a sequential activity parallel to walking in our sound-creating system. When we look at the world, we see and experience sequence all around us; walking, talking, time, the seasons, the calendar, day and night are sequences which give meaning to our life. Without the ability to perceive sequence we would be a very static creature.

Sixth-Order Perceptions— Control of Relationships

Relationships are the way things go together; they keep our world predictable and prevent it from being fragmented. What is most puzzling to us in a foreign country are relationships which are different from what we have learned. Driving on the left side in England is a typical relationship which we have to learn quickly to avoid disaster. Almost all scientific experiments are an attempt to predict whether A varies from B. For example, is poverty the cause of crime? Or in everyday life, please turn off the light when you leave the room, or what is your wife's brother-in-law to you? From simple to complex we continually perceive and attempt to control for relationships. Try to think of living in a world without relationships, where everything seems separate, where all are parts and no larger wholes appear.

In his study of the patient Zharetsky,* Alexander Luria, the Russian neuropsychologist, who worked over twenty years with this brain-damaged victim of World War II, reported that after about three years, when Zharetsky, who had made progress

* Alexander Luria, *The Man with a Shattered World* (New York: Basic Books, 1972).

in the familiar hospital, seemed able to go home, he was able to deal sensibly with almost nothing on the way. That is, he knew a street was a street, a house was a house, a cafe was a cafe, but he couldn't figure out how they related to those who used them. For example, do you go into a cafe to eat or to sleep? None of the common relationships meant anything to him. When he finally entered his house and saw his mother he did recognize her (her configuration). He was then able to see her rise and move toward him—transition and sequence—and he knew he ought to do something, but what? He stood there and did nothing, because he couldn't remember what it was that he ought to do. Later, much later, as he overcame the brain damage through prodigious reorganization and redirection, it came to him that he should have kissed her, but at that time, in his shattered mind, his ability to perceive relationships was shattered with it. More about loss of control caused by brain damage at this and other orders is described in the fascinating book by Howard Gardner, *The Shattered Mind.**

Seventh-Order Perceptions—Program Control

I want to go to San Francisco. I plan to drive. I have some idea of how to get there. To actually get there what I will do is execute my going-to-San-Francisco program. First I want to perceive that my car is filled with gasoline and ready to go, to make sure I have a road map and money. As I drive north I encounter bad weather, a bridge is out, and I take a detour. My car overheats, and I have to stop and get the radiator fixed. Finally, thirteen hours later I pull into San Francisco. I have made arrangements to stop at the Hilton Hotel. I pull my car into the Hilton garage, take my suitcases out, go to the desk, and check in. I have executed the go-to-San-Francisco,

* Howard Gardner, *The Shattered Mind* (New York: Alfred A. Knopf, 1975).

stay-in-the-Hilton-Hotel program. To get there I use all of the previous perceptual levels, especially configuration, transition, sequence, and relationship. And in using these, successfully controlling all of them, I eventually move myself, even through unforeseen situations, from Los Angeles to San Francisco. All along the way, as I executed this program, I had to open a number of comparing stations inherent in the program. When my car overheated, I got the radiator fixed. I dealt with bad weather and bad roads by slowing down and detouring. I consulted the map to perceive that I was on the right road after the detour. Even with variations my San Francisco program was flexible enough to be successful. Not only do I have programs that I execute, I can also simulate programs within my head and check them as a computer might in an attempt to pre-select one that is most usable or compatible.

Of course I am making it much simpler than it actually is. In terms of how our brain works such programs are extremely complex. There has to be, for example, a program point of view, or the best way to execute programs, which Powers suggests might be rationality or logic. Therefore, at the program order we not only have logic and deduction but also superstition; don't ever walk under a ladder, an obvious perception of our own making. We have grammatical rules, recipes, strategies, and by this time we are very far removed from the original perception of intensity that initiated the whole perceptual train of events that constitutes control of programs.

Many people operate inflexibly at the seventh order, even though it is "obvious" to us that it is detrimental to them. It is possible that Richard Nixon operated rigidly at this order when he could not bring himself to burn the tapes. To do so would have caused him massive error at this order of perception, because his program was to record every word he uttered for future historians to study. Even though he might have avoided impeachment he could not raise his order of perception and override his program. To burn the tapes he would have had to move up to the eighth order, but his redirection system was unable to do it.

Eighth-Order Perception Systems— Control of Principles

Although much of what we perceive and control is within the first seven orders, what makes us uniquely human is our ability to perceive beyond the seventh order. While it is possible that some animals may operate beyond the seventh order, most don't. The primates, propoises, and whales may be exceptions. At this order we are talking about morality, responsibility, and values, the fundamental perceptions that we have discovered that we must control in order to belong or to get along with each other. As our brain grew over the past 3 million years, we became both more and more dependent upon one another and also so concerned about freedom and personal worth that we had to develop at least one if not two higher-order perceptions (eighth and ninth) to help us to resolve the inevitable conflicts that occur when we want to belong and we want more for ourselves. At these orders we perceive the world in terms of right and wrong, good and bad, moral and immoral, just and unjust, all concepts which we find necessary if we wish to satisfy our constantly conflicting needs. Morality is an obvious example. Every moral decision is at the eighth order, where, for example, we say it is wrong to steal or cheat because we have no right to take from others to gain an advantage. With most people there is little problem with stealing; not stealing is an easy value to accept. But problems arise when we try to get a right and a wrong for behavior that doesn't lend itself easily to what we call right and wrong in our world. Basically morality is an attempt to tell all people that in their internal world they should believe certain standard things for their own good and the good of everyone. Fanatic anti-abortionists claim that all abortion is wrong: a woman should bear the child whether she was raped or even when she is carrying a proven defective offspring. She should take responsibility to preserve the life that she has even unwillingly helped to create. Obviously this is an extreme moral position with which few agree; morality is hardly cut and dried. As with all perceptions starting with warm and cold and extending up to the eighth order, we will attempt to control for what best fulfills our needs. And if having an abortion fulfills our needs we'll get one if we can, legal or illegal. People will fight and die to continue to perceive their world, a world that they believe is right, good, or moral and they will often change sides, because, as we live, our specific needs change. Ronald Reagan once a left-wing Democrat became a right-wing Republican as his specific needs changed. As cultures evolve they also change; the eighth order therefore is constantly changing and will continue to change. Even so, characteristic of this order is the desire not to change what we believe, because when we do we suffer a huge, painful error. I believe Charles Darwin suffered serious psychosomatic illness most of his adult life because he could not resolve his eighth-order conflict between his belief in Christianity and his belief in Evolution.

Animals don't suffer high-order conflicts; they function mostly at the seventh order and below. They don't concern themselves with how long they should support their children, as we do. They have a built-in program that tells them, after a certain time, to throw them out on their own. The young who survive continue that program. If not enough survive then the species will become extinct unless it can reorganize and change its program. Creatures without the ability to perceive values need fixed behaviors. Otherwise they would be in a constant state of indecision which would cause them to suffer a severe evolutionary disadvantage.

To some extent we too, like animals, find it very hard to move up and perceive the world at the order necessary for our own benefit. In our unwillingness to reduce our consumption of gasoline how much different are we from a monkey who can be captured if we put some nuts through a small hole in a hollowed-out coconut? The monkey thrusts his hand through the hole, grabs the nuts (seventh order), and then, locked at this order, is trapped because he is unwilling to alter his program by opening his hand and releasing the nuts. He seems to have no more ability to perceive at the eighth order that opening his hand would be to his benefit than we seem to have when we are asked to alter our fuel programs and conserve.

There are times, however, when perceiving the world at too high an order can be detrimental. How many times have you seen policemen stop scruffy people or young people with beards because they see them not as people who are different (third order) but as potential criminals (eighth order). Police, of course, are trained to be suspicious, but we do many similar things with our own children, as when we scold them not for what they did, perhaps spilling the milk, but for being no-good brats who are out to make their parents miserable with irresponsible behavior. If we didn't constantly raise the order in dealing with "difficult" people we would have much less difficulty.

An ability to make value judgments, to perceive at the eighth order, is how we decide what to control for or what comparing stations to keep open. Obviously when we suffer a large error that our behavior is not able to reduce, we must have a mechanism to shut down the system or at least one or more comparing stations. It is too painful to keep them open and hope that a successful reorganization will take place, or in most cases, since we know nothing about reorganization, that we'll get lucky. Animals obviously have no mechanism to do this; if the monkey could stop comparing for nuts and start comparing for freedom he would be, from any standpoint except the trapper's, better off. Having high-order perceptions allows people to do this, as most of us will quickly surrender our money to a robber because our life is more important.

However, let's not make this judgment seem easy, because it isn't. At the eighth order, when we suffer conflict, we find it very hard to stop wanting either of the conflicting desires. Many a person has died defending his money. Recently we had our heart set on a car trip to the mountains, we planned it for six months; now the president says to use less gasoline. We had a whole value system and a complex program built on exercise and fresh air, a value system that had nothing to do with gasoline. Gasoline, which was at most a third-order perception, now is at the eighth order and conflicting with our trip to the mountains. How do we decide which program to run, the mountain program or the conservation program? We appeal to our eighth order, but no matter which way we move our thoughts there is error. Later, in Chapter 9, we will discuss this resolution in more detail, but here we must learn that to resolve the conflict we have to assign more value to one than the other. If we value both parts the same the conflict will last forever. There is another way, however, that we sometimes use to resolve this and other conflicts, which is to move up to the ninth order. At this higher order there may be no conflict, but this step up can be difficult to take.

Ninth-Order Control Systems— Control of Systems Concepts

In 1968 Lyndon Johnson surprised the country with the announcement that he was not going to run for re-election. No one knows what went on in Johnson's head, but few presidents seem to have relished the power of the presidency more. He also had a dogged nature. He had fought adverse political circumstances many times in the past, and to quit a fight seemed foreign to his whole being. In terms of BCP, what may have occurred in his brain under increasing criticism and political attack over his rigid stand on Vietnam, was a substantial perceptual error. In his head he desperately wanted to win the war, an eighth-order perception. This order was supported by a lower, sixth-order, patriotic relationship perception that the U.S. always wins wars. But even with the huge *seventh-order* power of the presidency to run military *programs*, he was stymied. Perceptions that we were going to lose flooded in, and he was busy redirecting, devoting all his energy to the war, little to other matters. His redirection system became inadequate to deal with the conflict between wanting to be re-elected and continuing the war. When none of the win-the-war programs seemed to work his error grew and grew and he may have at times experienced his reorganization system nudging his thoughts. If this happened, and I believe it must have, he probably became very frightened. It certainly frightens me to contemplate a president using this random, often destructive system in the age of the hydrogen bomb.

As long as he continued to control for winning the war there was no way to reduce the error in his I-want-to-continue-to-be-president control system, and the pain must have become unbearable. His only hope was to stop controlling for winning the war, and at the eighth order he could not do it. To do it he had to raise his order of perception and control for something even more important, in his case, I believe, his ninth-order perception of the office of president. His poor showing in the New Hampshire primary aided him in his attempt to perceive the presidency as more important than Lyndon Johnson, president, and more important than winning the war, both eighth-order perceptions. His ninth-order solution, not to seek office, produced a quick and welcome reduction in error by resolving the conflict. The presidency, a conceptual system as he perceived it, was greater than issues or men, and he could live with his stepping down as supportive of this ninth-order ideal. Some may argue that this decision was cowardly and self-serving, but in Johnson's world I am sure he did not perceive it this way at all.

What this example tries to illustrate is that above the eighth order we are in a very difficult, unclear, highly personal state of perceptual control. A conceptual system to you may not at all be one to me, as, for example, I'm a liberal, you're a conservative. Still when our eighth-order principles are in conflict we often try to raise the order to close down control systems that may be as powerful as remaining president and as winning a war. Some people choose to become Roman Catholics, a ninth-order perception that resolves many conflicts in their lives, but many people in conflict cannot find a ninth-order solution and suffer indefinitely. In a sinking boat how do you choose between your own life and that of a close friend when there is only one life preserver? Is there a ninth-order concept that will allow you to make that choice? Not likely! Nixon also tried to convince the country that the presidency, not himself, was at stake when he would not release the tapes. In his head this may have been so, but in the heads of the justices who sit on the Supreme Court this was an eighth not a ninth-order situation.

"Love conquers all" is an old ninth-order perception that works fine until you have to choose between your family and working day and night because you are so successful. King Solomon undoubtedly enlisted the ninth order from the true mother when he offered to divide the disputed baby. Henry VIII and Thomas More struggled to find a ninth-order solution to avoid More's execution. Perhaps if they could have waited long enough their reorganization systems would have been able to offer an acceptable ninth-order solution. Certainly this is a clue: if you need a ninth-order solution to an eighth-order conflict, try to stall for as much time as you can—it's hard to reorganize if you've lost your head. Ninth-order perceptions, therefore, are good for solving conflicts, but they are not the only way. Other ways will be discussed in Chapter 9.

Ninth-order perceptions are not always as crucial as some of the previous examples. An enjoyable ninth-order might be the loyalty that many people maintain to the "Brooklyn" Dodgers, who many years ago became the Los Angeles Dodgers. This loyalty is extremely abstract, but it is a very real ninth-order conceptual system to many faithful fans. In this case the team changed city, changed managers, changed ball parks, changed uniforms, changed players, changed announcers; yet many people still retain loyalty to the "Bums" as a reference level. They are upset when the Dodgers lose and happy when they win. They continue to follow the team day after day even though no part of the lower-order perceptual systems, except maybe the eighth order (loyalty) remains the same. From the ninth order they perceive themselves as good Dodger fans. They set reference levels all the way down to the second-order sensations of hot dogs and beer and the first-order intensity of the crack of the bat and the roar of the crowd.

Tenth-Order Perceptions— Universal Oneness—Meditation

Bill Powers speculates that there may be a higher order than control of systems concepts, an order which might be described as universal oneness. We can only guess at what this order could be, but perhaps the great eastern masters of Zen at times approach this order when they achieve Satori, which might be described as a place or order in which all perceptions of the world seem to be unified into one. Some mystics of other faiths also seem to reach oneness. I personally see the tenth order as a place where essentially we control for nothing but, since this is so hard, perhaps in practice we reach the tenth order if we can control successfully for one very special idea, as when we practice Zen or some other forms of meditation.

Under these very rare circumstances what we try to achieve is a situation where our only active control system is operating with no error. In this no-error situation my guess is that we actually become aware of our reorganization system as it idles along in the background, because with no error we are not redirecting or acting on new information. My concept is that our reorganization system never turns off completely, and when it alone is operating, as it may be during deep, peaceful, no-error meditation, we experience it as a creative sense of oneness with ourselves and the universe which we call transcendant. I think many of us who believe we have experienced transcendant or meditative states of mind may have indeed had a fleeting direct glimpse of this creative system in its pure, nondriven form. Therefore, with no error when we become aware of our own reorganization system while it is peacefully idling along, we are at the tenth order. There are I believe some powerful applications to our lives if we can experience this high order, a subject that will take up almost all of Chapter 14, where we discuss meditation and Positive Addiction.

8

The Worlds We Live In

Of the bits and pieces of history that we still remember few
are better retained than Marie Antoinette's statement, "Let
them eat cake." How stupid and insensitive we thought she
must have been not to realize the effect of her remark on
peasants who had no bread. Yet, in a lesser way we are all
Marie Antoinettes and give foolish advice constantly. How often, for example, do we tell our husband, wife, children, or
friends what they ought to do and how they ought to do it,
never realizing that what we say may make little sense to them.
This is because we tend to live our lives as if there is something
in the real world called sense and we are endowed with it.
But as we have explained, sense is at least a sixth-order perception; it does not exist in the real world, and what we call sense
may mean nothing to anyone but ourselves. In extreme cases,
like "Let them eat cake," it certainly seems as if Marie Antoinette should have been more "sensible," but in the totally aristocratic *personal world in which she lived,* she thought she was
making sense, and certainly many around her who lived in
similar personal worlds would have said the same.

We underline *personal world in which she lived* because,
as we have explained, we live only a small fraction of our lives
in the first-order outside world or real world. Most of our lives
are lived in a higher-order, unique personal world that we
create in our head from our needs. We may have personal

worlds that *seem to us* to contain much more of the outside real world than Marie Antoinette's, but they do not. The reason that we think they do is that as students we saw ourselves as closer to peasants than aristocrats. Therefore, when we or Marie Antoinette talk about the outside world where, for example, we believe cake or sense exists, we are never talking about that world. We are talking about the world in our head where these exist because they fulfill our needs. For all practical purposes it is the only world we will ever know.

We are *always* aware of this world, but we think it is the real world. Only on rare occasions are we aware that it exists only in our head, for example, when we whisper an instruction around a group, as we described in the last chapter. When the instruction comes back changed we know one or more people must have changed it according to their needs. But on occasional "artificial" demonstration like this means little, because there is nothing in the way our brain is set up to make us aware of our inside world. We have no built-in gauge to tell us that when we perceive the world at second order and above, the world that we perceive is in our head.

It follows logically that if we believe our in-the-head world is the external or real world, then we also make the mistake of thinking that our world is the same as your world and everyone's world. But, because it isn't, when we attempt to fulfill our needs we are constantly frustrated. Since we assume that our son lives in the same sensible world that we do we cannot comprehend how he could have joined that horrible cult. *He* must have gone crazy! And if Marie Antoinette had known that her advice came from her personal world, not from the real world as she thought, she might have made an effort to find out about the peasants' access to cake before she said what she did. *Therefore, because our false assumption that our world is the real world can be so devastating, we need to learn as much as we can how to avoid making this almost universal mistake.*

Our in-the-head world is built from all the successful perceptions that have satisfied our general needs. Everytime we successfully control for something, we build the perception of that success into our personal world. For example, when we cry as an infant and our mother comforts us we build the idea of a comforting mother into our personal world. If she continues to be around to comfort us we also have no reason to doubt her existence in the real world. We have no way of knowing that all that is out there is some energy that we have put together in our head that we call mother. If that energy disappears we suffer a painful error, because now we cannot perceive the mother we want. But if we continue for months and even years to bemoan our motherless fate then our suffering is less and less due to the fact that the real world has deprived us of a mother. More and more it is because we are not willing to remove mother from the world in our head, but we have no way of knowing this. Lacking this vital information we may not make the necessary effort to change the world in our head, for example, to try to gain the comfort we believe we need from someone else. If we continue to control for our lost mother we will suffer a large error and eventually begin to reorganize and perhaps do something drastic that we may regret. To prevent this from happening *we must learn the difficult lesson that we always live in two worlds, our personal world, over which, once we learn it is our world, we have a great deal of control, and something out there called the real world, over which we have much less control.* No matter how good our control system is, when our mother dies and her energy disappears from the real world there is nothing we can do to bring her back. To avoid suffering we must, in a reasonable period of time, remove her from being an active part of our personal world. She can and should remain as a pleasant memory, but if we continue to want her active presence we will be miserable.

We know, of course, that the reason we control for mother

and build her into our personal world is because she fulfills our needs. If we had no need for love and comfort mother would not be in our world. But when we built her into our world then *the outside world where she really exists and our in-the-head world where she exists for us became one; they coincide, and this coincidence makes it impossible for us to perceive them as two worlds.* It's like looking through the viewfinder of a split-image camera: when it is in focus all you see is one image. You have to *know* there are two. There is no way just by looking through the viewfinder that you can find this out. Therefore, because we don't know of our two-world existence, we assume that what we see is the one and only real world, when in fact it is both the real world and the world in our head. When our needs are fulfilled this inability to see both worlds may cause problems in getting along with others, because any information we pick up from the outside world that does not interfere with fulfilling our needs may mean nothing to us. This is why the plight of the peasants meant almost nothing to Marie Antoinette; starving peasants did not exist in her satisfactory coincidental worlds which to her were the real world. If Marie Antoinette had been told that she would never again have cake and she had believed it, then she would suddenly have thought that something was wrong in the real or outside world. She still would not recognize her two-world existence; she would not be aware that what was wrong was not so much that in the real world she would no longer have cake *but that in her personal world she still wanted it.*

Ordinarily, unless we are aware of our two-world existence when we detect a perceptual error we attribute it to the outside world not to the world in our head. Even so, we become more able to appreciate others who are having similar problems with what to us and to them is the real world. We have no way to know that what is wrong may be caused by what we want in our world. Still, if Marie Antoinette had lost cake, or anything else, she might have gained an inkling of what the starving peasants were complaining about. As long as our needs are fulfilled we are remarkably insensitive to anyone else who complains about the world. If we knew of our in-the-head world, and therefore our two-world existence, we would be much more sensitive to the needs of others.

Knowledge of our two-world existence would also help us to have more understanding of why we and others seem to have so much difficulty learning from experience. Remember that in this situation experience is unhappy or frustrating, like losing a job, failing in school, or getting an unexpected divorce. Pleasant, need-fulfilling experiences are no problem; we learn to spend money easily if we have a windfall. When we talk of someone not learning from experience, like a failing student who doesn't buckle down and study, the reason he doesn't is that in his world studying does not fulfill his needs. If it did, the experience of failure would cause him to study as it does motivated students. When we say he doesn't learn from experience what we are really saying is he doesn't learn from our experience in what we think is the real world. We don't understand that his world is different from ours. So we may make mistake after mistake trying to teach him from our "real" world instead of trying to reach him in his world with a need-fulfilling experience which might motivate him. Review the examples in Chapter 4 and it becomes apparent that neither the manager nor the teacher knew of our two-world existence. If they had they would have been able to handle the situation much better from the start. Keep in mind that we always learn from experience; in fact, it's the only way we do learn. But because I live in my world and you in yours what each of us learns is as different or similar as our personal worlds.

Also, as explained in the last chapter, the higher the order of the world in our head the more it fulfills our needs. The reason we object strenuously to being overcharged in a restaurant (eighth order), but don't care if they substitute carrots for peas (third order), is that the higher-order perception is much more important to us. The world in our head won't accept this insult. Carrots and peas, however, are at the same low order and at this unimportant order the world in our head is much more flexible. Animals have few values. They perceive the world below the eighth order and learn more easily from experience because at lower orders they are much more willing to change the world in their head. Buy a grown dog from a good home or kennel, feed her and pet her, and in two days she is yours. This is because the dog perceives her owner more at the sixth order (relationship), an easy order to transfer, than at the eighth order (love), which is hard to give up. Marry a man who still grieves for his dead wife, and you may never have him for your own. To him you are a sixth-order "companion" who cannot replace the eighth-order wife who still exists in his head. He has not learned enough from the experience of losing his wife to be able to love again. If he knew he was living in his personal world, not, as he thinks, in the "real" world, he would not complain of his new wife's inadequacies; he would make an effort to change himself. Therefore not knowing of our two-world existence and thinking that we always live in the real world handicaps more of us than Marie Antoinette.

We realize this is confusing and that as you sit thinking about which world you live in right now you might ask, "Is not the world of this book, the chair I'm sitting in, the room, the house, the city of Chicago, isn't this world that I can see, hear, and touch, the real and only world? Why are you attempting to confuse me with all this discussion about another world, the world in my head? I know I'm in Chicago, and I'm only in Chicago; it really exists, and it would be here whether I'm here or not."

No, we are not telling you that your house in Chicago does not exist. Of course it exists. Look around; there it is. But, following BCP, if in your head you want to be sitting in a chair, reading a book in a room in a house in Chicago, *and that is where you are,* then, as we have explained, the actual world and the world in your head coincide. What you see and believe is the real world is actually both the world in your head and the real world, but again we must stress there is no way for you to perceive this coincidence. When you see what *you want to see* (or hear or touch) you are not, as you believe, confirming the real world, *you are confirming the Chicago world you want, which is the world in your head.* But that confirmation means much more to you than just confirming the existence of a chair, book, room, house, and Chicago in your world. It means more because when we easily confirm any part of it, we extend our *false* belief that the real world *is not just this part of our world. It is all of our world.* Therefore, the more comfortable we are in Chicago, the more we may also believe we are smart, or our wife loves us, or other parts of our personal world which we may find more difficult to confirm. Every time Marie Antoinette ate a fancy cake she not only confirmed the existence of cake, she falsely reconfirmed the existence of her whole aristocratic personal world as the real world.

To explain further how our unawareness of our two-world existence complicates our lives, suppose when you are in Chicago you would rather be riding the surf at Malibu. Then, as soon as you put Malibu into your head, Chicago will be unsatisfactory. Now it is not where you want to be, and while it is still in your head it satisfies your needs less and less. When this happens you begin the task of removing Chicago from your head. The longer you stay in Chicago when you don't want to be there, the more you gripe that the people are no good, the weather lousy, and the politics corrupt, but since you are still in Chicago doing the best to fulfill your needs, you can't easily get it out of your head.

Then you make the move to Malibu and it's a good move. Now Chicago, which was recently so real, will begin to fade, because it no longer has anything to do with fulfilling your needs. Chicago will be like your old elementary school where you struggled as a child. It's there, but it's no longer real. It's a ghost, a bit of shadowy reality that was once so tangible as you learned to read and write, but now hardly exists except as a building on a street. Or Chicago will become like a happily rid-of ex-husband, who, although you once loved him, now hardly seems to exist at all. Even when you see him, the only way you can really confirm his existence is to reach out and touch him. And even that touch, once so intimate, might now feel strange and unfamiliar—he is no longer in your head.

Probably the main reason that we tend to think the real world is the same as the world in our head is that we routinely deal so much more with things than people. Unlike people, things like a chair, table, or house do not interfere with our needs, but remember they are only there because they already exist in our head as at least a third-order configuration, chair, table, or house. Since we have no way of knowing this we automatically assume they exist in the outside world. And because this happens so often, that is, because most of what we see when we look around is already built into our head to help us fulfill our needs or at least not interfere with them, we tend more and more to assume that our world is the real world, when in fact it is not. As long as we deal mostly with nonfrustrating things that most of us have and use the same way, this *false* assumption works, and we can live in our own world reasonably well. When we carry this assumption over to people, we're usually in trouble, because people, unlike chairs, have needs of their own. The more we deal with them the more they tend to interfere with our needs. This is why, when we deal with people, we must keep our in-the-head and their in-the-head worlds in mind, or we will suffer constant frustration. But even when we become aware that all of us live in our own world it is easy to forget, especially with people who for a long time did fit well into our personal world because they satisfied our needs.

Jane was a compliant child who for years lived comfortably

in the world in our head. Because it was so comfortable for so long we have forgotten that she actually lives in a world of her own. Now as a teenager she turns "defiant" and where she had existed comfortably in both our worlds, now she suddenly becomes a very uncomfortable reality, because she does not fulfill our needs. We complain she has no right to do and say the things she does. We do not understand or accept that she is trying to satisfy her own needs in her own world. If we accepted from the start that Jane lives in her own world, not ours, we would understand how unrealistic it was to expect her to continue to behave as we want her to. She is not a chair, she is a person. From this we would then try to work out a compromise between how we want Jane to fit into our world and what she wants from us and others in her world. We might have to do a good bit of negotiating, but this would be sensible, because we would know that she will probably never again "live" in our world. What we are trying to find is enough overlap between our world and hers so we can get along. If we refuse to remove the old "good Jane" from our world then her "bad" behavior will cause us a huge error, and we will never find the compromise overlap between worlds that we need for Jane and everyone else we want to get along with. Dealing badly with that error, which is caused by our inability to recognize that she does not now and never has lived in our world, has cost many a family their Jane.

We are in for a lot of misery if we don't realize that people were not put on earth to satisfy our needs. If we try too hard to force others to live in our world, because we think it is the real world, we are doomed to disappointment. And even if we do recognize that others live in their own world we must also learn that with people, unlike things, we must continually compromise and negotiate if we wish to find common ground in our personal worlds. It takes a long time and a lot of pain, and still many of us fail to realize how hard it is to get our world even partly to coincide with their world when we are dealing with people. Or as Humphreys succinctly put it, Crusoe's real problems did not start until Friday showed up.

This also explains why no matter how many times we tell others to face reality, they rarely want to face it. From their standpoint, to face reality really means to face our reality, and for them our reality is almost always uncomfortable. Not too many people admonished Einstein with "Face it, Albert; you're a genius, and we've got to give you the Nobel prize." Those who demand that others face reality are more often saying, "Face it Snodgrass, you're a fool," a bit of our reality that has done little to lighten the burden carried by the Snodgrasses of the world. When we ask people to face our reality we must also take into account whether this makes sense to them in their world, an effort not often extended by those who make this demand.

The idea that we care little about anyone else's world unless it is similar to ours may sound selfish. For example, unless I like roses I may not want to listen to my neighbor's endless talks on the subject. But the reason that many of us are not selfish is that we, unlike Marie Antoinette, are usually unable to come even close to satisfying our needs the way we would like to. This makes us open to learning that we can compromise and share our personal worlds, and because I like my neighbor and he likes me, I listen to roses and he listens to tennis. In a sense, however, driven by our needs, our personal world is always a selfish world except—*and this is a strong exception*—part of our selfishness is to fulfill our built-in need for love and belonging. Viewed in this way even altruism could be seen as selfish, but it hardly works that way in practice. I don't mind if someone selfishly saves my life by risking hers. I would be happy if I could do the same for her.

There are many obvious practical applications of the knowledge that we live in two worlds. The first is that if we wish to get along with someone else we must find common ground within our personal world that we will agree is the "real" world.

If we can't find this common ground then we will never be more than passing acquaintances. Differences cannot be reconciled until we do, and marriages which are built on only a small overlap of common ground, perhaps initial sexual attraction, will rapidly dissolve into acrimony unless more can be found. We tend to get along with people who not only like the same things but who also dislike or hate the same things. In fact, at times hatred can form such a large sharing of worlds that people who ordinarily would have nothing in common get along well. War and even religion tend to pull people together to share their hatreds, although families too often also do a good job of uniting in bitterness.

Because our present affluent society provides so many options for fulfilling our needs, we tend to create such dissimilar internal worlds that we find it hard to locate the common ground necessary to maintain long-term relationships. When people talk of the good old days they are often talking of a time when, with less affluence and less opportunity, it seemed to them that we shared more common ground.

Finally, although we will cover this later when we talk more of marriage, to keep it or any close relationship viable we must not only share a large overlap in our personal worlds, we must also develop a tolerance for the parts which do not now and probably never will overlap. If I like sitting home and my wife likes going out and if I control strongly for sitting home, I put our marriage in danger because this part of our personal worlds we do not share. A compromise that may work is to encourage her to go out alone or with friends, so that the parts of our world we do not share do not cause error in either of us. But if I insist that my world is the real world and that in the real world women stay home with their husbands, I'll soon hear from her lawyer.

None of us lives to any extent in the real world, because all that's out there is bits and pieces of energy, the first order. Even though there is nothing in the way our nervous system is set up to give us this information *the world we mostly live in is the world in our head.* The more we concentrate on learning (and using) this almost unlearnable fact, the more we will negotiate and make the compromises necessary to fulfill the needs of our basic social nature.

9

Conflict, Control, and Criticism

❦

Recently I spent a cold winter evening with some Arizona friends in front of their fireplace, relaxing, talking, and eating homemade candy. Next to me on the couch was Princess, a fluffy cat who alternately slept, stretched, or just rested by the fire. I occasionally disturbed his toes (Princess, it turned out, should have been Prince, but the discovery came too late to change the name), but he did little to control for this disturbance except push gently against my fingers. As I shared the couch with this relaxed creature, I could not help thinking of how little error he seems to experience. His family confirmed that tonight was typical; he leads a life in which he is more than capable of controlling his perceptions.

In this chapter we explore why it is that so many of us, unlike Princess, experience errors we cannot control. We will not, however, concentrate on the obvious causes, such as poverty, discrimination, broken homes, poor schools, corrupt or insensitive political leaders, and misuse of drugs, legal and illegal, which affect the brain. No one reading this book is unaware that all of these lead both to large errors and to our inability to control effectively to deal with them. To take just one example, in a society where education is a necessity if we wish to fulfill our needs too many children learn almost nothing in school, and many drop out. Probably the main reason is that, at an early age, when they do not learn as quickly as our standards dictate, the school labels them failures but still moves them ahead where they have less and less chance to learn. Most of these children, when they experience increasing failure errors, shut down their whole school control system and give up trying to learn. Without education, without even a comfortable place to spend the day, their error increases and is handled badly, too often through the familiar behaviors of delinquency and drug use.

The obvious remedy of eliminating failure and instead teaching each child to reach competency in a no-failure situation, no matter how long it takes, is not yet acceptable in our traditional time- and failure-based system. We mention this one example here to make sure that no reader criticizes us for being insensitive to social ills, but the focus of this book is on the individual not the group. Here we will concentrate on the three major sources of all the error we as individuals experience, *conflict*, *control*, and *criticism*. Singly or together, we get almost all of our error from the inability of our control systems to cope with these three very common human experiences. Here we use the term control to mean our attempt to control or dominate ourself or others. If you tend to get confused, substitute *dominate* and you should have no problem.

Simply defined, *conflict* occurs when we try simultaneously to control for two or more incompatible reference levels, like being torn between the desire for love and money. *Control* (or domination) is experienced when we try to force ourselves or someone else to do what we or they don't want to do. *Criticism* occurs when you criticize someone, someone criticizes you or, at times worst of all, you criticize yourself. Sooner or later control or criticism leads to conflict; if not resolved it can continue indefinitely, defying all of our attempts to solve it. As we will learn, it is the most difficult situation our control system has to face.

Conflict

As we first described in Chapter 2, there is in all of us the potential for conflict among our basic needs. In Chapter 7 we explained how this conflict tends to surface at the eighth order of perception when we attempt to find a value or principle that will allow us to satisfy opposing needs. We gave the example of two close friends in a sinking boat with a life preserver buoyant enough for only one. Could you float comfortably and watch your friend drown? What principle could either person find that would resolve this conflict?

Fortunately, most of us will never experience this situation, but all of us frequently experience conflict. In fact the stronger and more adequate our control systems are, the harder we struggle to fulfill our needs and therefore the more intensely we will experience any conflict that arises. Typically in all of us there is the conflict between freedom to do what we want to do and our belief that we have responsibilities toward others, as in a failing marriage. From tiny upsets such as "should we eat at home or go out to dinner?" to major conflicts like risking disruption of our marriage when mom and dad threaten to give up trying to live if we don't open our home to one or both. In all these miserable situations there is no way to escape a large perceptual error. In fact if it were not for the error caused by conflict, most of us could deal with our life almost as well as Princess. We envy him because his needs never seem to be in conflict, and if they ever should be, he solves the problem by going to sleep. Not a bad way to reduce a conflict, but a way not open to those of us who have strong control systems.

Conflict is so frustrating because no matter which way we turn there is error; what we do is work very hard to go nowhere. What goes on in our head is analogous to what happens each year in Petaluma, California, when the world arm-wrestling championship is held. In match after match two contestants lock hands and at a given signal attempt to push each other's arm to the table. There is unbelievable straining and sweating. Every muscle in the contestants' bodies tense, but for a long time their arms remain upright. Here is a perfect model of what happens in our heads and in our bodies when we are trying to redirect or reorganize our perceptions for two or more incompatible reference levels. Struggling to move in two opposite directions at the same time we feel tired, dragged out, drained of energy or ambition, as if we had carried a load of bricks on our back, even though physically we have done little. We are tired because no matter what we do to reduce the error in one comparing station we increase it by that same amount in the other. And unfortunately, we can't relax as the arm wrestlers can when the match is over. In our head we can wrestle for years, go to sleep exhausted, wrestle half the night in our dreams, and wake up exhausted, involved in a contest where we can neither win nor quit.

To resolve a conflict we must accept that one side is more valuable than another or that neither side makes sense. How can you win when you bet against your home team? If your team wins, you lose money. If the other team wins, you feel lousy. But you might decide that you really enjoy the money more, and when you make this decision there is no conflict. Or you might decide to stop betting—again no conflict. The other possibility is to stop following your team altogether, saying that watching football all day Sunday is a waste of time. When you do that you remove the conflict by moving up to a higher order of perception where there is no conflict.

Suppose a married woman with children falls out of love with her husband and into love with someone else. Simultaneously she has a strong reference level for sexual love and personal acceptance and an equally strong reference level for loyalty to her marriage and family. Under these all too common circumstances, she may find her redirection system in the position of the locked arms of the two struggling wrestlers. Each arm is an attempt to control her perceptions toward a different reference level; one towards personal love and the other towards loyalty. She will waver in each direction, move heaven and earth to see her lover furtively, yet steadfastly refuse in her mind to consider a divorce or separation. Obviously there are as many variations on this theme as there are redirection possibilities, but regardless of which she chooses, any movement toward one reference level will increase her error toward the other, so she wavers back and forth unable to resolve the conflict. Driven by error she desperately tries to find a compromise or in-between reference level where there is less error. But what in-between reference level can she find? How can she be loyal and disloyal, or loving and nonloving at the same time? Unwilling to decide which way to go, she is redirecting with every bit of mental energy available to reduce an error that cannot be reduced. We see her, as she gets deeper and deeper into the conflict, perhaps choosing as a compromise reference level to do less and less, becoming discouraged as every move to resolve the conflict is unsuccessful. She may even begin to redirect by sitting around the house, listless, passive, responding very little, eating erratically, sipping wine, and almost fading away. This redirection to withdraw reduces the pain, because she already knows that any energy she can summon up will be expended on the conflict; why push further? It is as if two of the arm wrestlers were so perfectly matched that finally, with no strength left at all in their arms, each just supports the other. A gentle breeze would blow them over, but still their arms remain upright as they continue the struggle in their minds.

The distressed wife also may become exhausted by the never-ending error and develop one of the many illnesses of reorganization, a process we will explain later. Or she may redirect with depressing, which allows her to perceive herself as not only helpless but miserable. All these solutions are faulty, but

all in some way reduce the conflict through disabling the conflicting person. Just today, as I discussed a conflict with a client,
she suddenly became dizzy. It was a desperate attempt on
her part to redirect right then with an old symptom to avoid
the discussion, which was painfully focusing on the conflict.

While conflict may affect one's whole life, this is not necessarily the case. The undecided wife may have a job which she
intends to keep whether she stays or goes. Her perception of
her work is that she is doing well; on the job there may be
little or no error. She may even work harder and more effectively, throwing herself into her job in order to spend most
of the day successfully controlling the part of her life which
is not in conflict. She may tend to stay longer and longer at
work, take work home, do everything possible to avoid the
perception of the conflict. This may indeed help her for a while
until her lover gets too persistent, her sexual needs grow ur-
gent, or her children demand her time on the one Sunday
that she had planned for weeks to spend with her lover. Here
there is true conflict because the opposing reference levels
are equally strong and at the same order, the eighth, between
her value system of love and her value system of loyalty.

On the other hand, there may be discomfort but little actual
conflict when the opposing reference levels are not at the same
order. For example, another woman may have a husband who
pays less attention to her than she would like, so at social gather-
ings and parties she flirts to get attention. She may even have
a casual affair and enjoy it, but the thought of leaving her
husband for a lover never crosses her mind. Here she has a
conflict between an eighth-order perception of loyalty that will
bind her to her husband and family, and flirting, a lower-order
perception. Flirtation is sixth-order (relationship) because it is
little more than the biological interplay that will always occur
between a flirtatious female and an approachable male or the
other way around, a relationship that is as clear-cut as a cup
in a saucer. While she may fantasize, even have moments of

guilt, as she toys with raising her order of perception above flirtation, the higher-order marriage perception will prevail in the way she generally redirects her life.

Another option for the woman torn between eighth-order love vs. loyalty is to try to resolve the conflict by attempting to perceive the whole situation at the higher ninth order. To do so she may go to a psychiatrist and attempt to talk abstractly about the need to resolve the conflict in her life. It is too much effort, it is going nowhere, she is above such mundane carrying on. Here at the ninth order (system principles) she can talk quite dispassionately about whether either her need for romantic love or her "excessive" loyalty to family is really that important. What is more important are her "higher" needs, to live her life to its fullest potential. She decides that she'll tell both her husband and her lover that it's their problem not hers and let them work it out; just let her know when they do. Then she'll decide if she agrees. Now it's all at the ninth order, and as she discusses this with her therapist she feels good for the moment.

But weeks go on and she just talks, until finally the therapist says to her, "Fine, just how exactly do you plan to do this?" and she may quickly step down to eighth-order reality, back to the conflict. She may become mute, yell, scream, or cry. To attempt to avoid the conflict she may run out of the office or bitterly accuse the psychiatrist of being inadequate because he can't solve her conflict. It's very hard to move a strongly personal eighth-order conflict up to the ninth order. It's not even that easy to give up watching and betting on football. It's like people who talk about giving everything up for art or shipping out on a sailboat for Pago Pago, but never do. But with time it may happen, and when it does the conflict may be resolved.

There is also the possibility that the therapist may persuade the woman to do something about the situation by lowering the order of perception of one side of the conflict. For example, to force herself to try for a month to relate exclusively to her husband and avoid her lover. If she can follow this arbitrary seventh-order program, it may allow her some time off from the conflict. If she cannot perceive her husband as more or less valuable than her lover during this month it may not work, but arbitrarily trying to live for a while on one side may make that side more or less attractive. Or she may try the same approach with her lover, seeing him exclusively for a month and hoping that he will become more or less important than her husband during this time. Obviously this is difficult, but getting people actively to live a seventh-order program for a trial period, even though in the beginning they don't feel like it, will often resolve a conflict.

Another way to solve a conflict is the way of the arm wrestlers. Try to hold out until one side runs out of strength and the other prevails. The woman may not have the strength to continue to see her lover and to carry on with family responsibilities. As she grows tired, the lover, who seemed so loving, so necessary, and so appreciative when she overwhelmed him with her love, loses some of his luster. More and more in her eyes he may take on the lower-order perception she had assigned to her husband, and as he does so there is less conflict. The higher, eighth-order value of the marriage prevails, and she gives up her now sixth-order lover.

Further, she may redirect by persuading her husband to join her at a marriage encounter weekend where they have the chance to open up to each other. If she is able to talk to him she may find him as romantic and interested as her lover, and suddenly there is no conflict. Time and a resourceful redirection system resolve many conflicts. It is as hard to keep two opposing reference levels exactly equal indefinitely as it is to have a draw in arm wrestling.

Another possibility might be that she throws herself so passionately into her work that she begins to get a lot of recognition, even quite a bit from her husband. She then realizes that her lover's recognition was a great deal of his attraction, but she no longer needs it, and the conflict resolves in favor of her husband. Or one of her children gets sick, and both the husband's and the wife's order of perception moves up to the unconflicted, we-love-our-children-more-than-ourselves, ninth order, during the sickness. During the necessary lull while the child is sick, the love affair may drop all the way to the second-order sensation, hardly a sufficient perception to keep it going.

It is also possible that the wife could get sick, depress, or become crazy, all as a result of the conflict, which could get her husband's attention or cause the lover to lose interest. Few lovers are as understanding about sickness or disability as Robert Browning. There is also the possibility that her lover, who also must share some of the conflict, will recognize that she just can't handle the strain and quietly leave. She might grieve for a while, but separation usually resolves the conflict. Time, changing circumstances, chance, good redirection, or a lucky reorganization all can act to resolve conflict. We don't, however, want to intimate that conflict resolution is easy. It isn't, but it is not impossible either. It only seems that way when we are in the middle.

Obviously today, in the affluent western world, where there is so much we can do, there are opportunities for large areas of conflict between friends, husbands and wives, parents and children, grandparents and grandchildren, bosses and employees, teachers and students, and administrators and teachers. There is even conflict between pet owners and their pets, as many people who both love and hate a Siamese cat or a French poodle will attest.

Areas of disagreement tend to pile up as we live our lives. As we know people more and more intimately we find out that more knowledge leads to more places to disagree. People we meet casually on vacation seem so compatible because we only see them and do things with them which we find congenial. But if we try to maintain the friendship after the vacation, when there are fewer things to do that are fun we often find that they are so different from us that we wonder what we saw in them on the vacation. The couple who did everything so freely on vacation seems so rigid afterward, and the friendship flounders over where we should go to eat. Conflict mostly occurs between people who are intimate and in situations where we can't escape as easily as we can on vacation. We grudgingly give up our lover, but we are grumpy and unloving toward our husband, so we gain little. Our husband starts to drink a lot, and then we yell at him to stop drinking. One conflict replaces the other because we never really resolved the first. We try to settle for unsatisfactory or compromise reference levels, but all we accomplish is to drain our energy. As this occurs we get more and more tired, redirect less and less efficiently, and are forced to turn to our reorganization system; almost all painful reorganization is the result of conflict. It is no wonder that minority groups tend to reorganize with high blood pressure and many chronic illnesses (we explain this later), because to be a minority is to be in almost constant angry conflict between what you perceive you must do to get along. and what you would like to do to satisfy your own needs.

But member of a minority group or not, as time goes on we become more and more aware that conflicts exist between ourselves and the others we need. It seems as if conflicts tend to multiply, perhaps because as we grow older the limited time we have starts to concern us. We more and more want to do what *we* want. When we do it, however, often it causes us to be in more conflict with those around us. The success of many consciousness-raising programs, assertiveness training, and other such popular psychological diversions, especially among middle-aged people, is often based upon the attractive message: pay more attention to your needs and less attention to the needs of others. In other words, see yourself at the center of the world (ninth order), and the rest of the world at the eighth order or below, and you will have no conflict. As long as this is done by only a few people, it may be helpful to them. If, however, everyone were continually assertive or looked out mostly for themselves, there would be a lot of lonely people trying to convince themselves they didn't need others. In time, the self-centered person turns even his friends away. I am not knocking assertiveness, just saying that like all forceful behaviors it must be used with caution. It is, for example, a good way to protect yourself during casual encounters with people who try to push you around, but unless it leads to compromise, it doesn't work well among intimates for any long period of time. Think of it as a great way to sell a used car but to be practiced cautiously on your next-door neighbor.

As we grow older, among the people we live with we strive for a perceptive balance, to find a compromise value that minimizes conflicts. That is why there is always strain among people who live and work closely together, because life with our family or other intimates must be filled with compromises. It is impossible that we share exactly the same reference levels, but if we as intimates practice openness, negotiate our differences early before we get locked into defending our position, we can learn to live together successfully. There is no other way. If we don't learn to do this, we become more and more anxious as time goes on, fearing that each new demand will unbalance the control systems that are keeping us from conflict and disrupt the relationship with blowups that may drive a permanent wedge between us and a loved one. For example, a child who was so cooperative at ten becomes a terror at sixteen, doing things which upset us and threatening to run away if we get too restrictive. Our behavior therefore becomes a combination of rigidity and permissiveness as we buzz back and forth among a variety of conflicting (eighth-order) reference levels regarding our child. Here it is necessary to raise the perception of the child to the ninth order, decide upon a long range plan, and stick to it. If we can look at the child at the ninth order, as a whole human being trying to grow up in a tough world with needs of his own, and keep in mind that to us the child lives in his world not ours, we may be able to tolerate a lot of behavior that at the eighth order would cause us conflict. It's hard to stand by and see the child get bloodied up, but usually it's the best way.

If we are unable to resolve conflicts through active compromise and negotiation they tend to pile up as we grow older. Then, when something is asked of us, we too often give a quick *no* for an answer, because more and more we perceive that anything we do might disturb a whole series of rigidly controlled conflicts and unbalance the system. Therefore, when we are walking a tight line in our job, in our marriage, and with our family, the thought of doing anything as simple as lending our car to a neighbor becomes a big deal. We're afraid our husband or wife would criticize us, and our marriage, already full of conflict, might explode, so we say no. But then we get upset about our selfishness, and this triggers another conflict. Conflicts tend to build up, so we should resolve them if we can before they accumulate. This is why it is so extraordinary to deal with an adult who is gracious, flexible, generous, and laughs a lot, an unconflicted person who mostly has little error between her reference levels and perceptions and who has a good redirection system to deal with conflicts when they occur. Unfortunately, conflicted as many of us are, we often find it painful to deal with such individuals. They seem so free, so unconflicted, that our perception of their freedom of action, which we want so desperately, increases our error. Rather than attempt to be like them to reduce our error we may try to avoid or destroy them; they represent a threat to our rigid control systems. History is replete with religious and political witchhunts to seek out and destroy the unconflicted, like Joan of Arc, who communed freely with both God and the powerless peasants. When these rare people are safely dead we try to resolve our conflict over killing them by honoring them as saints or heroes.

Control and Self-Control

It follows, therefore, that to reduce conflict and to keep order most cultures traditionally attempt to control people who might place their personal needs above the needs of those in power. They do so through laws, customs, and the liberal use of punitive sanctions. They continually attempt to educate people to the virtues of self-control, of overcoming one's weaknesses, of keeping one's desires in check, of holding to the right path. This is an attempt by political leaders at the highest level down to bigger brothers or sisters at a far lower level to control potential conflict through getting weaker people to follow seventh-order programs without eighth-order questioning of whether or not these programs are good for them. We are taught early to eat the spinach before the dessert, to study our lessons before we go out to play, to respect our elders and above all our flag. Every civilized society has a series of do's and don'ts to reduce conflict and keep order by attempting to convince us to follow these programs whether it suits us or not.

But denying our desires and conforming to the rules decreed by others usually sets up within us a conflict, which if not resolved may ultimately spill over into society. If we believe nuclear power plants are dangerous, should we picket and risk going to jail? Most of us control very strongly for freedom, and jail is a tough choice. It is possible to do as the ant did— to pay total attention to business and work all summer long while the grasshopper is outside fiddling and enjoying himself— but it's hard. Most of us want a summer off once in a while, and there is no record that the ant ever got one. In time, we believe that even the ant will fight for a summer off. So while it seems easy to praise the virtues of self-control and self-discipline in ants and grasshoppers it's hard for people to control their desires. We should not be deluded into thinking that to control ourself all we have to do is grit our teeth, buckle down, and try a little harder. Or ask someone else to do the same. We don't realize the immense difficulty of this process, that when we attempt to deny our own needs, as in the case of most self-control, it takes a huge amount of strength, more than is available to most of us. What people are talking about when they expound the virtue of self-control is somehow or other to gain the strength to make no effort to get what we want, *in BCP terms to deny the existence of a large-error signal.*

Self-control or self-discipline, as most of us believe in it, is a myth. *It cannot exist, because if we cannot reduce the error, the error signal will cause us to reorganize.* Few authors understood this as well as Somerset Maugham who, in the story "Rain," depicts the married but passion-starved missionary, Rev. Davidson, desperately attempting to control his own sexual frustrations through zealous religious redirection. Until he was aroused by the prostitute Sadie Thompson, praying and proselytizing kept the conflict under tenuous control, but his unexpected passion for her, which he frantically tried to repress, made him desperate. He redirected with prayer for hours on end to maintain the behavior of repressing, to try to keep unconscious the desire for her that was causing him to lose control. His efforts to convert her seemed to be succeeding when suddenly his self-control broke and he succumbed to her sexually. When this happened his conflict was so severe he reorganized by killing himself. What Maugham knew is that we cannot stop the system. One can pray, condemn, damn, or entreat, but repressing will eventually fail and we will either redirect or reorganize. It may be that when we talk of self-control, self-discipline, or repressing in the sense of completely stopping our behavioral system what we are really talking about is suicide, murder, psychosis, or serious illness, desperate reorganizations that destroy one or the other or both sides of the conflict.

So when we say to ourselves, "Stop," as Davidson desperately tried to do, we are invoking the impossible. We must learn that we can't simply stop anymore than King Canute could stop the tide. We can, however, learn a more effective behavior, or we can seek help. If we continue to try to exercise self-control we will eventually reorganize. How much better it would have been for Davidson, and for his wife, if he'd had available a fellow minister or counselor to whom he could have poured out his heart. In time he might have learned to find love in his marriage or get divorced. But if this had happened, there would have been no story. It is reorganization, good or bad, that makes great literature.

What often distinguishes civilization from most primitive cooperative societies is that in the former the strong and the clever *exploit* the weak and the less clever. In primitive societies, even gorilla societies, the strong *dominate,* but they do not usually exploit. In democratic societies this is done a little less, because in any democracy there are nonviolent pathways for the weak and the less clever to get some control over their own lives and avoid exploitation. Protecting the rights of the weak and the less clever has never, however, been popular, even in democracies. Most civilizations have followed Clarence Day's little poem, "Might and right are always fighting,/In our youth it seems exciting,/Right is always nearly winning,/Might can hardly keep from grinning."* History is replete with instances of one man controlling a whole nation; perhaps Chairman Mao controlled more people than any man in history. He did so, of course, "for their own benefit." All successful dictators soon learn the ways of big brother. Even in the little dictatorships of parents and teachers, after the administration of corporal punishment the punisher may with feigned sincer-

* Clarence Day, *After All* (New York: Alfred A. Knopf, 1936), p. 277.

ity remark, "It hurts me more than it hurts you." It helps the punisher's own conflicting needs to believe that he is compassionate as he seeks the control of others. *Compassionate or not, however, it is not possible to control another without causing conflict in that person, unless through some miracle the reference levels in the controller and the controlled are identical or very close.*

But that doesn't stop us from trying. Husbands attempt to control wives, and wives husbands, parents children, children parents, big children little children, boys girls, girls boys, teachers students, bosses workers—the list is endless. Just review in your mind and see how many times in one day someone attempted to control you. And how many times you attempted to control somebody else. Look around and see; attempts at control are all around us. *What we must learn is the hard fact that most of us dissipate much of our strength in attempting to control others, strength that we urgently need to compromise and negotiate, to ratify our needs and theirs.* But can you picture many people willing to stop trying to control someone? Are you? Even if you agree that it is desirable, are you willing to be first, or must you wait for me? Is it any wonder that democracy is so fragile? How could it be robust if in our personal lives, especially as we grow up, we almost never experience it?

But if we are not concerned about the conflict we cause, there is no doubt that we *can* control other people's behavior. This has been done since time immemorial and will continue unabated regardless of the misery it causes. I can control you (at least for a while) if I can control something you desperately want to get or to avoid. For example, if I want you to dig a ditch that you don't want to dig and I point a gun at you and say, "Dig," you will likely begin moving dirt. It is important, however, that I keep the gun on you and that you be convinced that if you don't dig, I will shoot. If I relax for a moment you may take control by bashing in my head with the shovel. Therefore, one of the basic principles of one person controlling someone else is that the controller has to be there all the time. You can be physically present, that is, hold the gun over me, or you can be mentally present by causing me to feel guilty if I put down the shovel. In most cases the physical comes first but for long-lasting control the mental is by far more effective. No one expressed this better than George Orwell in his book *1984*. If your approval is extremely important to me, then you can control me through the idea in my head of your disapproval. Our old friend guilt is probably the most powerful interpersonal control that we have, but even guilt has its limitations. If you feel guilty enough you may just decide, "What the hell, I feel so bad I may as well bash your head in." Controlling others even through guilt is a very chancy business.

To control people successfully we have to guess what it is they desire (what their reference levels are) or in general what gives them pleasure (what causes them pain). Then, well aware of the ancient force of reward and punishment, all a good controller or operant conditioner has to do is to fine-tune his control so it focuses on specifics. What causes the most pain or the most pleasure with the least effort to me? To be most effective, however, a good controller must discover how to apply these forces in a way that does not cause conflict, that makes the controlled person happy to be controlled. *This is never possible when the controller uses punishment, because (except perhaps for masochists) it always causes conflict.* Giving you what you want in trade for what I want is the most effective form of control, but *even reward*, the usual way of doing this, can cause error and is often unsatisfactory.

For example, I offer you money to do something for me, but you don't want money, you want more of my time. I don't know that, so when you don't do as I ask I offer you more money, but you do less because you wanted time. You don't quit for a while, because you are hoping eventually to get more time from me, but the more I give you money, the less satisfied you are. If you try working harder in the hope that will get you the time you wanted, I may mistakenly assume it was the money that you wanted and still give you little of my time. Then, if you slack off, I offer you more money, and in disgust you quit. What I offered you seemed to me to be a reward, but it was not what you wanted, and the error became too painful. I failed to control you because I took money for granted; I didn't know what you wanted.

In another case, you want money but I offer you too much. This is inappropriate; it causes mild conflict and you redirect with guilt. Eventually you slack off or quit if the guilt becomes too painful. Again reward didn't work, because I didn't guess the right amount. Equally ineffective is the far more common case when I don't offer you enough, but here there is little conflict.

In none of these examples of controlling you with reward have I caused you serious conflict. Serious conflict does occur through the use of reward when, for example, I give you money but you resent it. You want money, you want it very much, *but your resentment arises because you perceive that I have the power to control you with money.* Even though you want money you don't want to be controlled. This is for many of us a puzzling concomitant of reward, but it explains why even well-paid people go out on long strikes or indulged children are so ungrateful. Basically it gets down to your resentment, even when you are well paid, of the fact that I have what you want and to some extent you must do what I want to get it. Although most managers haven't the faintest idea of BCP psychology, they understand the conflict being discussed here. When they are involved in a negotiation they often set up straw men that their employees can knock down, *in order to give the employees a sense of control that is important to them.* While this might be viewed as manipulation, there is really very little else a manager can do, because in any organization, whether it is as small as a family or as large as General Motors, there has to be some sort of control, or in BCP terms some common reference level that everyone will agree to, or there will be chaos. Nevertheless, the more the people being controlled share in their control, and the more the controller recognizes their other needs by treating them humanly and fairly trading what the manager needs for what they need, the more control they will accept. Even explaining why management does things the way it does helps people to suffer less conflict when they accept reasonable control. All of these factors, however, are beyond simple reward and punishment. They are an attempt to balance conflicting needs with compromise and negotiation, and they are becoming more and more important as we move into an identity society* where people generally seem to be demanding more control over their lives.

Punishment is still the most widely used and advocated way to control others, probably because, unlike reward, there is never any doubt that punishment will produce error, pain, and almost always a change in behavior. But most punishment produces only short-term control. There is no good evidence that punishment will control people to do what you want them to do over any long period of time, because when you hurt people, you always increase their error. Since pain is generally not considered desirable, in most cases you provoke an immediate conflict between what the person would like to do and the fact that if he does it he will be hurt. As in all serious conflicts frantic redirection and occasional reorganization will occur, but there is no reason to believe that it will be in the direction of the punisher's desire. For example, a child curses a teacher. He is paddled severely and told if he does it again he will be paddled harder. If he dislikes the teacher strongly, he will be inclined to curse him again, but if he does he will be hurt again. He may solve the problem by stepping up to a higher order of perception and vandalize the school, perhaps

*William Glasser, *The Identity Society* (New York: Harper & Row, 1972).

burn it down. At this order he solves the conflict with the simple no-school, no-teacher, no-punishment route. Much vandalism and senseless destruction is redirection against the controlling establishment.

Basically what we are saying is that when you attempt arbitrarily to control yourself or others you are on chancy ground. It may work if it is what you or they want, but it is rare that we or others want what we try to force ourselves or them to do. With ourselves or with others compromise and negotiation are the only reasonable courses of action. Newspapers are filled with articles on wife and child abuse, almost all of which results from the faulty reorganization that constantly occurs when people attempt to control others, in this case people with limited behaviors because they were beaten instead of taught. If there is a place that S-R psychology has a universal hold, however, it is in the area of punishment. Unfortunately we are a long way from getting rid of this affliction.

Criticism

Finally, it seems to us that we suffer much more error than we need to because we don't understand how much error criticism causes in our lives. For example, yesterday's sports pages were filled with UCLA's victory over Notre Dame in basketball. UCLA had lost earlier in the year in a game that was almost a carbon copy of the game they won. Both games were decided by free throws in the last few seconds, the UCLA player missing in the first game and hitting in the second. Gary Cunningham, the UCLA coach, said that in the first game, during the time out that the opposition always takes before a critical free throw to rattle the free thrower, he talked to his player and told him to be sure to concentrate. He missed. In the second game, fighting back the urge to repeat his mistake, he said nothing. Tyren Nauls hit and UCLA won.

What made the difference was the most common error-producing behavior we engage in, criticism. In the first game the coach said, "Concentrate," and the player perceived this, as we all would, as "coach is nervous, he doesn't have confidence in me." It increased the player's error, and likely this caused him to press a little and miss. The coach meant well; most criticism is sincere, but it rarely works, because it always increases error. There is no way that criticism can be added to our perceptions without increasing our error unless the critic is totally unimportant to us. Since this essentially never occurs, criticism is most likely our largest single source of error. When Coach Cunningham kept quiet the second time, his player had only his own error to contend with, not enough in this case to cause him to miss.

We live in a world of too much criticism and we suffer from it. From the time we are small, "wiser" people tell us repeatedly that we do wrong or that we could do better. In school, criticism, especially in the form of low grades, very quickly causes huge numbers of children to redirect by giving up. For all practical purposes they close down their comparing stations for academic learning to reduce painful error. School, perhaps even more than the home, is where we first run into major criticism for not doing as we "should." But destructive criticism pervades far more of our life than school. It occurs in every area. How many of us have seen the disastrous effect of criticism in little leagues. Here adults with adult standards berate kids, sometimes even hit them, for failing to play like Reggie Jackson or Roger Staubach. Driven almost to madness by the error of losing, coaches crucify little children for their inability to perform under high pressure. Many young players learn to hate the game they play because of the pain caused by disapproving coaches and parents. At the age when they need compassion and support, when they don't need the adult win-at-all-costs standard, they are loaded with so much error that they can't perform. This is strongly illustrated in the 1976 movie *The Bad News Bears*.

Work, marriage, religion, government are all vast arenas in which excessive criticism flourishes unchecked. How many people learn to hate their jobs because they receive so much criticism? How many marriages fail—from the backbiting and carping that seems so constant in our culture? Masters and Johnson have gained fame through the simple expedient of getting lonely husbands and wives to relax and accept each other, couples for whom criticism and self-criticism have disrupted not only the marriage but the old-brain function of sex. Driven by the error that they can't satisfy their mate themselves, many people find sex tedious or impossible. Religion, especially as practiced by zealots and cultists, has reduced thousands of people to frantic redirection and even reorganization in a desperate attempt to please critical leaders who will relax their criticism only if followed blindly. Examine in your own life what too much criticism has done to your feeling of confidence, to your ability to get along with those around you. If you have escaped unscathed you are fortunate.

Criticism is constructive only when two conditions are met. *First*, when it is directed less at us personally and more at our behavior and, *second*, where the critic stays with us and in a friendly, caring way helps us to correct the criticized behavior. When we are being criticized we find it very difficult to believe it is not directed personally, because our behavior is the most visible, the most conscious, and therefore the most personal part of us. We will believe that we are not being personally criticized when we know the critic either cares for us a great deal, or has no personal feelings toward us at all. For example, we all know that we can accept a lot from a stranger or a casual friend. Under these infrequent circumstances we will tend to focus at a low order on what is being criticized, and it may be helpful. We, also, suffer excessively if we are criticized for something we cannot correct. It's no use telling your son he should have filled the gas tank after the car runs out of gas. Regardless of the critic's intent, that kind of criticism is always personal and can only be taken personally. If the goof has been made, the only course to follow is to work out a plan to correct the problem. There is no sense crying over spilled milk. Spend your energy helping to get more gas in the tank; nothing else will help. And everything else will increase error and make it more likely to happen again.

Unfortunately, the most serious criticism does not come from others. We can avoid them, at least in theory. It comes instead from someone whom we can never escape, ourselves. For example, most of the people who have fallen prey to cultists were drowning in self-criticism long before they met their leader. Why do we do this to ourselves? Why do we engage in this destructive, error-producing behavior? Why can't we, as Princess does so well, accept ourselves, our needs, and our behavior without constantly saying to ourselves that we are incompetent, that we don't do enough, well enough, often enough, and with enough things or people?

The source of self-criticism is an abortive attempt to reduce error. When we kick ourselves for forgetting our lunch, hitting a bad shot, failing to perform while making love, or when we blame ourselves for a child's running away, we do so in an unrealistic attempt to change behavior that has already occurred, sometimes to enlist the sympathy of others, often both. Essentially, what we do is to act as if we were someone else and criticize ourselves as if we were they. This self-abasement reduces the error in a comparing station for self-improvement that is usually open in most of us, but unfortunately it creates more error, because we must take it personally. It's the most personal criticism there is. We may briefly feel better saying, in a sense, we deserved what we gave ourselves, but then we have to deal with the increased error that we have added to our already less than acceptable self-image. We not only suffer from what we did poorly, but as we criticize ourselves, we suffer even more from the fact that we don't accept ourselves for doing it.

Take the common word "shit" heard continuously on a golf course or a tennis court immediately after a bad shot. It makes the one who says it feel better because it is a quick, natural call for self-improvement; we are admonishing ourselves to do better, and in our self-improvement station admonishment is a desirable perception. Done occasionally it is a good way to deal with a short, painful error, because it reduces tension that hurts our play. But if we do it too often, it diverts our attention from the game, which requires a low-order perception, to ourselves, a much higher-order, distracting perception. We psych ourselves out, and instead of reducing tension we increase it, we play badly, and quickly the error becomes even larger in our golf or tennis station. Since we also always have a comparing station open for sympathy, "shit" is also a loud call for help, if not to people then to the gods who control the sport. But again, if called on too often, neither people nor gods (nor ourselves) respond. Perhaps when we were very little they did offer us solace which reduced our error, but this doesn't happen often after infancy. It's much more likely, after many expletive outbursts, that no one will want to play with us. Therefore, when the gods or more tangible creatures fail to respond, we are left with the perception that not only is the shot no good, but we also are no good, a high-order perception that starts a vicious cycle of increasing error.

This then is the core of self-criticism. It is, except with rare individuals, directed more at ourselves than at our behavior. Severe self-criticism can lead to error so large that we may reorganize by smashing our golf club or tennis racket. Accepting ourselves enough to criticize ourselves in the sense that we look for a better way is one of the best ways to reduce error in our lives. But this is not easy to do, and we are lucky if we learn how to do it as a child. If we are raised with little criticism, if when we err we are carefully shown or taught a better way, and if our parents and teachers don't treat each incident as the end of the world, we may have a chance to escape destructive self-criticism.

There is another form of self-criticism that is insidious, that is, we attempt to provoke criticism from others. For example, you come home discouraged after a tough exam, and to make you feel better I say, "Why don't you drop the course; this kind of aggravation is more than it's worth." You flare up and accuse me of trying to make you into a quitter. But, if I had said, "Hang in there," you would have flared by accusing me of pushing you too hard, and if I had said nothing you might have accused me of not caring. Here by keeping open conflicting or incompatible comparing stations, you put me in a position that no matter what I say it is construed as critical. This very common practice must be regarded as a form of self-criticism, because from the way you set things up you cannot escape the perception that you are being criticized.

From what is written here it would seem as if all criticism is bad, and we believe that most of it is. There is one time, however, when criticism is vital. This occurs when we personally are running little or no error, but our behavior causes error in others. For example, I drive down the center of the road and block traffic. I feel fine, the road seems clear to me, and I decide my speed is good enough for everyone. The policeman who stops me induces an error when he gives me a ticket, but this error is usually helpful, because how to correct my behavior is obvious and I should correct it. We can't let people go blindly on their way disrupting the world, but when we criticize them we must also show them a better way. Also in therapy, as we discuss later, if self-criticism is not present then it is important that the therapist get her client to take a critical look at what he does. No one will change his behavior without first accepting that what he is doing now isn't working. Therapy, however, is a special case where a caring therapist is there to help us to behave better, and because we recognize that she cares we are more able to face the fact that what we are now doing isn't working.

Try as an experiment not to criticize yourself or anyone else for a whole day and see how much more pleasant life becomes. Also see how much more you get done and how much better you do it. Trust your comparing stations and the reference levels in them—they are almost always set at reasonable competence, and as you succeed they can be reset higher. Without criticism you will find it much easier to move toward these reference levels (or goals) without increasing your error or anyone else's. You will find what seems so obvious if you understand BCP—that less error gets you there quicker and better.

Criticism unfortunately has come to be a way of life, an excessive part of our culture, wrongly thought to be constructive because we don't understand how our brain works. Any culture that understood BCP would never have woven anything as destructive as criticism into its fabric without making sure that it was not taken personally and that the wrong could be righted. But it is obviously here to stay. All we can do as individuals is to understand both its value and its danger and do our best to stop using it unless we are reasonably sure we can criticize in a way that will lead to less, not more, error.

10

The Misery We Choose and the Misery That Happens to Us

⋘⟨§⟩⋙

Every afternoon for three hours a Los Angeles radio station employs a psychologist to advise listeners on their personal problems. It's a popular program and I listen to it frequently. What never fails to surprise me is that the problems people call in about are so much alike. From the first sentence I can almost always predict not only the problem but often the words the caller will use to describe the difficulty. Whether they are men or women, young or old, mostly they complain that they are upset because the people in their lives do not behave as they would like them to. Less often they complain of a personal failure like overweight, but even this is usually related to their frustration with those near to them. Mostly they are depressed, anxious, or on rare occasions, if they view themselves as hurting someone else, guilty. Occasionally they are angry and destructive, but this too is unusual; it is usually others who are angry and destructive toward them.

What I hear are their intense needs and their inability to control their world to satisfy these needs. Driven by a chronic perceptual error, usually because of a conflict, they don't know what to do, so they call looking for answers. But the answer that most of them want is advice on how to make the world change, my husband love me, my child do better in school. Even when the weekday radio counselor, Dr. Toni Grant, points out, as she often does, that *they* must change they resist her guidance. But she is skillful and in a brief conversation does get many callers to see that it is their behavior that must be changed. What she can't accomplish on the air is to get those who call to understand that they *choose* all of their behavior, including the feeling behaviors they mostly complain about. Learning this difficult lesson takes time and usually personal involvement with a counselor, but understanding that we choose our misery in an attempt to reduce our errors may be the most powerful bit of knowledge that any of us can ever learn. As strongly as Bill Powers and I believe that this is so, we equally believe that few people, including most counselors, are aware that this is how our control system works. As long as most of us continue to believe that misery *happens* to us, that we are unfortunate bystanders struck down by runaway depression or anxiety, we will not learn that we must behave better if we wish to feel better. It is analogous to believing that malaria was caused by foul night air. It wasn't until the mosquito was implicated and we acted to get rid of them that it was brought under control. We don't claim that this BCP knowledge will bring misery under control as easily, but until we learn that, except for psychosis, we choose most of what we do and feel there is little chance that significant progress will be made in helping people to help themselves.

Today in my office I saw a woman who said she was depressed, but using BCP I would call her a woman who was depressing. As we know this is an active behavioral process not well defined by the usual, too passive, it-happened-to-me, I-have-nothing-to-do-with-it term *depression.* Considering the fact that so many people choose to redirect their lives by depressing, one is also tempted to believe it is genetic. It is not difficult to convince ourselves that this misery is built-in much the same as an ant and a bee have certain genetically built-in behaviors that they invariably follow to control certain perceptions. We believe that almost all of us have the capacity to depress, but, as with walking or mating, we still must learn to use this capacity. Certainly we have no shortage of examples to learn from as we grow, but even so I believe that our first experience with depressing comes as a result of an early reorganization. We desperately reorganized, perhaps searching for a way to reduce a large perceptual error, when another baby was brought into the house and we received less attention. Depressing worked and we got more attention, or at least it kept us from harming little brother. It may not have worked well, but it worked better than anything else at the time, so we put it into our redirection system and have used it ever since. Why so many of us have reorganized and found this same miserable behavior is that we are of the same species with the same needs, and we share a similar culture that frustrates many of us in the same way. We tend therefore to reorganize with similar behaviors. Depression, for example, by eliminating anger, does not cut us off from those around us; in fact for a long time, until people give up on us, it tends to bring them closer.

It was obvious in talking to my depressing client that she had no idea that she was *choosing* to depress, but she did tell me that before she "became" depressed she had tried hard to solve her problem, which she told me was an unsatisfactory marriage. What she had done hadn't worked, so now totally dissatisfied with the love-companionship part of her marriage she had separated from her husband and "said" she was through with men. In fact, she told me, if she were not so depressed everything would be fine. In BCP terms what she tried is almost always the first choice of a person with an uncontrollable error, that is, to attempt to close down the comparing station or stations which are the source of the error. If I am not living in the marriage or searching for love then I won't miss it and

I'll feel better. This step, giving up, is a typical human response to uncontrolled error. But it works only *when what is given up is satisfactorily replaced.*

For example, when the client had been separated for a while and felt better, she might reopen her love-companionship comparing station and again take a chance that someone new could satisfy her needs. Finding another lover is much more difficult than, for example, becoming frustrated with golf and giving it up for tennis, something many of us do successfully all the time. If her search was unsuccessful or she was rejected again, she might try to give up on love and companionship permanently, reasoning that it is just too painful to keep these stations open. People attempt this frequently, and they may even succeed in keeping them shut for a while, but because love is a basic need, at least one and almost always many more than one love station must be kept open (and equally so for *all* our intrinsic needs).We can attempt to close down all of our sex comparing stations, as Maugham's Reverend Davidson tried to do, but to keep them closed we must substitute something else for sex. Davidson was unsuccessful when he tried to pray away his sexual needs and also to convert Sadie Thompson to chastity so she would not be so tempting. Some people are able to do this; they can find an acceptable substitute for sex, perhaps in the love of God, but Davidson couldn't.

In the example in Chapter 4, when the teacher forced the nonreading student to attempt to read and in doing so made a fool of him, the student blew up. *He had given up in school, a specific need, but he had not given up on self-worth, an intrinsic need.* He was controlling for worth, not through a school station, but through a status station by being cool. When the teacher pushed him he had a huge uncontrollable error which he dealt with through an old behavior, anger. He had plenty of anger stored in his redirection system and he used it often.

But suppose for some reason he did not want to leave

school—maybe he had a girlfriend who did well in school—so to drop out would be uncool. Then he could further redirect by depressing, because to express the anger might get him suspended. Depressing also had been stored in his redirection system for a long time, not as long as anger, but it's an old behavior, because in the long run it usually reduces error better than anger.

But depressing, as all of us know too well, is neither satisfactory reorganization nor redirection; it is miserable, painful, and inactivating. Still, along with the woman and the student, once we pass infancy, almost everyone will choose to depress to deal with an error, because it seems to us the best of a group of bad choices. For example, when giving up on her marriage did not work, when my client felt the acutely painful error of living without love and companionship she didn't want to redirect with depression. But she also rejected anger, and try as she might she couldn't close down her love station, so she began to reorganize. Very quickly, as this sytem gained momentum, a whole series of possible behaviors flashed through her mind. Some may have been desperate, angry, hostile, even murderous; she may even have thought of killing her husband or killing herself. The thought of destroying her husband's car, injuring her children to spite him, perhaps murdering his girlfriend, all became conscious to her in bits and flashes. As these frightening thoughts flickered in her mind she also had the urge to run, to take drugs, to disappear from the face of the earth. At the same time ideas of how to regain her husband's love, to return to what she desired in her marriage, maybe to accede to his demands tossed and turned in her mind. Her reorganization system was both frightening her and encouraging her with a series of random, fragmented possibilities. Most of these thoughts she quickly rejected, because when she ran them through her redirection system, she perceived that if she acted upon them she would suffer more error (pain) than she was now experiencing. But as fast as she rejected these reorganization options they kept coming, because she had done nothing to reduce the error. I am describing this as if it were a long, drawn-out process, which theoretically it could be, but more likely it all takes place in a matter of minutes, maybe even less. Think of how much and in what detail you can dream in a three-minute nap, and you can get a picture of this rapid process. After the brief period, maybe a series of periods, between which she depressed, she finally settled upon depressing as the best way to reduce her error.

Later in life, even though we may initially reject it, as depressing becomes refined and available to us in different forms, we tend to use it more and more. Our new-information system is very sensitive, and it picks up nuances of depressing from so many of those around us that we learn to tailor it to the situation when we experience a large error. It does not turn off our reorganization system totally—it almost never reduces our error enough for that—but it is accepted as a compromise and protects us against drastic reorganizations that would be worse. It becomes a kind of miserable base line against which our reorganization works sporadically, and it will continue as long as the client can't reorganize (or redirect) with something better. She complains about her depression as if it were an alien invader that has slipped into her head, and it will test my skill to get her to believe she is choosing this misery. I keep thinking if only I could teach her that this is a chosen behavior she might be more active in finding a better one. But she is passive and accepting that she is a victim, a feature of this behavior that makes it so ensnaring.

We recognize that it is also possible that she might have redirected better and perhaps solved the problem by finding someone else and falling in love with him. She might also have gone to a marriage counselor, learned to talk more satisfactorily with her husband, got involved in marriage encounter weekends, or settled for the fact that her husband loves her and can give her some but not all of what she wants in the marriage.

I am sure if you listen to the Los Angeles radio station I mentioned, you will hear all of these possibly satisfactory redirections suggested over and over, because marriage problems are a constant complaint. *The advice given, like almost all advice, is good.* But what I must face is that regardless of what my client could or should have done—and I'm sure she listens to the radio—up to now she hasn't been able to do anything better than to depress, because depressing reduces error. We have mentioned briefly here and in previous chapters how it does this, but now let's take a detailed look.

First of all, it honestly allows us to perceive ourselves as helpless, because mostly we are. We are not quite as helpless as we feel; with a friendly push most depressing people can move and do something, but we don't want to move. We feel more comfortable because obviously, depressing as we are, "we don't have the strength" to solve our problem—in this case maybe what the client could do without her husband's help to bring companionship back into their marriage. Our helplessness gets us off the hook; we are no longer responsible or at fault, and these are powerful rationalizations that reduce error.

Second, depressing keeps the anger completely in check. Long before we learned to depress, we learned to be angry; possibly our very first reorganization is to learn to cry and to scream. Soon we learn to control this anger, because anger almost always drives away the people we need. It is rarely appropriate, and *it always increases the error in those around us who then may reject us.* Depressing protects us totally from this threat to our intrinsic need for belonging. While some people do continue to redirect with anger—we'll talk about them soon—most of us don't. We are frightened of the anger, and we would rather redirect with depressing or another symptom.

Third, depressing allows us to ask for help. Who is not moved to offer help to an obviously depressing person, and what depressing person does not feel helpless and therefore justified in asking for help? Could you as easily ask or get help if you felt strong and capable? Fourth, as we continue to depress we find that others who are close to us and who don't like to see us upset are easier to control. A husband who fishes too often and leaves us alone will cancel a trip and stay home because we are so depressed. These are the main reasons that our redirection system chooses depressing; there are probably more but all of these serve as an effective way to keep our error as low as possible.

We turn to depressing often when we are in conflict, or when we suffer rejection or criticism that we cannot handle, but we have also developed some other behaviors that serve the same purpose. For example, we can also choose anxiety or worrying, which is much like depressing except that it is more active. We experience tension and agitation and we tend to be less immobilized when we are anxious. Like depressing, anxiety—or perhaps "anxietying"—has the same benefits as depressing, such as allowing us to ask for help and to excuse ourselves for our failure. Where it differs from depressing is in its activity. It is often felt as fear and moves us to run away. Active anxiety, unlike passive depressing, often makes good sense. In danger it can be life saving. But mostly, like depressing, it does not seem to be a good way to reduce error. I believe that anxiety is created from a mixture of depressing and anger, that is, some anger is blended into depressing to produce what we experience as anxietying. Anxious people, even when the anxiety is not useful, do more than depressing people and tend not to suffer quite as much. Anxietying, also initially a product of reorganization, very quickly becomes a frequent way for many of us to redirect.

Another common behavior we experience, especially when we do something to help ourselves but hurt someone we care for, is guilt. With guilt or guilting we can rationalize that at least we are suffering from our wrongdoing, and it is this rationalization that reduces our error. "Accepting" the pain allows us to continue to behave "against" our principles; it makes what we do more acceptable to us. Even better than anxietying or depressing, guilting allows even more behavioral leeway, and very often it is a useful feeling behavior, because it does tend to cause us to rid ourselves of it by correcting what we are doing wrong. Contrary to what is popularly believed, if Rev. Davidson had felt even *more* guilty about what he did, he might not have killed himself. His problem was he didn't feel guilty enough, and because he didn't, he probably contemplated doing it again. This is what caused the severe conflict that he reorganized away with suicide. If he had guilted more he would have had less conflict.

Guilt also is the most correctable of these three behaviors because, unlike depression and less like anxiety, it is related more to our behavior, which we could learn to correct, than to someone else's behavior, such as a rejecting husband who won't accept his wife even if she loves him. Guilt, of course, allows us to weep and wail and ask for help, but unless we change what we do, it will continue. Like all the feeling behaviors, guilt is almost always associated with something wrong *now*, not in the past. It is possible to feel guilty about a past mistake, but more likely the guilt exists because we could do something now to correct it or because we are contemplating something similarly guilt making right now. Many of us dwell in the past because it is less painful than to face that we are tempted to do something wrong again. Most of our emotional upsets or miserable feeling behaviors are one or some combination of depressing, anxietying or guilting. They all serve a purpose in that they reduce error and prevent more destructive reorganization. They are also all useful at times, *in fact, for a while, all the time.* But if we continue to use them instead of finding better behaviors, they too may become so painful and destructive that they serve little purpose.

When we read the newspaper or watch TV we are continually confronted with another redirection behavior which is less common than the previous three but which receives a lot of attention. What I refer to is known as incorrigibility, delinquency, or angry crime. Far fewer people use this redirection, but those who do get so much publicity that most of us feel that we are living in a more angry, dangerous, crime-ridden society than we probably are. Nevertheless, there is a lot of anger around, and it is rarely a good way to reduce error even in the short run. This is because even under the most disciplined of circumstances, as in a protest or counterprotest, it is very easy to lose control and begin to redirect more violently as error increases. It is doubtful to me that Jews who had been victims of the Nazis could have watched American Nazis march in Skokie, Illinois, without violently redirecting, perhaps even reorganizing. Most of them could not have handled their astronomical error in any other way. Of course, the purpose of the Nazi march was to provoke this anger and to get publicity.

The common advice "vent your anger" is not good advice in most cases, because it so often triggers more anger in us or others. Walking, running, counting (waiting or delaying tactics), and getting involved in something new or different are all much better ways to reduce error than taking a chance with angry behavior. Very young children, who quickly become angry when frustrated, need to be taught some alternative ways to redirect at home and in school. Unfortunately, many of them when they express anger are forcibly squelched or punished, which leads them to reorganize and then to redirect ineffectively with depressing, anxietying, and guilting. Some children, however, are so neglected that they never even learn these ways to handle their anger, and they continue to use angry acting-out behavior all of their lives. Animals almost all learn alternatives to anger; for them it is an important survival skill seen as submission. Many people, however, seem to lack this knowledge.

Perhaps in the beginning, anger is like trying to ride a skittish horse. As long as we are able to keep the horse under control, we have no problem and our redirection system is working. But very quickly and unexpectedly we may lose control and begin a mad gallop, the horse trying desperately to get somewhere with no particular idea of where to go except somewhere different from where it is. Now we are reorganizing. We may ride to safety, but it's a dangerous ride and we hang on for dear life realizing the horse is apt to do anything, perhaps something so desperate that it might destroy itself and us too. For almost all people, this is a short ride. Some people, often those we read about in the papers commit horrible, senseless crimes of violence against themselves or others while they quickly ride to destruction. Most of us, however, quickly rein in the horse with depression, anxiety, or guilt, and once we take a ride like this we try to stay off the back of this kind of horse. We recognize anger is too hard to control, and we don't want to chance even a short ride.

We should be aware, however, that unscrupulous leaders understand how quickly angry redirection can turn into angry reorganization. They stir people up, hoping to attract people who are already angry and whose reorganization systems are triggered and ready to go. The leader *preaches calm redirection,* as did Marc Antony when he kept repeating that Brutus was an honorable man, and later, when the crowd madly reorganizes, he may even make whatever happened socially approved. History is replete with smaller Hitlers who ride to power on the murderous force of angry redirection. Sometimes, as in the French Revolution the leaders stir the people to reorganize, and when this happens even they may be caught up and destroyed in the process. The reorganization system has respect for no one.

Angry people become disruptive in school, engage in juvenile delinquency, and later branch into adult crime. They tend to use alcohol (to be discussed), and under its influence angry redirection is more pronounced. They often engage in a whole series of destructive, senseless crimes that we all fear and spend much of their lives in juvenile halls, reformatories, and prisons. Sometimes given time by prison, they redirect their lives constructively, but more often continue their angry behavior or learn to depress. Because prison does little to reduce the chronic perceptual error of most criminals, they may when free return to angry redirection because it's all they know. When they do, they repeat their behavior over and over again. Eventually many of them learn that this behavior does not reduce their error, and after years of frustration most of them turn to large amounts of drugs and alcohol to get rid of the pain sufficiently so they don't have to redirect this senseless way.

I think by now it is obvious that for most people who do not anger, angry redirection is intolerable. Already in some places in the United States, especially in some of our larger cities and in our central city schools, angry redirection has become for many a way of life, and these schools no longer function as places to learn. Unfortunately, angry redirection is also taught to some extent by the media. Television glorifies the use of anger and forceful redirection to attempt to reduce perceptual error because there is no drama in calm, sensible behavior. On television this isn't too harmful, because the bullets aren't real, the knives don't cut, and the cars are driven by stunt drivers. But in real life, as an emergency-room physician can testify, this isn't the case. Also when they watch TV, people who experience large perceptual errors are usually unable to understand or even care about the difference. To some extent it might be argued that seeing angry redirection on television might vicariously reduce perceptual error for people who might tend to be violent. And perhaps to this extent TV may cut down violence. Probably we'll never know, but it does seem as if exposing people who tend to use angry redirection to violence, even TV violence, is not prudent. We think it would be sensible for those who control the networks to attempt to show more satisfactory forms of redirection than anger and violence. Programs like *Colombo* or *The Waltons*, and even in its day *Bonanza*, where not all problems are handled either simplistically or violently, are good examples of what we mean.

Because our society would fall apart if any substantial number of people redirected with anger for more than a few moments, depression, anxiety, or guilt are the most common choices of those who suffer from a large perceptual error. There are, however, some other behavioral choices which are so common that they should be discussed. First of all there is psychosis, where we reorganize temporarily or for long periods.

Because our dealings with the real world are so painful we may treat what we have created within our behavioral system, for example, a hallucination, as if it were really the world. Because the psychotic perceptions are actually our own behaviors, we often create a new crazy internal world that satisfies our needs. For us our reorganization has replaced the "painful" world, and a psychotic person may drink his own urine and say it is wine or the elixir of life.

Some psychosis is much more benign than others. We have a whole series of mildly psychotic behaviors called obsessions and compulsions. These are situations in which a person for no obvious or sensible reason engages over and over in some sort of useless behavior like hand washing or having an obsessive thought that the front door is unlocked and then running back and forth to the door twenty times each night to make sure it's locked. Both of these common psychotic reorganizations, which are quickly accepted as redirections, reduce perceptual error because the false thought that the door is open causes an easily corrected error that is temporarily reduced by the behavior of checking the door. All this crazy activity which is now part of his internal world prevents the person from dealing with the real world and therefore having to cope with a real-world error that he or she cannot handle. As long as I continue to wash my "dirty" hands how can I possibly get into trouble? It's crazy but it works, and these behaviors, originally a product of reorganization, become psychotic redirection. It was a compulsion that caused Lady Macbeth continuously to wash her hands in an attempt to wash out the guilt of an act already committed, but it did prevent a further act of violence. It may also prevent a first act of violence or anything else that would produce error by taking up all one's time washing. All of these seemingly crazy thoughts and behaviors make sense; they are an attempt to avoid a world that we fear *we cannot control* through ceaseless mental or physical activity that precludes any other activity in that "fearful" world.

Besides obsessions and compulsions, there are also phobias. An unbelievably large number of people in our society control their perceptual errors through phobic behavior. They are afraid to leave the house. They are afraid to drive on the freeway, fly in a plane, go into a crowded room, get into an elevator, look out from the top of a high building. There are as many phobias as there seem to be Greek words to describe them. A phobia is an unrealistic fear, a fear which is created for the sole purpose of reducing perceptual error. When a person believes that if he leaves his house he will be tempted to do something that he shouldn't do or be rejected by people he might meet or harmed by people he fears to encounter, all of these possible perceptual errors can be eliminated by simply staying home. All phobias in some way serve the same purpose; they eliminate a part of the phobic world that people believe they cannot control. The fear restricts the phobic to a "safer" internal world. The fear may appear to be so absurd that even the phobic may, in relaxed moments, laugh at the senselessness of the fear, but this does not release him from it. The laughter is just a way to attempt to keep in touch with the people the phobic person needs by not seeming too crazy and by acting "sensibly," preventing even larger error.

Except for people who act out, the rest of us, when we suffer uncontrolled error, would rather choose to depress, to guilt, to anxiety, to compel, to obsess, or to phobe to stabilize our lives. In a sense all of these miserable behaviors are successful, because usually they prevent us from alienating those around us whom we need. While even these behaviors may eventually cause us to lose those people, they give us much more time than if we were to anger. And it is time that is critical, because given time we may learn a better way or even possibly our reorganization system may, in its random activity, lead us out of our misery. Few people will put up with angry behavior for any time at all, and too often, if we act upon our anger, we ruin our life.

Sometimes, almost always during conflict, none of these crazy redirections works. If we cannot solve the conflict we must reorganize. Here we don't choose what happens, we reorganize, even if it turns out to be against our interest, because we will accept nothing our redirection system offers. This is because when we are in conflict we can find no satisfactory redirection to reduce the error. Whichever way we redirect, our perception of the world is so painful, so empty of what we need, that rather than try to force it into reducing our error, as angry, acting-out people do, or accepting the incomplete error reduction of the other feeling behaviors, *we attempt to reorganize it away.* By this I mean that we don't stop reorganizing when we have reorganized a small part of reality away, as does an obsessive, compulsive, or phobic person. We reorganize away whole blocks of reality and, in some rare instances, all of it. But remember, as we explained in Chapter 8, when we talk of reality we are talking of our own internal world, which we believe is reality, and it is this world that becomes crazy. Here we are talking about psychosis, or more accurately, psychosing, *which is the most common way we can actually observe ongoing, long-term new-brain reorganization as it changes the internal world of another person.* Unable to find even a miserable redirection, the reorganization goes on unchecked. As we said, what we attempt to do is to remove the part of our world that we cannot control by offering our reorganization activities, thoughts, and feelings, our world, to our own perceptual apparatus as if they were the real world. Our perceptual apparatus accepts this offering and builds it into our internal world because it does reduce error. If it doesn't we are back in the conflict, which is worse—more error. Through reorganization we have even succeeded in replacing some or all of our lowest-order external perception, intensity. We are now capable of denying the outside world completely, denying that light, heat, or sound, for example, are reaching our sensory nerves and substituting for them a behavior which becomes an imaginary perception at the first order and possibly every order above.

To reconstruct our internal world takes massive and continuous reorganization, but that is what crazy or psychotic people do. As a young psychiatrist I saw a psychotic man take cigarette after cigarette and put them out by pressing them against his own forearm. The smell of burning flesh filled the ward, yet he seemed bemused by what he was doing. It doesn't take too much imagination to realize the power of a mental system that could cause us to deny the energy of the outside world to this extent, in this case even down to the first order.

Some psychotics, especially in the beginning, create a lot of noise or random psychotic distractions running around in their head to prevent them from seeing, hearing, or contacting the outside world. Many times this is how they begin, with a wild confusion and often a mixing of perceptions from the real world with those in their head, a mass of perceptual gibberish which effectively blots out the world. Later, as they continue to reorganize, their perceptions may become more structured and go beyond blotting out the world to create hallucinations or delusions which replace it. Initially their hallucinations may be horrifying, their voices may call them vile names, thus "proving" to them that indeed the real world, where they think the voices are coming from, is no good. When this happens the psychotic reorganization has developed a crazy, error-reducing personal world where they may think they are God, Jesus, the Virgin Mary, or Napoleon, a delusion of grandeur which will provide them with an in-the-head world where they have everything they could possibly want. Now psychotic reorganization is no longer necessary; their redirection system works well. They become serene and happy: how could God have a perceptual error? Once their internal world has become so different from those around them, then every effort to change it to "normal" causes error and more reorganization. This is why psychosing is so hard to treat.

It seems that for people to be able to become psychotic, that is, to undergo long-term, sometimes continuous reorganization and live their life directed by this system, they must have not only a large error but also some genetic predisposition. We seem to need some genetic psychochemical propensity for at least one or more of our major neuro-transmitter systems to be pathologically involved in this disruptive reorganization.

Possibly once a person has become psychotic the next time he does so it might be redirection, but I believe that more likely each time a person becomes psychotic it is again reorganization. I don't think it's ever exactly the same, but like a recurrent dream it can be similar. And it's much like living a dream, because I think that our dreams are a window through which we catch glimpses of our reorganization system. It is also important to realize that, except in rare cases, only high-error control systems are involved; there are many without error that work normally. For example some patients are perfectly normal in the safe hospital and only become crazy when they are visited by a family member. It is perhaps a love-hate relationship with their family that is the source of their conflict. Away from their family they have little error. Many psychiatrists believe that the craziness comes from a chemical imbalance much as a normal person becomes crazy under the influence of a drug like LSD. Perhaps in unusual instances this may be the case, but I think that it is the rare person, psychotic or not, who makes any of these symptomatic choices without a severe perceptual error caused by an unresolvable conflict. It is not chicken or egg, the conflict comes first.

For the most part the psychotic is so wrapped up in his own world, his own thoughts, his own false perceptions that he has little or no desire to deal with the outside world. The exception to this is paranoid psychosis. Here the reorganization extends to and includes what the psychotic falsely believes is the outside world. This false belief may initiate destructive behavior toward those around him. For the most part, however, crazy people are not dangerous. Their reorganization is intellectual and internal, and when it is behavioral, the behavior is ritualized, stereotyped, and pertinent only to the psychotic person as in catatonia or similar states.

Finally, there is another painful redirection or feeling behavior which is extremely common and belongs in this chapter, even though it seems to belong in the next, where we will talk about the diseases of reorganization. Here we are talking about the physical symptoms of pain and disability. *These seem related to the body and feel much different from the symptoms of this chapter, but actually they are much more related to depressing, anxietying, or guilting, because they have little to do physically with the body they are felt to be coming from.* Here we are talking about headaches, backaches, neckaches, chest pain, abdominal pain, paralysis, nausea, dizziness, weakness, insomnia, blindness, and deafness—aches, pains, disabilities associated with literally every part of the body. For reasons which probably could be figured out for any individual but which are hard to generalize, some people, when they suffer from a chronic perceptual error, are able initially to reorganize and after that to redirect their behavioral system into producing a chronic physical pain or disability that is not associated with any medically detectable pathology. And this is not to say that this pathology is not sought. Huge numbers of doctors and much research go into trying to find the physical cause of headaches and backaches alone. It is a source of great frustration to the medical profession that these complaints are really no more medical in origin than anxiety or guilt. It is important to stress that these are only symptoms, *there is no disease. There is pain or disability, but even in hysterical blindness or paralysis there is no physical involvement—the eyes and the muscles are normal.*

Driven by pain and disability people run from doctor to doctor in an attempt to get cured of something that is not medical but certainly seems to be medical. A leading expert on these symptoms is David Bresler, Ph.D., a psychologist who directs the UCLA pain-control clinic. In a recent book, he describes how many people suffer from these physical symptoms.* He claims for example, that over ten million people suffer from migraine headaches in some form and that low-back pain is disabling to seven million more. Bresler estimates that chronic pain costs our economy over $50 billion annually.

All of these symptoms seem to serve the same error-reducing function as depressing and in BCP language are best called paining or disabling. By causing the sufferer to be sick and helpless, they more than keep the anger in check, and above all they allow the disabled person, perhaps even more easily than any of the other symptoms, to be offered help, or to seek it. And as medicine becomes more organized and glorified, people tend to choose physical symptoms because with pain or disability you can go to a competent, respected professional person and ask for help. The added attraction is that in most cases the treatment is paid for by the government or an insurance company, even though the trouble is nonmedical. We may well bankrupt the country if we don't recognize that these symptoms are caused by uncontrolled perceptual error and

* David Bresler, with Richard Trubo, *Freedom From Pain* (New York: Simon & Schuster, 1979).

the more we treat them medically the less chance we have to get to the cause.

Lack of physical causes does not mean the pain is not real. It is just as real as if it were physical, perhaps in a sense even more real, because it comes from our behavior and therefore is not in any way diluted by an outside event. For example, if you fall down and wrench your knee you will suffer immediate pain, which, of course, is felt in the knee part of your in-the-head world. But the pain has to be initiated through the knee. Without injury there is no pain, and as the injury subsides the pain subsides. But if the pain is caused by the way you attempt to redirect to reduce a perceptual error, and your knee is sound, then we are dealing with a more perfect pain, really the behavior of paining that won't subside, because it is not related to an injury—it is related to an error. And it won't go away until we learn to control the error in a more satisfactory way. Pain and disability also have an additional advantage over other symptoms in reducing error because they reassure us (we choose them, of course) that we are psychologically sound, an important reassurance for many people who can't bear to perceive of themselves as psychologically weak.

Suppose at age forty-five we begin to suffer persistent, severe headaches and consult a doctor. Using all the resources of modern medicine the doctor can probe into almost every part of our physical functioning, but often, after he does so, he tells us that he can find nothing physically wrong. Puzzled, we persist and ask why it is we are having these blinding headaches several times a week, if there is nothing physically wrong. It is precisely at this question that much of the machinery of modern medicine grinds to a halt. Whether it is asked of the local general practitioner whom you trust or of the Mayo Clinic after they have examined you for three full days, the question is rarely answered satisfactorily, because there is no medical test for unsuccessful redirection. Further, medicine slavishly adheres to the S-R thinking that sickness is a reaction to something physical, external or internal, that has disrupted your biologic machinery. There is a specific cause (S) and your headaches are the specific result (R).

BCP psychology maintains that headaches or headaching are the way the patient is redirecting. While he is actively suffering the headache he isn't excessively angry, depressed, guilt-ridden, anxious, tense, or psychotic. These behaviors may be present, but the headaching predominates. He has headaches because there is something that he wants in life, and he is perceiving that he is not getting it. This perceptual error is driving his redirection, and his headaches, the product of a previous reorganization, are the result. It is not a question of whether he has real disease, imaginary disease, or psychosomatic disease. All of these labels obscure the main issue, which is that he has severe, blinding headaches three times a week because this is the best his own particular redirection system is able to do in its desperate attempt to reduce the perceptual error. For example, the man with the headaches could be going through a severe crisis at work. He may have reached the age where if he doesn't get a promotion he will be moved aside and spend his remaining years slowly spinning his wheels, no longer moving ahead, gaining little recognition, never reaching the goal that he has struggled twenty years to reach. Each day, fearing he is in a dead-end job, he perceives himself slipping further from where he would like to be. Each day he is burdened with a larger and larger error signal, and he redirects more and more desperately.

The redirection system, which has access to all of our mental functioning, is an intelligent system. It recognizes the basic fact that it can do nothing directly to get him the promotion, and also that anger would be inappropriate. It would increase his error and must be kept in check. The people who might yet promote him cannot be reached except by hard work and a good attitude. Therefore, still controlling for the promotion, his redirection must rule out angering, depressing, and anxiety-ing, as these would interfere with his capacity to work. Al-though we haven't touched upon the subject, let's also say that drinking is not his usual way to redirect, so that alcohol is not an option at this time. During this critical period he must try to keep clear minded, sociable, and friendly, work hard, and do the right thing. But even as he does so he perceives that each day the decision isn't made seems to him to be a step backward. He then begins to suffer the blinding headaches. They occur at home, but they leave him washed out. At work he looks drained and drawn, and when he mentions the head-aches he is given the advice that he ought to see a doctor. But we already know the doctor will find nothing physically wrong.

Probably he redirected with headaching because he desper-ately wanted to be able to go to someone and say, "Help me." Rationally he knows no one can help him, but that doesn't stop him from wanting to get help. He can't beg for the promo-tion; that would increase his error, so he develops blinding headaches, not only to get to see a doctor but also possibly to get some sympathy from his wife. Perhaps she will even say, "Relax, don't worry so much about the promotion," which may help if he feels that she doesn't want it as much as he thought she did. It is also possible that his redirection system believes that his superiors will say, "My God, this man is work-ing so hard he is having headaches. Maybe we ought to hurry up and decide on his promotion." Managers today are not naive about the fact that headaches could be related to the pending promotion. This common scenario could be easily duplicated in a hundred different situations. Almost all of us have experi-enced our own redirection system causing some kind of physi-cal sympton in an attempt to deal with a large perceptual error. Paining is probably as common as depressing.

If our man doesn't get the promotion he may eventually lower his sights, that is, reduce his reference level, and his headaches may leave. But it is also possible that he won't do this, and they may get worse and incapacitate him. He will then have to leave his job but in doing so will not have to face daily the uncomfortable reality that someone else has the job that he coveted so long. To get out of work, perhaps to retire on some sort of disability, he needs to have a serious physical complaint, and the headaches could serve the purpose. Retirement might reduce his perceptual error, but he has to pay the price of blinding headaches to get there. As we have already discussed the pain is real, but in almost all instances this kind of pain can be relieved by addicting medication, a subject we will take up in a further chapter. Nonaddicting aspirin is excellent for real physical pain, but does not seem to relieve the pain of symptomatic redirection. The aspirin test is a very helpful way to tell the difference between a physically caused symptom that aspirin will relieve and the symptom behaviors being discussed here.

A tremendous amount of time, effort, and money goes into the medical care of symptomatic redirection. If the care is perceived as making the world a better place, a more caring place, or a placebo is given with a strong suggestion from the doctor that this will help, medical care is sometimes effective. More often, however, medical care compounds the problem. Doctors who examine more and more, test more and more, medicate more and more are readily incorporated into the unsuccessful control system. The more they treat, the more we convince ourselves that we are sick. We enthusiastically cooperate with medical care by redirecting with more pain and disability as the care continues and we continue to do so to get the care.

These pains are not difficult to diagnose. The aspirin test is a good start, and often, even though it may seem facetious to say so, the pain can be diagnosed by the patient's constant complaint, "Look, doctor, before we start, I want you to know this pain is not in my head." That complaint is almost always indicative that the pain *is* a behavior, a symptom that we suffer to reduce our error. What the patient is asking is that we don't tamper with his symptom. It is keeping his perceptual error under enough control to prevent reorganization, but he would like a drug which would cause him to suffer less.

Years ago I treated many people with chronic back pain. Even though they had no history or complaint of difficulty with their eyes, I would ask them if they had noticed since the back pain that they just didn't see as well as they used to see. In their eagerness to convince me that they were sick most would answer this diagnostic question, "Yes, I have been having some trouble with my vision." I would use this question to help separate those who had physically damaged their back, who would almost always answer no, from those who had symptomatic back pain. Their immediate acceptance that their backbone was connected to their eye bone told me I was dealing with a person who was asking for care, for help, and most of all for me to accept him as sick. I did not consider this question unethical or a trick, because I was desperately trying to help those who didn't need it to avoid serious back surgery.

Unfortunately, physicians who do not recognize the eagerness of the redirection system to augment the symptom do not help their patients by prescribing complicated medical tests. Many patients are made worse and suffer more through medical testing and medical treatment than if they had no medical care. We are not saying they should get no care. What we are saying is that when there are no physical findings, medical treatment should be severely limited. We recognize that faulty redirection is difficult to treat, but unless we begin to do this, that is, treat the faulty control system, we are not treating the patient. We are blindly treating and often perpetuating the symptom.

Finally, there are no rules and regulations governing any of these symptoms. A person can be unfortunate and suffer from many of them, alternately and even at the same time.

Only psychosis seems to be mostly suffered by itself, but there are even exceptions to this. None of the symptoms in this chapter is easy to overcome, but the more that people realize their symptom is faulty redirection the better chance they have to work on their own toward more satisfactory ways to deal with the world. Here is a valuable suggestion that might help anyone: the next time, for example, that you depress, say to yourself, "Why am I choosing this miserable, painful behavior? What could I do to get what I need from the world that would be so much better than this?" Say these sentences to yourself for depressing or any other symptoms several times a day, and you will quickly begin to redirect more adequately, if you have a reasonably functioning redirection system. And since most of us have such a system, once we recognize that faulty behavior is at the root of our pain, we need not settle for the misery we choose.

11

Diseases of Reorganization

Not long ago a colleague told me of a man that he has treated for years. Now in his mid-forties the patient has suffered from chronic eczema of both hands since he was in high school. It weeps and oozes so badly that at times he must wear gloves. All treatments have been tried, from x-rays to cortisone, with no success. Recently, however, the patient was able to make a trip to his native Ireland, a journey he had had his heart set upon since he came here at ten years of age. Within three days after he arrived in Galway his hands were clear. The eczema melted away, and for the three weeks he was able to stay, his skin was normal. When he returned home, within a week his hands were so raw that again he needed gloves, and it was as if his hands had never cleared.

While there are some who might claim he encountered therapeutic air, food, or water, and a few cynics who might lean toward the healing power of native Irish whiskey, my guess is that what benefited him was some long overdue removal of a chronic perceptual error. I have, however, no more information than I have given. I don't know what his error was or how it was removed, but when it was, the cause of the eczema was removed with it. We believe that faulty reorganization is the cause of many chronic diseases ranging from asthma to heart disease, from stomach ulcers to rheumatoid arthritis. But this reorganization takes place, *not in the new brain* which has been mainly the subject of this book so far, *but in the old brain* discussed in Chapter 2.

To begin, let us explore further the relationship between the old brain, which controls all our body machinery, and the new brain, which deals with the world. In Chapter 2, the new brain initially was the servant of the old brain. It provided the contact with the world needed for survival, food, air, water, warmth, and safety as we began to move around. But to help us to survive the new brain then developed social and competitive needs of its own, which we have dealt with extensively from the first chapter—needs which at times can interfere with the physiologic-survival needs of the old brain.

An example of this interference is the psychosing new-brain symptom called anorexia nervosa (psychological refusal to eat), in which, typically, adolescent females starve themselves because they develop a reference perception that they should be thinner than they are. Every time they look at the mirror they see themselves as too fat, because their in-the-head image is to be thinner. Research shows that when they are shown pictures of their head superimposed on a series of thin bodies and asked which they prefer they choose the most emaciated and even say this is too fat. They totally reject a normal body as grossly overweight. Therefore to deal with their "crazy" error they refuse to eat and in a significant number of cases starve themselves to death. Why their internal world is so distorted that they can't even accept their starving body is not the point; reasons can usually be discovered in each case. What is important here is that the new brain in a crazy attempt to satisfy its own needs is even capable of refusing the basic old-brain demand for food. The victim may get sick and die of malnutrition, but this is not a disease of reorganization of the old brain. The crazy reorganization and redirection is in the new brain. The old brain is perfectly capable of regulating the digestive machinery if they will eat, and once they start eating most become physically normal in a matter of weeks.

The purpose of this illustration is to show that the new brain can reorganize to the extent that it can deny the old brain the food it needs to keep the body alive. This again illustrates that there is no absolute priority of one brain over the other; this is individual and is not predictable.

There are also times when the old brain takes precedence and can initiate reorganization in the new brain. Under the pressure of starvation the survivors of an airplane crash in the Andes were able to reorganize sufficiently to eat the flesh of their dead companions. This was not easy, but the pressure of starvation causes people to do many things that ordinarily they would not do. In this case, however, the new brain worked as it originally was designed to work. Driven by the old brain it provided food for the body even at the temporary expense of some of its psychological needs. Again, however, the reorganization was in the new brain. The old brain functioned normally.

We also need to point out that while many chronic diseases are caused by long-term old-brain reorganization, it is perfectly normal and also necessary for the old brain to be able to reorganize. For example, a person suffers a severe heart attack, and his heart begins to beat wildly and irregularly. The nerves that control the normal, regular heartbeat are disrupted by the tissue damage. But there is feedback to the cardiac regulatory centers located in the old brain; they detect the error and begin to reorganize in an attempt to regain control over the heart rhythm. This may not occur in every case, but the old brain, sensing the error, is perfectly capable of reorganizing to try to reduce it. Medicine is also filled with "miracle" cures after serious injury; the impossible occurred—the patient regained consciousness or walked, again most likely as a result of a fortuitous old-brain reorganization. In those cases the old brain, sensing an error in a vital physiologic control system, reorganized successfully and function was restored. It can rearrange our body chemistry, conduction pathways, hormonal control, and immune capacity rapidly but probably randomly until it corrects the error. We are sure that in many cases this reorganization is unsuccessful, and in many serious injuries or illnesses the person dies reorganizing, but the point is that when the old brain detects an error beyond its normal ability to correct, it will. If the error is corrected it will store this mechanism in its own redirection system to use again, and this is how its central capacity grows. If the man suffered another heart attack the old brain might redirect and quickly correct the arrhythmia. This process is, however, totally unconscious; it is completely physiologic, and it probably goes on continually as we suffer illness or injury, or make extreme demands upon our body.

When a person attempts suicide through what would usually be a lethal overdose of barbiturates and is found alive five days later, we are sure that the old brain reorganized massively and in this case successfully. I remember reading about ten or fifteen years ago the "miraculous" story of a small woman whose child became trapped under one of the wheels of her car. The mother actually lifted the car and pulled the baby out from under the wheel, perhaps lifting as much as 750 lbs. Here we are dealing with a rapid reorganization of her old brain. Ordinarily she would not have this kind of strength, but suddenly under the impetus of a tremendous error, of her child being crushed, she picked up the car. Initially the error was in her new brain, but the new brain cannot reorganize to lift anything. It can direct the muscles to do it, but it can't impart the strength of the muscles to lift a teacup much less a car. It's from the old brain that we get our physical strength. Remember, as we explained in Chapter 2, as soon as you wake, order yourself to leap out of bed and you'll see you can't move for a moment. That moment is the time it takes to reset the muscular reference level in the old brain from a resting state to motion. It is always a two-step process, new brain to old brain, although ordinarily most of us perceive it as a single step. What the muscles must do to get their strength is mediated through the control mechanisms of the old brain. This control system must augment the new-brain nervous impulse with blood, nutrients, oxygen, and chemicals, the whole complex machinery of muscular activity.

What happened with the mother and the car is that the tremendous demand she placed on her muscles instantly reset a reference level in the old brain for muscular activity far above what ordinarily is the case. When this happened, *although of course she would have no awareness of the process,* there was a huge error and error signal that triggered a sudden physiologic reorganization in her old brain directed toward her muscles. It went through a random series of physiologic possibilities until it fortuitously came upon a combination which briefly powered the muscles of that slight woman far beyond their normal capacity. Probably this was the only time in her life that she will be able to do this, and probably most people couldn't even do it the first time, because there is no assurance that this or any reorganization will work. What makes it newsworthy is that it worked for her, but it's not something most of us could count on if we were in a similar situation. Of course, once the baby was safe her perceptual error disappeared and the reference level in her muscles was reset to normal. This quick, one-time physiologic reorganization is described here only to show that the old brain can reorganize, often successfully, and do what normally it is unable to do. Also, because this reorganization is quickly shut down there is usually no damage to the body. If this reorganization had for some reason persisted, if she continued to drive her muscles with that extreme reference level she probably would have bombarded them with so many random chemical and electrical impulses that she would eventually have suffered muscle damage. As we will shortly explain *it is this mechanism, chronic old-brain reorganization, that often leads to disease.*

What she experienced is something that many of us experience, that is, short bursts of old-brain physiologic reorganization which cease as soon as the demand is over, but the demand originates in the new brain. The old brain knows nothing about what it must do beyond maintaining normal resting physiologic activity, homeostasis. But in times like these it reorganizes to attempt to reduce an error caused by a sudden change in physiologic reference level set by the new brain in response to some perceived new-brain need. *Thus the new brain, as it deals with the world and needs a non-homeostatic bodily response, gets this response by resetting a physiologic reference level in the old brain up or down from its normal state.* Setting it down, however, as in resting or sleeping, does not trigger active reorganization; it only reduces homeostasis to a lower, more restful state. Ordinarily this is healthy, but as we will explain later it can be set too low and contribute to disease.

So far what I have described is the normal reorganization that occurs constantly in the old brain under many different conditions. Ordinarily it is short-lived; it works and we survive, or it doesn't and we die. Or, as in the case of the trapped child, someone else dies. Neither the new brain nor the old brain is set up for chronic reorganization. When it goes on and on in the new brain we suffer psychosis, our interaction with the world is greatly disrupted, and without help at times we might not survive. In the old brain chronic reorganization is also highly abnormal. It disrupts the normal physiology (it could be viewed as a psychosis of the old brain) and almost always causes chronic physical sickness such as the eczema of the man described in the beginning of this chapter. Often, as in eczema, it need not kill us, but it can be fatal. Heart disease, an extremely common result of old-brain reorganization, is the leading cause of death in this country.

Initially described by cardiologists but by now common knowledge is the fact that there is a type-A driving personality who often suffers severe coronary-artery disease. A type-A person is someone driven by a high need for achievement, who strives constantly to get ahead. He is very competitive, rarely resting, always driven by his intrinsic need for self-worth, trying to perceive success but setting his reference levels very high. He is the last person who would want to be sick or disabled, yet often this is exactly what happens. His sickness is so frustrating that he may continue to drive himself and his weakened heart to an early death. He is a far different person from the symptomatic reorganizer of Chapter 8 who often suffers in order to justify lowering his aspirations. The type-A person will disregard circulatory symptoms if they occur, but in the beginning there are usually no symptoms. High blood pressure, a frequent precursor of coronary-artery disease is rarely detected by the sufferer unless it becomes astronomically high. In fact, it is often first discovered on a routine physical examination.

The type-A person has such high aspirations that he tends to suffer from a large, chronic new-brain error because he is never completely able to get all he wants. Most of the time his perceptions are significantly below what he would like and often he is in conflict because active as he is he keeps a lot of comparing stations open, some of them incompatible with each other. If he succeeds in reducing his errors he quickly raises his reference levels. It is as if he were in a lifetime poker game where he wins a lot but is never satisfied, continuing to play and to raise the stakes. His redirection system churns away, desperately trying to reduce all his errors, but if it offers symptoms like angering or depressing, he rejects them. He needs his wits about him, and feeling behaviors would increase his error. Even though he may suffer large and chronic error, he is never in danger of psychotic reorganization, because he is competent, his redirection system is highly functional. Sooner or later he may raise the stakes too high or continue the game so long that he suffers such error that he involves his old brain. Although he does not do this purposely and has little or no awareness it is happening, he raises the reference levels in his old brain much like the woman whose child was trapped under the car. But unlike her he raises the levels and keeps them high, *a chronic not an acute process.* When this occurs, although his first awareness of the process may be a heart attack, he has started a long-term old-brain reorganization of his cardiovascular system.

Physiologically, however, this process has good precedent. It is like a primitive man 50,000 years ago relentlessly pursuing a mastodon, trying to be the first of his tribe to kill one. But this pursuit would be over in a reasonable time; he would not continue to make this effort for years without rest. During the hunt he would have to raise a whole series of reference levels in his old brain, driving his body to its physical limits, usually redirecting but perhaps even reorganizing briefly in the last desperate struggle to dispatch the huge beast.

In a sense the type-A person, by resetting his achievement reference levels higher and higher, is hunting his mastodon, but like Captain Ahab in pursuit of Moby Dick he will not rest. As he relentlessly pursues "success" he suffers a chronic perceptual error, but because it's an intangible from his own in-the-head world he can neither kill it, nor escape, nor give up the chase. All the new-brain redirection that he attempts is unsuccessful because he sets his reference levels in conflict or beyond his capacity to reach, usually both. As we have said, he rejects angry redirection and other symptoms as he actively pursues his goals. He may feel good or bad in his pursuit depending on how close he gets to elusive success, but as he does so, unknown to him, the continual error of this chronic struggle is reflected in his old brain. To win the struggle he raises his physiologic reference levels to cope with "the physical demands" of a chronic error as if he were the primitive man involved in a perpetual hunt. The old brain is designed to monitor the error in the new brain, and to respond by raising or lowering its reference levels to provide the physiology needed to reduce the error, but *it never has any understanding of why*. And until modern times and the advent of chronic new-brain errors there was never any reason to know why; primitive mankind did not suffer significantly from diseases of reorganization. Perhaps if the human race survives long enough we will evolve to where the old brain will be able to "recognize" that its excessive unnatural reorganization is driving some part or parts of the body to disease. Until that time, however, the old brain, responding as if the type-A needed increased cardiovascular output, increases his heartbeat, his blood pressure, elevates his blood sugar, raises in his blood the fatty substances like cholesterol and triglycerides to give him long-term energy, and increases the clotting elements of his blood to help stop the bleeding which might occur if he were gored by the mastodon.

But unfortunately, while our new brain can handle chronic error and even at times enjoy its challenge our body was not designed to deal with the stress of chronic old-brain reorganization. In this case as our old brain reorganizes we may suffer a clot in one or more of our arteries. When they form there or in our brain, a heart attack or a stroke results. This may serve to warn the type-A person to reassess his aspirations, and in this way it may be protective, but too often our first warning is a fatal or disabling heart attack or stroke. There are many diseases of reorganization, all caused by a chronic error which, for individual or genetic reasons, causes other parts of our body to fail. What happens is that under the influence of a chronic new-brain error that it misreads as *prepare the body for some major change,* the old-brain control system goes berserk.

This disruption of old-brain control we believe is the cause of a whole host of chronic diseases. I have a little saying that any disease that doesn't kill you quickly or that the doctor can't cure is usually a disease of reorganization. Here we have, for example, diseases like asthma, emphysema, duodenal ulcers, ileitis, colitis, arthritis, polyarteritis, lupus, glomerulonephritis, and a whole host of skin diseases. Probably 80% to 90% of our medical effort goes into completely physical and, in my opinion, less than satisfactory treatment of these diseases.

At this point no one knows why some people's lungs break down, others suffer from heart disease, and still others from kidney or intestinal damage. What is believed so far is that this may be partly related to the kind of new brain error— cancer seems to follow the loss of someone close—and partly the disease may be the result of a genetic predisposition as in rheumatoid arthritis. Here they have succeeded in isolating a genetic arthritis factor that must be present for a person to break down in this way. It seems that many of us have this factor, but of course only a few of us ever experience enough chronic new-brain and subsequent old-brain error to get arthritis. If we don't have the factor, however, no matter how our old brain reorganizes it is unlikely, probably impossible, that rheumatoid arthritis will be the result.

Sometimes, as in symptomatic redirection like headaching, backaching, and stomach-aching, physiologic reorganization with a psychosomatic disease *seems* to serve a purpose. If we are sick enough it may allow us to escape responsibility for failure, which in turn may reduce our anger, and make it easier for us to ask for help. Psychosomatic disease does so, however, at too high a price, we believe. Most of us, if we understand BCP, would attempt to reduce our error through more satisfactory behavior or perhaps through changing our internal world so that we can function better. We would probably prefer even as painful a symptom as depressing if it would help us to avoid physical illness, but unfortunately we do not know how our brain works and we don't give ourselves these choices. Therefore, if we live too long with a chronic error that we cannot or will not correct, we chance breaking down. Once we are sick we can't go back and change the way we have lived our lives. We have to deal with the whole host of errors caused by the perception that we are sick, and things often get worse.

As we said, type-A people who keep driving may quickly have a second, fatal heart attack. But once we are sick we may possibly get the help we need to reevaluate the way we are choosing to live our lives. If we do, then our sickness has inadvertently served a purpose, *but these diseases are not "chosen" for that purpose, they are not chosen at all. We do not want to get sick.* Psychosomatic disease is the unforeseen result of a long-term new-brain error; ordinarily we haven't the faintest idea of why we are sick.

As we try hard to deal with our conflicts and our errors, we are unaware that we risk getting sick if we struggle too long and don't succeed. And we don't have to have a type-A personality to reject depressing and anxietying as poor solutions. I want to be mentally clear and functional, but if I wish to avoid illness I have to learn that allowing myself a little upset when I can't redirect better may be good for me. The point is *how much* and here there is no set answer; each of us has to try to learn for himself. But now I know that if I avoid using any error-reducing feeling behaviors like angering, depressing, anxietying, or worrying, if I almost never laugh, cry, or yell to reduce error, I risk illness. Most of all I should not whistle in the dark and try to kid myself that things are good when they are not. Even our feeling behaviors are good ways to redirect, at least for a while. If we fail to use these ways we become more vulnerable to heart disease, strokes, asthma, chronic allergy, arthritis, and other autoimmune disease. This claim is supported by a recent article which indicates that cancer patients who express upset survive longer.* If we do get sick with one of these diseases it is hard to get good care, because they are so physical, so related to bodily dysfunction that both we and our doctors find it difficult to believe that there are not clear-cut physical or "real" causes for the illnesses. It has taken medicine a long time to realize that rheu-

* L. R. Derogatis, *Journal of the American Medical Association* (5 October 1979).

matoid arthritis, a very common crippler, and its related autoimmune diseases are conditions in which our own immune
system, a system created to protect us against attack from foreign substances like bacteria, turns against our own body and
attacks it as if it were a foreign object. Our belief, however,
that this is initiated by new-brain error is far from commonly
accepted in the field of medicine. Most doctors are searching
for a more tangible outside agent to produce what they believe
is an S-R disease. Many, however, are relating these diseases
to stress, which to some extent, approaches the BCP reasoning
of this chapter even though most physicians see stress in S-R
terms as an outside event rather than an error, a BCP inside
event. While in arthritis there has to be some genetic component it is now well accepted that our immune system may
attack our own knee, wrist, or spinal column and destroy it
with acute inflammation. It's hard to believe that our own brain
would do this to us, would lead an attack on a perfectly functioning part of our body, but reorganization is random, and we
believe this is an unfortunate result of that random system.
Even in heart disease some doctors believe there is an acute,
"hostile" immune component. They hold that our immune system "mistakes" the early roughening of artery walls, perhaps
caused by high blood pressure, as a foreign body and attacks
it, causing inflammation, scarring, clotting, and finally obstruc-
tion. Therefore, for reasons for which are not yet known it is
our belief that a misdirected immune system, literally an immune system misdirected by crazy old-brain reorganization,
is at the core of many of these chronic illnesses. But as yet
there is little understanding of how this occurs.

It is well known that in infections such as typhoid fever and
tuberculosis, where a disease-causing foreign agent enters the
body, the sickness we see—for example, the fever, the pain,
and the weakness—is much more our body's normal redirection
as our immune system copes with that agent than any direct
toxicity of the agent itself. When the TB bacillus enters the

body our immune system swings into action immediately. It attempts to neutralize, destroy, surround, wall off, or do something to protect the body from what it perceives to be the dangers of the bacteria. In many cases the immune system deals successfully with the outside agent. There is a brief clinical sickness which includes fever, increased white-blood-cell count, increased antibodies, redness, swelling, and all the other signs during which the infection is overwhelmed and homeostasis is restored. What makes us feel sick is not necessarily the outside agent—that is often relatively innocuous—it is our bodies' frantic redirection to close the error which is induced by our perception of that agent.

What we experience as a common cold is not usually the invasion of a new virus, it is our attempt to control the error caused by our immune system perceiving a familiar virus differently. Quite often a cold virus can live symbiotically within us, and we experience a cold only when for some reason or other the virus multiplies, and our old brain now perceives this multiplication as an error. Sometimes this doesn't even have to happen. For unknown reasons we suddenly perceive a virus which has lived quietly within us for months or years as a noxious agent. Then, as our immune system attacks, *we experience this attack as a cold.* After a while the attack subsides, the cold is over, but the virus can remain. Something has caused this to occur, and we believe it is some upset in our life, some new-brain error which is misinterpreted by the old brain and causes the immune system to function abnormally. Personally I rarely get a cold, but when I do I am always aware of a severe frustration or disappointment that precedes the inflammation of my upper respiratory tract.

Occasionally there is a lethal outside invader that overwhelms our immune system, and we die of the infection. The great influenza epidemic of 1918 was caused by an invader that was so toxic that it overwhelmed most of those who were exposed to it. Those whose immune systems could not reorganize to cope with this lethal invader died quickly. For diseases like these we have learned to alert our immune system to some of the more virulent invaders like tetanus and polio through immunization. Here the immune system is taught to redirect specifically to resist an invader through previously exposing it to a small, nonvirulent, controlled sample of that invader. As long as the inoculation is taken for the invader the system works. Then when the real invader comes along, the alerted immune system disposes of it quickly through redirection, and we do not get sick.

Cancer is similar to an infection except that the "outside" agent is one of our own cells that for some reason changes its genetic makeup and acts in its own interest rather than in the interest of our body. This genetic change is often caused by some sort of noxious chemical, radiation, or perhaps an unusual bacteria or virus that somehow has the capacity to alter the genetic structure of some of our cells. There may also be in some of us a genetic predisposition or a hormonal imbalance that causes certain cells to turn cancerous under the influence of the outside agent. Somehow the foreign substance (perhaps through causing enough error in the cell itself so that it reorganizes) changes the cells, so that what was once an active, cooperating part of our homeostatic system, a cell with the same genes as the rest of the cells of our body and obeying the same genetic codes, now becomes an outsider, very similar but actually foreign to our body. This cell, driven by its own different genetic code, multiplies and feeds upon the resources of our body. When this happens, perhaps when only a few cells are involved, our immune system senses the altered cells as foreign bodies and attempts to destroy them, but ordinarily as it does so we feel no illness. Perhaps because the cell was of our own body it does not cause as much error as a *more* foreign outside invader, and our immune system doesn't attack actively enough for us to feel it as sickness. Nevertheless, the immune system is thought to become active and probably in most cases does destroy the cancer cells without our knowing. Many researchers believe that when we become clinically ill with any kind of cancer it is because somehow or other our immune systems were unable to immobilize or destroy these "foreign" cells. They have multiplied until they are present in sufficient numbers so we or our doctor detect them. In fact many scientists believe that we are besieged by so many carcinogenic agents that probably all of us have cancer cells within our body most of the time, but our healthy, active immune system continually eliminates these cells and protects us from their multiplying to the extent that we have cancer. These researchers advance a theory called immuno-surveillance, claiming that our immune system continually patrols the body, searching for foreign agents or invaders, and overcomes them before they can become too numerous. Whether this occurs or not—and many don't believe this is how it works—most doctors do believe that a healthy, active immune system does in some way protect us from cancer. This, much more than the futile effort to avoid all potential carcinogens in our industrial society, is what saves most of us from this disease.

It is also widely recognized that some cancers are so overwhelming that no immune system can protect us against them. Exposure to plutonium, an ingredient in atom bombs, will cause people so exposed to die of cancer in a few weeks. This agent is so noxious and so carcinogenic that no immune system is presently capable of reorganizing to cope with this kind of insult. Cancers also seem to be so "clever" that some of them are capable of masquerading as normal cells, at least on the surface. Cancer researchers believe that since our immune system deals only with the surface of the cell, it cannot detect that the interior of the cell has an altered genetic structure. If the surface seems to be normal, the immune system, sensing no error, is not activated. That cancer cells can masquerade like this is only one of the many complexities still to be solved in cancer research. It is our thinking that in most cancers we are dealing with either an active but ineffective immune system or an inactive immune system, maybe at different times both.

If people who get cancer have an immune system that, in one way or other, does not seem to be as effective as it might be the question must be raised: what causes it to be ineffective? One answer, which closely follows some psychological research on cancer carried on by Lawrence Le Shan,* is that many people who develop cancer have suffered an overwhelming human loss in the six months prior to their cancer's being diagnosed. Someone who is near and dear, someone terribly important has either died, moved away, or drastically rejected the cancer patient, causing in BCP terms a huge perceptual error. It seems as if the person then suffers some reduction in his actual will to live, or in BCP terms, he reduces his new-brain reference level for life. He begins to look at life as hopeless. While he may go through the motions, his old brain senses that the new brain makes almost no demands at all. He is almost the opposite of the type-A person in that he resets his homeostatic reference levels too low. For the old brain to function well, it may need ongoing and varying demands upon it by the new brain, almost like a piece of machinery which deteriorates if it is not used enough. The potential cancer victim may not admit giving up to others, as that would upset them and cause him an additional error, so he suffers in silent resignation. In a further effort not to upset others he may exhibit a false cheerfulness as if he is redirecting successfully to the loss. As he quietly gives up, the first indication that he is sick may be the discovery that he has cancer. As we said, his is a much different situation from that of a type-A person who is struggling optimistically agains his own odds (and reorganizing physiologically to stay in the hunt). The cancer sufferer continues to keep his stiff upper lip, but the message his old brain receives

* L. L. Le Shan, "An Emotional Life-History Pattern Associated with Neophastic Disease,"*Annals of the New York Academy of Sciences* 125 (1966), pp. 780–93.

is "it's all over; lower homeostatis." At this level he can no longer redirect effectively, much less reorganize to fight his cancer. And most important of all he is unaware of the severely lowered homeostasis; what goes on in his old brain, up or down, is almost totally unconscious to him.

Recent research* shows that men in their sixties whose wives were suffering from advanced cancer showed a markedly depressed functioning of their lymphocyte cells. Since these cells are an important part of their immune systems the researchers concluded that the sickness and death of their spouse had caused them to become increasingly susceptible to immune-related disease. Here is a direct relationship, between a large, almost uncontrollable perceptual error and reduction in physiologic capacity to deal with many diseases. It tends to support what Dr. Le Shan observed in his psychological work with cancer.

In certain cases this may be the answer to psychological death, that is, dying of no apparent physiologic cause. Here the drastic lowering of the old-brain reference levels may reduce homeostasis to such a low level that life is no longer possible. Even if this reduction is not in itself fatal, as it rarely is, any outside invader becomes potentially lethal. Infections are often overwhelming under these circumstances, and as we have just suggested, cancer, an "inside" invader, may grow unchecked.

It is also important to understand that, for many of these patients, learning they have cancer can be the last straw. *They may have given up, but they didn't want cancer. No one does.* At the news that they now have the disease they further give up, compounding a vicious cycle that augments the immune-system failure. To me this is a good argument for a doctor's not telling a cancer patient he or she has cancer. The patient may realize that it is possible, but still, even with the greatest

* "Stressing the Immune System," *Science News*, 5/24/80, vol. 117, no. 21, p. 335.

tact, telling him could initiate the final give-up cycle. Almost without exception, people find it hard to struggle against the grim knowledge they have cancer. Not knowing may prolong their life. Once they know, or if we decide it is wise to tell them, then helping them psychologically to make the struggle is very good treatment (see Chapter 14).

It is not within the scope of this book to examine medical treatment in any detail, except to point out that medical care is aimed at either pharmacologically or surgically restoring homeostasis or blocking the pathologic effects of altered homeostasis. For example drugs to relieve hypertension may work centrally, directly on the old brain to lower the blood pressure to normal (or even below) or they may work peripherally to relax muscles in the arteries, causing the arteries to enlarge, which lowers the blood pressure. Surgeons attempt to restore heart function by attempting to replace blocked coronary arteries with veins taken out of the leg. In almost all of the immune diseases, like arthritis, cortisols are used to block the attack of an overactivated immune system, and if the arthritis subsides, surgery may be used to replace the damaged joints. In the case of cancer, augmenting the immune system by killing the cancer cells with chemotherapy or radiation while retaining the integrity of the body's normal cells, or activating the immune system through drugs such as BCG, are all accepted treatment.

We also recognize that even when the doctor is aware that she is confronted with a disease of reorganization, there is nothing she or anyone else can do quickly to help the patient cope with new brain errors. You don't talk to a person in the midst of a serious heart attack about how he is getting along with a mate or a boss. Certainly this discussion wouldn't be appropriate either for a person with a bleeding ulcer, acute rheumatoid arthritis, early lupus, or any of the many other diseases of faulty reorganization in their acute beginnings. These people are sick and they need prompt medical treatment or they may die.

Eventually, however, medical treatment should take into account the fact that the person likely has a chronic unresolved problem in life that must be dealt with more effectively to help him or her get better.

One of the difficulties that confront both doctor and patient is that in the beginning of any acute illness, even though the illness may later become chronic, almost everyone who is sick temporarily will reduce their aspirations. Few people are able to continue to consider themselves as unsuccessful or unfulfilled when they are critically ill. Temporarily almost all of us revert to the basic reference level for staying alive, and if we are able to perceive we are receiving good medical care, it will certainly help us to reduce our new-brain error and to allow our old brain to function more normally for the time being. This is why so many people do so well after a sudden, unexpected heart attack.

Perceiving oneself as acutely ill and lowering one's reference levels also may help us to be clear, warm, compassionate, and seemingly psychologically sound as we cooperate with the doctor's treatment. This, and the fact that before we got sick we often seemed to function well psychologically, that is, we weren't terribly depressed or anxious, makes it especially difficult for most doctors to see the heart attack, for example, as a disease of reorganization. It's not that doctors don't recognize psychological upset, they do. Like most of us, doctors control for upset, anxiety, depression, anger, and guilt, but their acute or chronically ill patients may show few of these symptoms after or even before they get sick. As we have said, if they had, they might not now be sick.

In most cases, however, the homeostasis temporarily gained with reduced aspirations and good treatment is again upset when the patient survives the acute phase and begins to deal with the world much the same as before. When this happens, as it often does, the errors return and the disease may become chronic. In many cases if the patient can perceive herself as sick, but receiving good treatment, she will stabilize at some life-preserving level. The treatment won't be curative, because her homeostasis is chronically upset, but at least the reference levels for care and her perception of getting good care may reduce her error enough so she'll stay alive, perhaps even do pretty well while "enjoying" poor health. In relationship to the medical care she continues to receive, she is charming, cooperative, and helpful, but in the rest of her life, dissatisfaction or conflict keeps upsetting the old brain and driving the disease process. Typically, this kind of patient may go to doctor after doctor and become an excellent patient. She willingly becomes involved in major medical procedures, sometimes as heroic as coronary transplants and, in doing so, gets puzzling symptomatic relief from these now-common operations that seems to be far above the actual increase in coronary circulation. There is no doubt that they have value, but possibly some of their value lies in how the patient receives this drastic treatment. After surgery, even when she has recovered and looks at her scars, she is more easily able to see herself as someone who has received heroic care. This reduces her new brain error, and if she also reduces her aspirations the error will be further reduced. Homeostasis is then more possible because she does not drive her heart so hard, and the pain is reduced or disappears. The operation has been not only physically but also psychologically successful.

Each sick individual needs study, but if one gets to know people who have chronic diseases of reorganization, it is usually not too difficult to find the source of the main new-brain error or conflict. It is usually also fairly clear why a person is willing to be sick rather than to redirect more effectively or not to redirect better until he or she gets sick. As implied previously, it is because *those who reorganize with sickness would, albeit unknowingly, rather lose physical than mental control of their lives.* They don't want to face their psychological problems, they want to live with a chronic error and tough it out. We repeat: *they don't want to get sick,* but when sick they may prefer their sickness to facing their problems.

Getting people who suffer diseases of reorganization to accept psychological help is difficult. Many sick people resent the implication that having psychological problems means they are to some degree, even if indirectly and unwillingly, responsible for being sick. They feel this is an overwhelming and unnecessary burden, and obviously when the person is in the acute phase of the disease they have a point. This is not the time to talk about their troubles. However, we believe that people who are at least taught the basic knowledge that sickness can be the unwanted and unconscious result of faulty new-brain redirection can help themselves or get psychological help to prevent or to fight many sicknesses. This is one of the tenets of what is now called wholistic or integral medicine, and probably it was always a part of good medical care. In Chapter 14 this will be discussed in some detail. Here I only wish to point out what should now be obvious: that to be healthy we need to redirect successfully. We should not be led to believe that our health is unrelated to the way that we fulfill our needs.

To me it is fascinating and "reassuring" that psychosomatic disease is neither necessarily nor only a human problem. A recent research carried out on rabbits in the attempt to establish the much discussed relationship between high-cholesterol diets and arterial clotting and scarring took an unexpected turn.* Rabbits who were fed diets high in cholesterol did develop arterial lesions, seemingly proving the S-R theory that cholesterol intake and heart disease are cause-effect related. It was noted, however, that one group of rabbits who were fed the diet showed only 50% of the artery problems of the other rabbits. Careful investigation led to the discovery that a compassionate lab technician had taken these animals from their cages each night and petted and fondled them. Evidently, like us, caged rabbits control for love, attention, and freedom

* Fred Cornhill, *Brain Mind Bulletin* 5, no. 6, (4 January 1980).

from confinement, and when this error was reduced this group's old brain was able to cope much better with the huge intakes of cholesterol. The simple S-R research has now turned into much more complex BCP research because Dr. Cornhill, the investigator, tried petting and fondling other rabbits and over and over got the same result. It was the petting, not the particular petting technician, that seemed to be necessary. To me the message is clear, be you rabbit or human: eat sensibly and get petted daily if you wish to avoid heart trouble.

12

Negative Addiction and the BCP Effects of Drugs

❦

One night about ten years ago I found myself in a hotel room in Tokyo deathly frightened because each time I breathed a strong pain shot through the middle of my chest. I had suffered an upset stomach the night before and felt a little below par all day, but I was totally unprepared for the chest pain that started after dinner and got steadily worse. By 1:00 A.M. I was beside myself, convinced I was in the midst of a severe heart attack and sure I was going to check out 5,000 miles from home. Finally, when I could stand the pain no longer, I got over my reluctance to call a foreign doctor, and the hotel provided a physician for me almost immediately.

He queried me, examined me, and told me that I was not having a heart attack, that all I had was a light case of stomach flu, and asked if I wanted something for the pain. From his manner I could tell he also suspected that I was some sort of drug addict, but when I told him to give me anything, he relaxed. If I had been an addict I would have told him exactly what I wanted and in what quantity. He then injected me with a drug in the morphine family. He did tell me what it was, but I paid no attention; all I wanted was relief.

What next happened was so completely pleasurable and so totally devoid of the pain that had racked me for hours that

I would like to describe the experience. Let me explain that ordinarily I use no drugs except an occasional aspirin—no caffeine, nicotine, or alcohol except at most five or six glasses of light wine a year. I don't like the effects of drugs and I don't feel I need them. But, of course, this time was different.

About ten minutes after he had given me a shot I began to feel good, then great, then ecstatic. Physically every part of me felt unbelievably pleasurable. Any motion at all provided a feeling of physical euphoria in whatever part of me I moved. Even running my hands along the back of my arms caused a feeling as if each hair provided individual and sensational pleasure. It seemed as if every part of my body was alive with pleasure. I am sure that part of the good feeling was the complete contrast to the previous fear and pain, but it was much beyond relief. It was as if I was experiencing a constant, intense, but diffuse orgasm, as if my body were a large sexual organ in the midst of a slow, prolonged climax. This came to a peak in about thirty minutes, maintained itself about three or four hours, and then slowly tapered off. I have never felt anything physically like this before or since.

But that was only the physical part of the experience; there was also a mental part that I can still remember clearly. First of all, I recall telling my wife that this was so good I didn't want to go to sleep. I stayed up all the rest of the night, not only feeling physically ecstatic but also hallucinating a trip to the planet Jupiter, lying on my belly on a tiny flexible-flyer, sledlike spaceship that I could control. I flew around Jupiter for hours, diving and climbing into mountains and clouds that were the most beautiful shades of reds and oranges. I remember wondering to myself why it was all reds and oranges and occasional yellows, the warm colors of the spectrum. But since it never changed, I just accepted what it was. I would dive into valley after valley and then swoop over the mountains that separated the valleys, and as I swooped over them I went right through erupting volcanoes, soaring through the clouds and the smoke, all of which again were reds and oranges, brilliantly colored and filled with fire. Each valley was different. Each was a new, exciting visual experience, and this too went on for hours. I must have circled Jupiter completely two or three times.

Then it slowly wore off. The visions drained away; I was no longer circling Jupiter, I was back to the reality of my hotel room. It was, however, a beautiful, quiet room, and I rested peacefully in it until afternoon. I ate a little and felt wonderful. There were no aftereffects; there was no tiredness from staying up all night, and I felt totally nondrugged. I was well for the rest of the trip.

I often joke about that experience by saying I never want to know what that drug was, but, in truth, I have had no desire to take it or anything like it again. It was a unique experience. I am happy I had it, but that was it for me.

I can understand, however, that if I suffered a chronic perceptual error, if I were miserable, frustrated, and depressed, I might be very interested in trying to get this feeling again and then again. I understand the heroin addict better now, because if this is what she gets instead of misery it is a good trade-off, but it is not one that I want. I don't want my perceptions drugged, good or bad, but after this "trip" I am certainly able to understand how another person, perhaps less fortunate in her ability to control her perceptions, would be more than willing to settle for this, or even one percent of this, if her life were filled with pain and misery. It has changed me from the glib professional attitude that too many of us fall into when we think an addict will be "better off" without the drug. I can now see that to get an addict to be better off requires a massive redirection of the addict's life, a task that many addicts, even with much help, fail to achieve.

It has been known for some time that if a micro-electrode is implanted precisely in the old brain of a rat, and then connected so that the rat can press a lever to stimulate its brain through that electrode, most rats will press the lever repeatedly. The rat will stop eating, drinking, lose interest in sexual activity, and seem to be interested only in pleasuring his brain with the current. Since he is no longer concerned with anything except this activity he dies, probably with a feral smile on his face.

This indicates that in rats, and now it is also known that human beings have a similar place, there is within the brain at least one, if not more than one, pleasure place. Obviously all creatures with advanced nervous systems have a capacity for ecstasy, and stimulating this place in the brain seems to tap that capacity. Continuous stimulation causes it to attenuate; this is true of all nervous systems, so the rat stimulates itself intermittently choosing the timing to get the maximum effect. The pleasure is so powerful that the rat presses the lever over and over again to the exclusion of all else. Obviously, this could be the basic mechanism of addiction, since addiction involves taking some drug which, for the addict, usually reduces pain but, most important, *always provides pleasure.* The most addicting drugs, like morphine, provide pleasure that is so euphoric that, while it has little direct effect upon pain, it makes the pain unimportant. The euphoria is strong enough to render inconsequential even the strong anxiety, terror, and physical pain that can occur during a severe heart attack. Aspirin, which is nonaddicting, seems to reduce physical pain directly, perhaps better than any other known chemical, but is almost totally lacking a pleasure component. It, for example, does nothing for a terrifying pain like a heart attack, where the fear and the pain are so mutually supportive that it is impossible to get relief by treating the physical pain alone.

Most cultures place a negative value on any pleasure gained through drugs. It would be a "bad" rat who presses the shock lever until he dies, bad because he gave up his health, his sexual activity, and his friendly association with other rats, all for greater pleasure. For an addiction almost all addicts will give up community-accepted values; they no longer care whether they belong or not and those of us who struggle to live by these values say that this is wrong. To the addict, however, the pleasure of addiction may be the ultimate successful life. "After all," they claim, "everyone searches for pleasure; why pick on us because we have been lucky enough to find it?" Most human addicts also see to it that they continue eating, drinking, and sleeping at least enough to stay alive, recognizing that it does require minimal health to experience and prolong the pleasure. Plenty of addicts, however, have a life of such misery and they pursue their addiction so diligently that, like the rat, they die. Further, since we all have a need to belong, few addicts can totally deny community values. At one time or another, usually when drugs are hard to come by, most would agree that addiction has its flaws. At this time some even enter treatment, but most don't, because they don't want to give up the drug. *It feels too good.*

Heroin Addiction

The most addicting of all drugs are opium and its derivatives morphine, heroin, dilaudid, demerol, percodan, and darvon, the so-called heavy narcotic drugs. The drug I was given in Japan was undoubtedly in this group. These drugs seem to act much like the electrode in the brain of the rat, that is, they seem to have the capacity to produce pleasure directly. Considerable study has been done to locate the action of these drugs, and the consensus at present is they act at certain places in the old brain by mimicking the natural pleasure chemicals or neuro-transmitters which seem to induce what we recognize as pleasure. Called enkephalins or endorphins our "natural" opiates bind to large molecules which lie on the surface of certain neurons in our old brain. This binding is analogous to fitting like a euphoric key into a keyhole-shaped molecular slot on the surface of these neurons. Morphine and its relatives all fit the same lock, so when we take them we feel euphoric. They mimic nature, which is, perhaps, how many "unnatural" drugs work. Exactly how this binding to these neurons causes pleasure, natural or unnatural, isn't yet known. *But* when we feel the pure pleasure associated with the sudden elimination of a perceptual error something must happen chemically in our brain to give us that good feeling. Probably the morphine drugs mimic all or part of this natural process. *We still have the error, but we feel so good that the error is meaningless to us.*

Therefore, in negative addiction, what happens is that people who usually have felt badly for a long time suddenly feel good through the simple activity of injecting heroin. Very quickly they come to the conclusion that there is no sense in controlling for anything else than the pleasure-producing drug. At this point the person is an addict and has drastically reduced the number of comparing stations that we ordinarily keep open. He does so because *in his case* these stations had filled his life with painful error. Think of living your life, after years of pain, with no hassle, with just a few comparing stations open, with nothing to want, because much of the time you are relaxed, peaceful, and euphoric. Think of learning to gain that feeling repeatedly through an activity as simple as injecting a drug. If one of us could easily get that feeling would we exercise ourself to try to keep comparing stations open for love, sex, recognition, or fun? Would we even care if we had freedom?

The truth is that most of us would care! Most of us don't want to give up controlling for these specific needs, because we enjoy knowing that usually we are able to control successfully for them. We enjoy doing what we do; our needs are too important to us to give them up for chemical pleasure. Even though I enjoyed my one drug trip I'm not about to give up all else that I enjoy in the hope or even in the knowledge of taking that trip again. I want the activity, I want the sense of human involvement, even though at times the pure physical pleasure of drug use may be more intense than the varied activity that I use to fulfill my needs. Heroin addiction is analogous to an oil company drilling for oil but, instead of striking oil, finding gold. Would the oil company continue to try to find, refine, ship, and sell oil under these circumstances? Would they pay attention to the argument that the country needs oil if it were more profitable to drill for gold? Unlikely! Therefore since an oil company really controls only for money, oil is incidental; a heroin addict controls only for pleasure, all else is incidental. For you and me, however, the money would be insufficient; we want the chancy work of drilling for oil because we recognize that the oil is the love, worth, fun, and freedom that we need. Feeling good by itself is not enough.

Therefore, the heroin addict is much different from most of us. All his or her reference levels become replaced by one overwhelming reference level for heroin in a wide-open heroin comparing station. All redirection is devoted to getting the heroin, because without it there is huge error, with it euphoria. Few people redirect as frantically as a heroin addict lacking heroin. Once the heroin is obtained, his perceptual error starts to diminish the moment he wraps the tourniquet around his arm and prepares the fix. When the drug is injected the addict feels a rush, a beautifully descriptive term of a quick move toward closing the perceptual error in his one open station. The gap snaps shut and in doing so provides a small burst of natural ecstasy, in addition to the main pleasure he always feels when the unnatural heroin molecules lock to the surface of pleasure neurons in his old brain. Now much like the "electric" rat, the heroin addict replaces food, shelter, family, friends, and health with heroin, often dirty, impure heroin. Nothing else is important.

There are, however, other physical effects, as this unnatural but powerful neuro-transmitter upsets the homeostasis of the old brain. Initially we may vomit and later become chronically constipated as our bowels become sluggish. Urinary difficulties arise as bladder muscles relax and sphincters tighten; breathing slows because the drug inhibits our respiratory center. For most addicts these effects are not serious enough to stop the drug, and they adjust to these difficulties because they don't care that much about what happens to their body anyway. But for nonaddicts who care about their bodies these effects would be alarming and would cause us to question the value of this drug even if we had periods of euphoria. Therefore, even if the drug were widely available, its use would not sweep the country, although I'm sure more people would use it than now.

Alcohol Addiction

Unlike heroin and the morphinelike drugs, which could be called directly addicting because they mimic the natural pleasure chemicals of the body, alcohol, the most common addicting drug, does not work that way. It seems to affect the whole brain, and it both reduces pain and produces pleasure. But it neither mimics any natural pleasure chemical nor specifically reduces physical pain like aspirin. What it does, however, it does so well that at least ten million people in the U.S. are alcoholics. Why this very simple, unnatural chemical provides so much pleasure and pain relief for so many people, as well as where and how this drug works in the brain, is still unknown. But from talking to many alcoholics, and following BCP theory it seems possible to conjecture how this may happen.

First of all, alcoholics and ex-alcoholics agree that alcohol seems to make whatever is wrong with their lives right. They claim, for example, if they are lonely and miserable alcohol makes them feel less lonely, less miserable. Without this pain they are then able to be more gregarious, to feel more wanted. If they are angry, alcohol in some cases calms them down, in others allows them to act upon the anger without feeling the sensible restraint that ordinarily accompanies angry behavior. If they are overly controlled, alcohol allows them to release their inhibitions and move aggressively through the world. Or, if they are frightened of the world, alcohol allows them to withdraw passively, to let the world go by while they enjoy doing nothing.

Second, it is a fact that alcohol reduces the precision of all behavior, physical and mental, yet under its influence we deny this loss. For example, we stagger when we walk, but we don't realize our gait is affected. And we realize neither that our speech is slurred nor that we make mental errors that would not occur if we were sober.

From this evidence, following BCP, it seems that alcohol addiction can be almost completely explained by one simple but profound effect which occurs at all of our open comparing stations, that is, it reduces our ability to sense a perceptual error. It is as if it acts like novocain on the error in an open comparing station; for all practical purposes it knocks the comparing station out of the system. Our speech is slurred and we can't walk a straight line, but without the ability to compare we are not aware of the error, and the more alcohol we consume the less it registers. Not only do we not sense the error, but with the comparing station disabled the error signal which is generated from the error is also reduced, so we do not behave properly to reduce the error.

It is as if we were an autopilot set to fly a plane at 10,000 feet. The plane drops to 5,000 and the autopilot does not sense the error. There is no signal sent to the engine or control surfaces and no correction. Perhaps if the plane were to drop to 3,000 feet there would be some sensing of the now-large error and a signal sent to the controls to correct, but with the comparing station disabled the control system lacks the ability to control properly. For example, the plane may be brought back up to 10,000 feet, but it keeps going higher, perhaps rising to 15,000 before the error is large enough so that it initiates correction. And again it will probably overcorrect and fly erratically through the air. Therefore, control is lost, and whether the error is the mental pain of our lover leaving us or the physical sloppiness of straying from the lane while driving, in both cases, without the comparing station working, we do not detect the error. Our behavior to correct either situation is as erratic as the defective autopilot. It usually makes things much worse, but without the ability to compare we have no way to sense they are getting worse. I may, for example, when drunk, break into my ex-lover's house and force my attentions upon her, not realizing I am not wanted. Or I may fail to negotiate a curve and hit a tree, again not realizing that I had lost control.

Obviously most people drink to get rid of pain of loneliness, rejection, or worthlessness; the loss of physical control is accepted as an unfortunate but usual side effect of the drug. Probably if we drink enough to become an alcoholic we are suffering from more than the simple error of losing a job or being rejected by a friend; we are alcoholic because we are suffering a severe conflict that we cannot resolve. If there is no conflict most errors are reasonably correctable, and while they may cause a few alcoholic bouts we eventually correct them rather than become alcoholic. It is the long-term, irreducible pain of a conflict that drives most people to alcoholism. For example, the woman who, in Chapter 9, was in conflict between her desire for her lover and her loyalty to her family might have attempted to deal with that conflict by drinking. Caught between conflicting needs, she is in constant pain, her error is huge no matter what she does, and even if she does nothing it continues. When she drinks she feels better because the alcohol removes the pain of the error. The conflict remains, but she doesn't hurt nearly as much. It becomes increasingly hard to predict what her behavior will be; she will act upon the impulse of the moment and do one thing or another and for a short time feel much better as she does so. Usually she will do something that she could not do when sober (it would cause too much error) like abruptly leaving her family and moving in with her lover. But to stay with him she has to continue to drink. She has not resolved her conflict, she has just changed her behavior; therefore, she still needs alcohol. Without alcohol the pain of the conflict will cause her to be miserable.

It is unlikely, however, that both sides of any conflict are exactly equal, that, for example, the desire to remain with her family exactly balances the inner force attracting her to her lover. At any time we tend to be inclined one way more than the other. Under these common circumstances, when the error is removed the conflict will be resolved in the direction of what was the greater desire at the time. This is what we see in alcoholics all the time. When they are sober they don't even want to face up to which side of the conflict is more desirable, but once the error attached to both sides is removed they move rapidly toward the preferred side. If her attraction to her lover is stronger that's the way she'll go. In the analogy to the arm wrestlers it is as if one wrestler were winning and had the other's arm bent back close to the table but could not put it down. The alcohol would be analogous to removing some strength (error) from both arms, and the stronger arm would immediately prevail. The match would be over as long as the effect of the alcohol lasted. The opposition would be defeated, there would be no more pain, it would feel wonderful. But when the alcohol wore off the arm which was pinned would come up from the table, and the conflict would be back in force.

In many alcoholics there is a very high-order conflict between their need to belong and therefore to conform and their need for personal achievement and personal recognition even though some toes may be stepped on as they struggle to get it. This conflict exists within all of us to some extent, but it seems to be unusually prevalent in alcoholics. Or if it is not more prevalent, what is typical is their inability to negotiate a reasonable path between these two always-conflicting needs. Also, we live in a society that seems to encourage personal pleasure and places little sanction on deviating from the belonging needs of the culture. But even with all this emphasis on personal fulfillment, cultural ties are still strong; we do not sacrifice them easily, so when sober we remain in conflict. When drunk, however, the story is completely different. Not to belong doesn't hurt anymore, and without the restraint that the need to belong ordinarily places on our behavior we do what *we* want and the hell with the world unless it agrees with *us*. In theory the resolution could be the other way around, that is, when drunk we might say, "The hell with our needs, we'll do what the world wants." And some people do, for example, the English navy, which exercised brutal control over its men, gave them grog to help them follow orders and disregard their personal misery. Many a corporation executive or married person drinks to stay on the job or with their family. They, like the English sailors, use alcohol to move toward a belonging they don't desire, but alcohol is completely democratic, it will work either way.

There is also the possibility that alcohol will not "resolve" the conflict, for example, when the forces are close to equal. Now when the error is removed the alcoholic will move erratically in both directions. When drunk the woman may bring her lover home with her and see nothing wrong with it—or take her children, move them in with her lover, and tell them their father is no good—and then quickly reverse this behavior. There is no predictable pattern, because there is no longer any control. There is no error, and while feedback will continue it will be meaningless because, like the drunk walking the line, she has almost lost the ability to compare. It will take a lot of error to break through the alcohol barrier and cause her to correct. This is why when counseling alcoholics we must at times be brutal enough to break through and cause the alcoholic enough error so that she senses something is wrong. This is hard to do because this rough, forceful counseling causes error in the "caring" counselor, but it is the only approach which will work. AA, for example, makes the new member stand up, say he is an alcoholic, and repeat the miserable, stupid things he did while drunk. AA may not know BCP, but they do know alcoholics, they have been there. And obviously, all alcohol rehab programs have to be alcohol free; it is not possible to give it up while using it.

The pleasure associated with drinking is probably the natural, pure pleasure we feel when we quickly, although usually briefly, remove perceptual errors that have been present a long time. The temporary alcoholic resolution of a long-term conflict must be ecstatic, and this euphoria is probably induced through the secretion of our own natural pleasure chemicals, our endorphins and enkephalins. Because we were miserable for so long before we began to drink the sudden appearance of these long-dormant natural chemicals acts as a euphoric shock to our system. We, of course, ascribe this pleasure to the alcohol, not realizing that it is not a direct process, as in heroin addiction, but a two-step process, the first part the unnatural alcohol block of the error, but the second part the perfectly natural release of our own pleasure chemicals. That's why alcohol works so well for misery, because it indirectly allows us to re-experience our own long-dormant innate pleasure mechanism. In fact, while alcohol is not a particularly good physical-pain remover, it is an excellent psychologic-error remover. Under its influence we are able to move to where we "want" to go, the conflict is "resolved," and the natural opiates take affect.

Heroin use does not remove error; it just causes us to feel so good that we don't care about anything but heroin. But because it does not reduce or eliminate error, under its influence we can perform precise acts. We still have our control systems intact, but except for the precision of injecting the drug we ordinarily care very little about doing anything precise. A heroin addict can walk the line precisely if he wants to, but under the influence of heroin he might feel so good that he wouldn't want to. The only precise thing that most heroin addicts do is buy, sell, or inject heroin.

The more we drink, the more the people we need don't like the self-centered way in which we tend to deal with them, and they reject us. Or if we drink to stay with those we don't want to be with, they may reject us because we drink. In many instances alcoholics' spouses are very tolerant of alcohol, because they fear that if their spouses stop drinking they may lose them. Eventually, one way or another, if the drinking becomes continuous no one will accept an alcoholic. As this rejection is painful they drink more, experience less error, and the cycle becomes tragic. As the drinkers lose those they need the only behavior that gives them any semblance of life without error is to drink. At this point, drunk but unconflicted, they are controlling almost exclusively for alcohol. Like heroin, the drug has become almost their sole reference level, that is what they want, and drinking is their most successful perception. The move to this position takes a while, but, when there (and millions of people are there), they are alcoholic.

Through all of this the alcoholic, because he feels no error to tell him otherwise, will maintain that he is okay, nonaddictive, that he enjoys alcohol socially, who doesn't? When sober and confronted with what he did when he was drunk, he may in truth be amazed, but this error, like all of his errors, will be solved by using more alcohol. In large quantities and over a long period of time alcohol does cause brain damage and memory loss, especially immediate memory loss. Exactly how this happens is not yet known, but even in people who have no memory loss when sober, alcohol seems to interfere with their ability to recall what happened when they were drunk. For example, it is common for an alcoholic to say things were going great until suddenly he awoke in jail or found himself lying in a smashed-up car in a ditch, thrown out by his wife, or fired from his job. The reason that all this aberrant behavior is difficult to recall is classically explained by BCP psychology through the basic idea that we control for our perceptions not for our behavior. Therefore when we are drunk, with no error and no effective feedback, our perceptions are okay, so why in the world would we pay attention to what we do? Our alcoholic perceptions are, unfortunately for us, "controlled"; there is no error signal to drive the behavior of remembering.

It sounds as if there should be even more alcoholics than there are, since most of us suffer from conflict, but there is a trade-off in alcohol that stops nonalcoholics from drinking too much. This trade-off occurs when the loss of physical control caused by the drug becomes more upsetting and outweighs the pleasure gained by the resolution of the conflict. For most of us, when we feel this effect we stop. Alcoholics, however, don't stop until they are drunk, because the reduction of conflict error is so much more important to them than the loss of physical control. Besides, when they are drunk they don't notice the loss of physical control, but they may notice it along the way. They just drink faster to get through this "barrier" and then there is nothing to stop them.

So far we have discussed addicting drugs that have as their main action simulating, directly as in heroin or indirectly as in alcohol, the pleasure we feel when we are able to control our perceptions. Probably there are other drugs that work in a similar manner, but only one, Valium, is used widely enough to warrant mentioning. Latest research indicates that Valium may possibly simulate a natural brain chemical in the neurotransmitter category, in this case some sort of anti-anxiety agent.* Since our emotions are complex there is every reason to believe that natural "drugs" are associated with how we perceive many feeling behaviors. When you use Valium you don't reduce the error, but you reduce the anxietying that is

* Benzodiazepine drugs; see *Science News* vol. 16, no. 19, p. 325.

associated with the error and this makes it an addicting drug. It is probably not as addicting as heroin, but it is well recognized that it does reduce pain and in doing so induces enough pleasure so that people prefer to use it rather than getting help or helping themselves to solve their problem. Like alcohol the physical side effects both of using Valium and of trying to withdraw from it can become disabling, a situation well described in *I'm Dancing As Fast As I Can* by Barbara Gordon.*

While all addicting drugs furnish chemical pleasure they also cause us to suffer painful withdrawal symptoms if the drug is stopped. There are two kinds of withdrawal, psychological and physical, and most withdrawal is a combination of both. The psychological is easy to explain. By the time we are addicted the drug dominates our personal, in-the-head world; it is mainly what we control for. Take it away and there is the pure pain of a sudden error, which is soon augmented by a painful feeling behavior initiated by the accompanying large-error signal. During withdrawal addicts try almost any form of painful feeling behaviors that their system can generate in the hope that their misery will get someone to give them the drug. Since it is hard to stand by and watch them suffer these behaviors often work. Addicts who are able to remove the drug from their personal world—physician addicts are an example of a group that can do this because they have potentially a satisfying life without drugs—suffer much less, often very little.

On the physiologic side, for a drug to be addicting it must be accepted by the old brain and become a part of, even at times augment, its control systems. First the old brain may reject the foreign drug because it causes a physiologic error, but if the addict continues to take it for the psychological pleasure the old brain may reorganize and reset reference levels to accommodate and then accept the drug. If the old brain cannot accept the drug, then no matter what the drug does it will not become addictive; strychnine, which some people

* *I'm Dancing as Fast as I Can* (New York: Harper & Row, 1979).

use for sexual pleasure, is probably an example of a pleasure drug that is not addictive. Too much and it is fatal, for the old brain cannot reorganize for strychnine. Once the drug is accepted by the old brain and becomes part of the brain physiology, then if it is withdrawn there is again an old-brain error. To reduce it we must reorganize with sickness as our body readjusts to life without the drug. For example, before one gets addicted to heroin vomiting is frequent as the old brain rejects the drug. Then the old brain reorganizes and resets the reference levels of our vomiting center to accommodate heroin. Then when the heroin is withdrawn we may vomit again as the reference levels are reset to life without heroin. Depending upon how we reorganize for this drug, and vomiting is only one example, there may be many different physical effects as the homeostasis of the old brain readjusts to life without the powerful drug. Withdrawal from alcohol and Valium also causes a lot of sickness and upset in long-term addicts for the same reasons. To stop, the upset addicts again take the drug, which immediately stops the old-brain reorganization that is causing their sickness. This physical withdrawal may cause them to take the drug after it ceases to be as pleasurable as in the beginning. Alcoholics especially report that in later stages they drink as much not to get withdrawal sickness as to gain pleasure.

Besides alcohol, heroin and Valium, there are two other drugs, cocaine and amphetamine, that people take to gain a pleasurable perception that they cannot achieve through competent behaviors. Called stimulants they provide a feeling of clarity, power, and lack of fatigue that those who take them find hard to duplicate naturally. While they are highly addicting to those who can obtain them in pure form or large quantities, both have an important effect that limits their use over a long period. This is the ability they have to increase the strength of the error signal and give our behavioral system a push which is initially felt as a powerful lift. It seems as if we are energized beyond belief and this seems wonderful. Cocaine, for instance, improves our sexual stamina. It increases our response and is valued for this quality especially. But, like running your car past the red line on the Tachometer, if you use these drugs too long you will push your behavioral system into reorganization, which in most cases means psychosis or crazy acting out. Once the user becomes psychotic then the capacity to continue the drug ceases; the person is too crazy to get it and no one will give it to him. PCP, another drug which is now widely used because it provides a quick high, also often produces reorganization and psychosis.

Therefore these drugs, which have, according to those who use them, extremely pleasurable effects, are self-limited in use because they tend to drive the behavioral system to reorganize. Until they do, however, the taker may use them almost nonstop in an effort to achieve and maintain the desired perceptual high. Once the user fragments into psychosis then he requires psychiatric care and immediate separation from further use, because in the crazy state of reorganization he may kill himself through exhaustion or suicide, and he is always dangerous to others.

Similar but much less active (they never trigger reorganization) are the common stimulants caffeine or nicotine. These wake us up, give us pep, and are easily accepted into the old brain as helpful to many of its control systems. When we try to stop these drugs we get a mild psychological withdrawal but a severe physical withdrawal as our old brain reorganizes to try to get along without them. Nicotine especially is hard to kick, and many heroin addicts report that the physical craving for nicotine is stronger than for heroin. Nicotine seems to get involved in every synapse of the body, and smokers report that craving may continue for as long as twenty years after they quit.

There are also many sedative drugs that can become addicting because they calm down anxiety and reduce tension. Barbiturates especially fall into this class and can slow down our behavior so much that we become unconscious. They are addicting for those who like their effect and they are also easily accepted into the old brain, so when they are stopped their withdrawal is both psychological and physical. All of these drugs fool us into thinking that because we feel better, we are functioning better, but of course we are not. Barbiturate sleep is not sleep at all; it is unconsciousness, which may be physically restful but is not as mentally restful as natural sleep. This is because those sedative drugs all tend to stop our dreams, which are the healthy way we reorganize while we sleep. It is this reorganization that seems to rest our mind; when we wake from a barbiturate sleep we are still mentally tired or in popular terms hung over. If we continue to take them to sleep or to overcome the mental fatigue that their use has caused we get into the vicious addictive cycle of drugs, fatigue, and more drugs.

One of the main medical uses for stimulants like amphetamines or synthetics like Ritalin is in the treatment of hyperactive children. People who do not understand the nature of this disorder claim that these stimulants have a paradoxical effect, because instead of further stimulating they seem to act to calm these children and to improve their behavior. I believe that the name *hyperactive* is a misnomer, that a better description of these children would be *hypo*-behaviored. They lack the necessary behaviors to control their perceptions at a level where they can even minimally fulfill their needs. Their pressing, demanding behavior is an infantile cry for attention; they have no confidence in their ability to do much more than breathe. What we see is the limited behaviors of a long-drawn-out, sophisticated tantrum more appropriate to a year-old than to a school-age child. The stimulant works as it should work; it gives them the sensation of power and confidence that is common to the way we all perceive these drugs. The slowdown or calming of the behavior is a result of the perception that their error is reduced. There is also a side effect, or more accurately another effect, of these drugs that is also beneficial, that is, they drive the behavioral system or perhaps make it more receptive to learning. Since these children desperately need to learn more behaviors, these drugs in activating the system may make it easier to teach them what they need to learn. If the teaching part is neglected, if we depend upon the drug alone to "cure" them there will be no lasting benefit. The drug, used properly, gives us a chance to help, but if the child fails in school, is neglected or left to watch too much TV he will not learn the social behaviors he desperately needs. Used for a short while and coupled with attention, firmness, teaching, and minimal TV watching, these drugs can help us to deal with these difficult children, but we must not be misled by the initial calming to believe that needed behaviors can be learned from a drug.

Today, to treat psychosis it is usual to employ drugs that depress our total behavior but do not, like barbiturates, cause us to lose consciousness. These are the major tranquilizers like Thorazine, Haldol, and Prolixin, all powerful drugs that in moderate-to-large doses can almost totally paralyze the patient. Many psychotic people are given them until they are indeed almost unable to move. They are also used specifically to counter the psychosis (psychotic reorganization) that is caused by overstimulation with amphetamine or cocaine (barbiturates are also useful but much less effective here). In large doses these powerful drugs totally stop the delusions and hallucinations which are the way many people reorganize in an attempt to deal with the huge errors that lead to psychosis. Too many psychiatrists believe that we must tranquilize away the delusions and hallucinations no matter how much drug we have to use. But getting rid of the delusions and hallucinations only stops reorganization; it does not provide the behaviors needed to resolve the conflict that started the process. Slowing down reorganization so that we may reach the patient makes sense, but to get him functional we must teach better behaviors, a subject we'll talk about in Chapter 15.

If we paralyze the whole system and turn the patients into nondeluded, nonhallucinated, nonbehaving unfortunates we have drugged them to where *they cannot learn the new behaviors they need because they cannot behave.* But because they cannot delude or hallucinate anymore, people with little understanding of what psychosis is call them cured. It's interesting that many families of people who are given massive doses of phenothiazine-like drugs wonder if, in this paralyzed state in which they can hardly walk across the room, they are not worse off than before the treatment. It is my belief that many are and that the so-called psychiatric drug miracle is too often just another way that psychiatrists have devised to put large numbers of "crazy" people back into chains, deluding ourselves that what we do is humane because it's "scientific." Moderate and gradually reduced doses are useful, but there is little justification for paralyzing people who have the misfortune to be unable to solve their conflicts and have begun to reorganize to try to do so.

There is another group of drugs—led by marijuana, perhaps the most widely used recreational drug outside of alcohol—that makes us feel good or at least different by altering our perceptions. Marijuana, which for most users is the chemical equivalent of rose-colored glasses, makes what we perceive look or feel better. According to those who use it, its action seems to lower the orders at which we perceive the world and especially to add a lot of pleasant second-order sensation to what we perceive. Music sounds better, pictures look better, sex feels better. It is not that we don't perceive high orders, we do, but the lower orders seem to take on more importance. We care less about values, programs, or even relationships, and more about intensity and sensation. This may be partly artificial, because marijuana is mostly smoked under relaxed, pleasant, low-error conditions. But even on noisy, boring assembly lines, where it is used a great deal, it seems to make the senseless cacophony more pleasing and the monotonous work less onerous. In doing this it may also reduce perceptual error through releasing some natural pleasure chemicals, because the lower the order at which we perceive the world the less error we experience. Marijuana is not a high-pleasure drug like alcohol or heroin, but it makes things a little better through reducing boredom by helping to focus on low-order sensations rather than the high-order perceptions which like boredom may cause us errors. It is also a social drug to the extent that it helps us to perceive each other at lower orders, where we tend to accept each other with less criticism. It does not reduce pain or cause enough pleasure directly for it to be psychologically addicting, although in large quantities it might be mildly addicting for a few people with large errors, because it does reduce error. It does not seem to affect the old-brain functions one way or another, and there is little discomfort in becoming used to it or giving it up. It is also used a great deal by people whose control systems are adequate, who enjoy its restful, perception-lowering effect but do not try to use it to solve conflicts or escape pain, because in those situations it has little value. People in serious conflict or in great pain will turn to alcohol, Valium or a morphine derivative; they will get little relief from marijuana. Because it does lower the order of perception it may decrease the effectiveness of precise behavior, but it does not in any way reduce our ability to compare as does alcohol, so physical control is at worst minimally impaired. *Its danger is in its seductive ability to get us to accept a limited, low-order status quo in which our needs are not well fulfilled. When we do so we don't make the effort to learn the behaviors required to live in the high-order world that most of us have to live in.*

The other drugs that work on the perceptual system, like LSD and mescalin, jumble and distort perception and produce a markedly disordered world. We call these effects hallucinations, but they are not the same as the hallucinations caused by our perception of ongoing reorganization seen as psychosis. Under their influence we may, for example, perceive the bowl of flowers on the table next to us start to move around, and tiny faces may appear in each flower and start to speak. LSD will produce effects like this; in fact, it will produce *any* effect, because what it does is to jumble and totally alter the careful hierarchy of perception that we have built. People take these drugs to get a new look at the world and in most instances they certainly do. There is, however, nothing necessarily insightful or creative about this "new" look, but it is random, different and to some people it might have value. For most people it's just a "trip," a look at things in a different way that those who take it often report as frightening.

What LSD may also do is provide such a disturbed perception that we immediately begin to suffer huge perceptual errors, errors so large that we start to reorganize because our redirection system is not able to handle this marked alteration and jumbling of the way we perceive the world. Therefore by drastically altering our perception, the length and variety of the "crazy" experience can be as much our attempt to try to re-establish control as the perception-altering effect of the drug itself. When the drug wears off we usually regain control, but sometimes, especially for people who have large errors before they took the drug, the additional drug error triggers a reorganization that does not stop when the drug wears off. It is like the straw that broke the camel's back, and for this reason LSD should not be taken except in controlled, low-error situations with friends around and a phenathiazine drug available to turn off any reorganization that may occur.

Even then it seems to me that there are no therapeutic uses for this drug. It may provoke a research interest in that it does give us a way to study our perceptual system when it is distorted, but it's hard to think how this could be valuable. The LSD experience is definitely not a meditation, a valuable reorganization experience we'll discuss in detail in Chapter 14. Instead, it is a high-stress experience that can cause people who have large errors to lose temporary and often long-term control. It is, of course, not addicting. It is not accepted by our old brain, and I'm sure part of its physical effect is the old brain desperately reorganizing to try to accommodate this powerful substance.

Food

A word about food as an addicting experience. Food is, of course, potentially addicting because eating provides pleasure and that pleasure can be regained easily just by eating more. Most people, to feel worthwhile when they look in a mirror, control their food intake at some reasonable level. Perhaps the too-thin look that present fashion dictates is below most people's reference levels and causes for many a continual struggle, but still most of us adjust without overeating. Some people, however, who suffer conflict turn to food and use it in large quantities because for them it does seem to release the natural opiates that make us feel so good. They get involved in a vicious circle. The fatter they get the more error they suffer and the more they eat to get rid of the pain. These people need group support or programs like Overeaters' Anonymous or Weight-watchers to help reduce the loneliness that causes many of them to eat. It's a difficult problem and one which was of no concern until the coming of agriculture made food so readily available. Food is, of course, the perfect old-brain drug because it is accepted by our old brain completely—it causes no physio-logic error at all. The old brain has no way of knowing that the new brain is using food as a drug, and it redirects to the physiologic demands of an obese body remarkably well. There-fore, while there may be psychologic withdrawal there is never any physiologic withdrawal. From the standpoint of the old brain excess food is a good hedge against the hard times we all experienced before agriculture, and it busily directs its storage for future "hard times" in its most economical and compact form, fat.

Gambling

Finally a word about gambling. This is for many a highly addicting activity because the gambler has so much tangible control as he constantly sets and resets reference levels and then tries to gamble to reach them. When he does or when he wins he feels the intense pleasure of an error being rapidly eliminated. And gamblers often get a lucky hit and overshoot their reference level, which for them is pure ecstasy. *Their systems must be flooded with our own natural opiates (enkephalins) at these moments.* There is no more clear-cut reference level than trying to hit the jackpot, to roll the big 7, or to beat the dealer at blackjack. Addiction occurs when these hope-to-win reference levels dominate our lives. But winning is such a socially approved perception (certainly we all try to win) that gambling is a very accepted activity. Even where there are laws against it these laws are almost totally unenforced. Certainly few activities are as clearly BCP as gambling. The setting of the gaming level and the constant redirection to attempt to produce the winning perception produce a remarkably clear-cut addiction control system.

Most gamblers are not addicted. They gamble as another person might drink socially or overeat once in a while. To an addicted gambler, however, there is no greater pleasure than the snapping shut of the perceptual error when the bet is won. What makes it so addicting is the constant resetting of the reference level higher and the fact that the thrill is very short-lived. To get that thrill over and over again and to get more of a thrill with a bigger wager or a greater risk, usually both, is what makes gamblers into real addicts. Unlike with alcohol or heroin, there is also the possibility that someone will become a successful gambler, which means to win enough so that the game can continue indefinitely. Gamblers don't like to lose, they like to play, but because the odds are usually against them, if they play too long most lose. Many business-men, however, gamble and do so quite successfully. They be-come so involved in the game called work that they become addicted to their job. When this happens, and the rest of their life becomes insignificant, they become what are commonly called workaholics. Mundane jobs, however, do not produce this kind of people. Few file clerks are addicted to their "thrill-ing" occupation.

If workaholics are a type-A personality and set their levels so high that they begin to lose, it is likely that they may reorgan-ize with heart disease. This is probably fairly common, but since workaholics are so much within the system (in some cases they *are* the system), they are often praised by all except their family, making this a very difficult addiction to break.

Perhaps the best way to end this chapter is to tell a story about a man I treated in a neurology ward years ago. He came in with a paralyzed shoulder and was at a total loss to explain what had happened. He was a young, healthy man and claimed he had done nothing to harm his shoulder. He just woke up one morning and could not move his arm.

Careful questioning, however, brought out the fact that he had spent the night before in Las Vegas playing slot machines. What happened is that he pulled the handle hard, long, and with such concentration that he paid no attention to painful messages from his shoulder. In BCP terms he was not control-ling for shoulder pain, he was controlling for a jackpot. Until we questioned him he had no conception that he had redi-rected so excessively the night before that he had injured the nerves that operate his shoulder. With a little rest he quickly recovered, but his paralyzed arm still stands in my mind as a graphic example of how much we control for our perception, how little for our behavior.

13

Using BCP Psychology in Our Personal Life

❧ ❧

Not long ago, when I was in a restaurant, a family was eating nearby, and its youngest member, a boy about a year old, was fussing. The parents were trying to get him to keep quiet. They obviously didn't want a disturbance, yet the more they tried to get him to stop, the more noisy and upset he became. They started to yell, and finally, in an irrational effort to quiet him, the father slapped him rather hard. At this point the baby went berserk. He screamed and carried on so that the father had to pick him up and take him outside.

It seemed to me, from my comfortable vantage point of an observer, that the parents should have known that what they were doing was making the situation worse not better. Certainly the final slap had no chance to accomplish its purpose. But why didn't the parents see what I saw?

Probably they did vaguely understand that what they were doing wasn't working, but, driven by a large error, they used the angry S-R redirection, punish the child and he'll keep quiet. Only when this became obviously ineffective did they change. Had they known BCP psychology well enough to use it, they would have tried to figure out a better behavior as soon as their error started to escalate. They would have known that as they had many more behaviors than a year-old child, they had a much better chance to change than he did.

The purpose of this chapter is to encourage people to use BCP psychology in everyday life, in their dealings with husbands, wives, lovers, children, mothers, fathers, bosses, and friends. It is our belief that the more we do this the more successfully we will fulfill our needs.

Our example illustrates a sound BCP principle, which is always to make *a thoughtful and forceful effort not to increase your own error or the error of people you deal with unless you have reason to believe that you or they have adequate behaviors to cope with that increasing error.* If there is an axiom in BCP, this is it. In the example, driven by their own errors, the mother and father increased the child's error until his primitive redirection system had no behavior except screaming to cope with this increase. When the screaming worked he was picked up, removed from the restaurant, and probably comforted. But because an angry behavior works doesn't make it good. In fact, the more it works the more the child will use it and fail to learn more complicated behaviors that are socially acceptable. If the parents had used the axiom, and in the very beginning hadn't increased the baby's error, they would have fared better and maybe taught him a new and more useful behavior.

While children tend to have limited behaviors to cope with errors, even an adult who experiences an increasing error is unlikely to deal with the situation well. Therefore, the first corollary to the axiom is that *we don't learn well in a high-error situation.* The parents probably didn't in this instance, and it was obvious that the child learned nothing of any value. Therefore, as soon as we detect an increase in error in someone we are dealing with, an increase which we should sense when others become tense, show discomfort, or shift to an inadequate behavior, we must alter what we do and attempt to reduce the error. In most situations, we easily detect this increase, but occasionally, as in the case of Marie Antoinette, we lack that sensitivity. This usually happens when we fail to realize that our world is not the real world. Therefore if we wish to use BCP in our lives, we must constantly remind ourselves of the fact *that our world is not the real world, that we always live in two worlds and so does everyone else.* The fussing baby was not living in the parents' world, and even if he had known what their world was, the more they yelled at him, the less inclination he would have had to accept it.

There may be times, however, when, to reduce our error we purposely increase the error in someone else, for example, in today's jargon, when we choose to be assertive. The purpose of being assertive is, as calmly as we can, to cause enough error quickly, and usually when it isn't expected, to get the other person to back down, or in BCP terms to become aware that our worlds may be different. Our hope is that the sudden increase in error that we cause may get the other person to stop controlling for something he wants that is getting in our way. For example, *I tell* the mechanic he must have my car repaired by 5:00 P.M. If I ask politely, it may not be ready, but if I demand in a strong, assertive voice it likely will be.

To reduce his anticipated error if he does not have my car ready, he may move it ahead of someone else's. The danger is that instead of the increased error's scaring him, it may anger him and cause him to move my car to the end of the list or repair it badly.

Assertiveness assumes that I have the behaviors to frighten people so they will back down. It will work, for example, with someone like a salesperson who is not controlling for anything very important to her, but it's a dangerous technique if you use it with people who are controlling for what they believe is very important. If you need, work with, or live with these people you may win a lot of small battles, but assertiveness tends to increase little skirmishes into big wars. Like all error-increasing behavior it should be used sparingly. Those who teach assertiveness well understand that its best use is to take a firm attitude toward negotiation and compromise, rather than to force your will on others. For example, ask firmly, "What are my chances of getting the car at 5:00 P.M.?" Tell the mechanic it's very important that you have it but you understand he is busy. Compliment him on anything good he has done for you in the past. Say, "I'll call at 2:00 P.M. to see where I stand." If it is ready at five thank him and compliment him again. This approach initially will slightly increase his error, but at the same time leads him toward a good behavior to reduce it by fixing the car on time. If he does he'll feel good and then even better because of your thanks. In all negotiations the process is delicate. Try to keep the ups and downs of the other party's error in mind, and be aware of the danger of opening it too wide. Remember, it's worthless to be assertive in a world where no one will compromise, and the larger the other party's error the less compromise there will be.

During the past two years, in which I have almost completely incorporated BCP into my life, it has seemed that I am surrounded by suffering caused by people increasing their own errors and the errors of those around them through using stimulus-response psychology. I think of two instances that I recently heard about. In one case a young couple had moved back into her parents' home and expected the elderly parents to take care of their small, active three-year-old boy while they worked. When they lived apart, they had always been on good terms, but after only a few weeks in the parents' home, the couples were barely speaking. The error caused by this unexpected move and by taking care of the child was so great that the grandparents were distraught. They didn't have the behaviors to cope with this situation. Because in their world they think they should be good grandparents and accept this burden, the real world is now more than they can handle. The young couple is upset because they feel parents should not only be able, but eager, to accept them and their child. If either or both couples understood BCP they would quickly realize that there is a real world which is much different from their world and because of this difference everybody is in an increasing error situation. The young couple would also see that the grandparents do not have the behaviors to cope with the grandchild, and they would make another arrangement, or the grandparents would tell them they don't have the behaviors to handle this burden at this time in their lives. Knowing BCP does not tell people what to do, but it does make apparent that the increasing error calls for a change. Look for a better behavior to reduce the upset. The two couples are trying to use the inadequate stimulus-response behavior of barely speaking to each other, a far cry from the negotiation and compromise that BCP would call for in this situation. Not knowing how people function has locked them all into this deteriorating situation; the error is increasing and if angering builds there could be an explosion. More likely all parties will control their angering—not speaking is at least helpful in doing this—but if the error continues too long one or both of the grandparents will likely reorganize with sickness. The boy will also suffer because in this tense, high-error situation he will not learn behaviors he needs at this age.

The other example I heard about is a dispute, which may end in court, over one neighbor's dog messing in front of their next-door neighbor's house. It may be that, in the world of the dog owners, all people should love dogs, even messy dogs, but in this case the complainer does not have a dog and does not live in that world. He is on the verge of going to court to resolve the problem. Court, which is always a high-error situation, will cause the errors in all parties to increase, and while the problem may be legally settled, the neighbors will probably no longer be on speaking terms. If the dog owner understood BCP, he would quickly realize that right or wrong in his world, the dog's messing has caused a huge error in the complaining neighbor. There is no reasonable way to reduce this error except to obey the law and keep the dog away from his house. Refusal to understand this and do it, that is, really live BCP psychology, has led to the present debacle. Ultimately the owner will keep the dog away from the neighbor's house but how much more easily this could have been accomplished had the owner understood that his dog only lived in his world; she will never live in the world of the next-door neighbor. This conflict caused by "let the dog mess" is very similar to "let them eat cake."

If it is hard to learn better behaviors in a high-error situation it is obvious that we learn best when we have a small error, an error that drives our behavioral system gently. It takes time to learn to run trial behaviors through our control system and speculate on their ability to reduce an error before we actually use them. Under the pressure of a large error, we must act. There is no time for this deliberate, internal trial process. We don't learn in a panic, we learn in calm, quiet times of reflection when we take a look at the whole situation and run alternatives through our mind to see if it seems they might work. Therefore, *another corollary* to the first axiom of BCP psychology is *don't increase the error if you want yourself or someone else to learn better behavior.*

When I first was asked into public schools because children were becoming more and more difficult to discipline, my initial suggestion was: if you want children to learn and to follow rules, don't threaten them with failure. Failure causes huge, uncontrollable errors in students, most of whom deal with these errors by acting out, giving up, or using drugs. Unfortunately, too many schools still stick firmly to stimulus-response psychology, that is, that the *stimulus* of threats or punishment will cause students *to respond* with hard work and sticking to the rules. When this does not succeed, many educators increase the stimulus by continuing to threaten and punish until the students' error has increased to where violence in the schools is common. BCP psychology would predict this result through another corollary: *increase the total error in any organization, and that organization will steadily deteriorate in function and usually also in purpose.* Look around at high-error families, schools, and work situations and you will see this happening all over. In ghetto schools this is now the rule, not the exception.

Therefore, to use BCP in your life, don't increase your own error or the error in those around you. Remember that you live mostly in your world and only a little in the real world, and don't look for or try to teach yourself or others better behavior in high-error situations. Reduce the error first.

Assuming that by now you believe that BCP is valuable for you, you might ask, "What can I do to make it a part of my life?" To start, we believe that there is no better way to learn to use BCP psychology than carefully to reread Chapters 3 through 8 of this book. As the ideas become familiar, the first thing to do is simple; whenever you are relaxed and your needs are fulfilled try to observe the world around you in terms of BCP. *Using* BCP will come later. Now just see how many situations you encounter each day where BCP would make much better sense than the S-R psychology you see employed around you. The next time you see parents scolding a child, the child screaming, the parents scolding more, watch how the errors and the ineffective behaviors grow. Then perhaps, from your nonerror position as an observer, say to yourself, "What is at least one thing that I could have done that would not have increased the child's error?" Keep observing! Watch people hurt, bicker, backbite, carp, and criticize in an attempt to control others, and see how much of this behavior ends in frustration, friction, and acrimony. Keep saying to yourself, "What would I do differently?" Think about the personal world that each of us lives in and how the people you observe act as if they live in the real world, and as if, since it is the "only world," everyone else lives there also. See how many times a day you hear the equivalent of "let them eat cake." See people try to teach in high-error situations and observe the devastating effects of conflict on usually sensible people. Look at people getting drunk to reduce their growing errors or using addictive drugs to make it seem as if their errors do not exist.

William Powers says it takes about two years of hard work to change from seeing the world in S-R terms to BCP, and in my experience his estimate was very close. It has taken me two full years to get to the point where, at least, I now *see* almost everything this way. I still can't *behave* this way as much as I would like to, but I'm working very hard to reduce the amount of ineffective S-R that I still use.

After observing for a while, perhaps a few months, make a plan to use BCP in a situation that you have not handled well in the past. Perhaps your first opportunity will arise in something as simple as how you handle your wife's request, "please take out the rubbish." In your world you don't want to take the rubbish out just then, and the untimely request has caused a small but significant perceptual error. But remember, it is from these small errors that larger errors grow, and the course of that evening at home can be sharply altered by how large an oak tree you want to grow from that night's acorn. First of all say to yourself, "I don't want to take the rubbish out, but there is no doubt that I do know how to take it out successfully. I am not deficient in rubbish-taking-out behaviors." Then ask yourself, "Do I have the time right now to take the rubbish out?" Although you are watching a football game, you know that momentarily there will be a 60-second commercial, and it takes less than 30 seconds to run out with the rubbish. As you think these simple but important BCP thoughts, your rubbish error starts to diminish, and driven by less error, you get up from the television, walk to the kitchen, grab the rubbish, go outside, dump it, come back, and watch the rest of the commercial. You only missed 15 seconds. Your perceptual error is gone, and your wife has not experienced any rubbish-in-the-kitchen error. Whatever happens the rest of that evening will happen more smoothly because you have avoided an opportunity to deal with an error badly. And in the course of any evening these opportunities are frequent. For example, later, as you continue to watch the game you remark, "I'm hungry, could you make me a snack?" She doesn't care that much for football, but with little error, none where rubbish is concerned, she makes you a tasty snack. Had you not taken the rubbish out, she might have said, "Make your own snack," which you would have done grudgingly, and each of you would then be suffering an error. Relationships between people are dynamic. Errors rapidly increase and decrease, but in a good relationship anyone who knows BCP works to keep the total error low. As errors increase, relationships deteriorate; the statement "the honeymoon is over" is really another way of saying the errors are larger than we now have behaviors to reduce them.

Suppose your wife had said to you, "I don't want to sit around the house tonight watching you watch football; let's go out to a movie." This creates a much more substantial error than rubbish; you had looked forward to this game for several days. Here, understanding BCP, you know that if you sacrifice the game and take her to the movie, the error will be too big to dissipate and you'll be a bad companion that evening. You recognize that you must negotiate and try to compromise; there is really no other way. At this point you say to her, "I've looked forward to this game all day, but I'm free every other night this week; how about a movie tomorrow night? Tuesday night is a good night; neither of us has to get up too early Wednesday morning; how about that?" If she has any understanding of BCP psychology at all, she will probably accept that compromise and things will work well. She would recognize that you didn't have a behavior that would allow you to give up the game that night. To have forced yourself into a behavior which would have increased your error wouldn't have worked. You did, however, have plenty of behaviors to go to the movies on another night, and you quickly brought them into operation when you suggested the compromise. Therefore, a further corollary to the first axiom is: *if either party recognizes that an error-reducing behavior is not available, work toward a compromise; it is the only way.*

Let's take this a step further and try an extreme case to see how BCP psychology might work. Suppose your wife says, "OK, you've watched Monday-night football for half the season; that's enough. I've joined a folk-dance group and I would like you to come with me. It meets on Monday nights until summer." Now you have a huge error in your head. You don't mind folk dancing, but you don't want to give up football. You are in conflict because you realize your wife has a point— she did compromise and wait for half the season. Now she wants your companionship, and the folk-dance class meets only on Monday nights. How do you deal with the error of this conflict? The urge to return to S-R behavior and start an argument is strong, but you restrain yourself. In this situation you realize that you have no argument that will get her to change. Arguments will not work unless they lead to a compromise. And arguments tend to increase errors and make compromise more difficult. Therefore, following the don't-increase-the-error corollary, you know you must negotiate. One way to start that might work is to explain to your wife exactly what's going on in your world, that is, you are in conflict and to reduce the error of a conflict will require a little work on both your parts. Here if she understands the serious BCP implications of a conflict, you have a much better chance. You have no simple behavior to reduce the error of a conflict as you had for the rubbish. You also know if the conflict isn't resolved, if she continues to try to force you to choose between folk dancing and football, the error in your marriage will increase to the point where the other errors that always exist in a marriage will escalate. Therefore, you *both* must face the fact that there is a conflict and it must be resolved. Any other course is courting disaster. Replace football with any other conflict, large or small; they all work the same. There is no way that any relationship can endure a conflict and not be severely damaged. In the end unresolved conflicts destroy relationships, and the longer they exist, the harder they are to resolve. As we said in Chapter 8, time does tend to resolve conflicts, because things change in time, but there is no guarantee this will happen.

A possible resolution might be that, recognizing the seriousness of the conflict, she offers to go on Monday nights without you, even though it's much more comfortable for her to have you there. You then say you'll come with her as many Monday nights as you can—not every game is that important—and add that as soon as the season is over, you will come every Monday. You talk it over and accept that there still will be some tension. Perfect solutions are rare if not impossible. It takes a while for each of you to accept the errors associated with this compromise, but at least you recognize that once you have a conflict-solving plan these little errors tend to be short-lived and diminishing. If tension continues, review the situation to see if the plan is working or if the conflict is still lurking, very much alive, and both of you are trying to avoid facing this unpleasant fact. When two people live together, conflicts must be brought out into the open, and recognized as conflicts. They must be discussed, negotiated, compromised, and a solution attempted. If that solution doesn't work, renegotiate and recompromise. Time may work, but someone who understands BCP will attempt to help time along through negotiation.

While this is good advice, often we will be in high-error situations where there is literally nothing we can do to compromise or negotiate. No behavior will work. For example, you are at the airport, you have to get to another city soon, and your plane is delayed. There is at least one situation like this every month of your life. We are constantly faced with the fact that the real world is different from the world in our head and we can't change it. Knowing BCP we have a chance to suffer much less if we can apply this knowledge. Assuming that at first we don't want to change the world in our head (we may never want to), then we would know and also feel that our behavioral system is being forced into action. Any of the behaviors mentioned in previous chapters, from angering to depressing to drinking, is possible, and one or more will be what we do. Becoming aware of BCP teaches two very important facts about this common situation where there is no way to reduce the error: (1) our behavior (or feeling) is not happening to us; we are choosing it. (2) whatever we initially tend to do, think, or feel we can probably choose another behavior that would be more effective and more comfortable. In other words, the third axiom of BCP is: *we are not locked into any one behavior; all we are locked into is that we must behave.*

BCP teaches us that what we ordinarily call feelings, and therefore think *happen to* us, are in fact *chosen* behaviors like angering or depressing in which the feeling component seems to us to predominate. We have to give up the idea that we are the victims of outside forces which cause us to feel this way. BCP teaches the difficult lesson that we both choose the world we want and choose the behavior that is our attempt to move the real world closer to the in-the-head world we want. Therefore, we are not *depressed* because Susan rejected us; we are *depressing* to try to deal with our perception that Susan is not what we would like her to be. Understanding this gives us the insight to ask ourselves, "Couldn't we choose a better behavior than depressing?" Or, "Why are we choosing to depress when maybe something else would work better?" Or maybe we should take a look at our world and change the way we want Susan to live in it. It takes active dialogue with ourselves to make us aware that while it's hard, we can choose a better behavior. If we are too passive we tend to lock ourselves into our "stimulus-response," Susan-rejected-us, misery.

We also must realize that we choose miserable behaviors like depressing because they do work for us, and we won't easily give up what works. We can't expect just to say, "This isn't working; I must do something better," and then do it. But as unhappy behaviors like depressing tend to drag on and grow less effective and more miserable with time, we might say to ourselves as part of our active BCP dialogue, "I've been depressing long enough! Now it is time for me to do something better." And then add, "What can I do now that will be a little better." After you say this to yourself then remember that as miserable as you may feel, your behavior always has *three* active components—*doing, thinking,* and *feeling.* Keeping these three components in mind, even though the depressing seems to predominate, both from my personal experience and as a reality therapist, I have found that it is easier to force myself to *do* something different than to think or feel something different. For example, if I've been sitting at home depressing, as miserable as I may feel, I can get off my chair, go outside, and walk for an hour. I am capable of doing that; walking is in my behavioral system and does not increase my error, because I have no conflict where walking is concerned. But if I change any component of my behavior I must affect all of it. By that I mean we cannot change one component of our behavior without affecting the other two; they are linked together. If I walk and increase the doing component I will necessarily, at least while I'm walking, depress less. I will have the same rejection error (Susan doesn't love me) but by deciding to walk, and suffering less because walking hurts less than depressing, I get the idea I am in better control of my life. I get this idea because I feel better, and with the idea that I am in better control I may now remove Susan a little bit from my world. As I do this I reduce my error and I cope with Susan's rejection that much better because I need her less. Nellie Forbush washed that man right out of her hair in *South Pacific.* I have walked Susan, at least a little, out of my hair.

It's a small start, but if I didn't understand that depressing is a chosen behavior I probably would not have started to walk at all. Many people don't, because they think "I am depressed" in the old S-R terms as specific helpless response to the stimulus of Susan's rejection. They believe they are depressed because Susan won't change, not that their depressing is an active but ineffective way to try to change her. She may change, but BCP tells us that if this has been going on for a while it is unlikely I can change her. My best chance is to change myself. If and when I change, Susan may see me differently, which could help, but if she doesn't, as I change I will also change my world and may not need Susan as much or in the same way.

Finally there is also the possibility that to decrease your error you may be able to learn to change your world to a world that is easier to control. The way to accomplish this is to try to keep your in-the-head world at as low an order as possible, and to do this you must try to perceive the outside world also at as low an order as you can and still fulfill your needs. This means you have to learn to rely more on yourself and less on others. For example, you are unhappy and frustrated because your daughter smokes marijuana and refuses to stop. In your world marijuana is illegal, immoral, and dangerous; your child is incorrigible for defying you and continuing to smoke it. To you as a parent, marijuana, which could be as low as a third-order perception, is perceived at the ninth order; it dominates a whole value system that your daughter is violating. Because in your world it is a dangerous and corrupting drug your daughter now becomes a bad girl (eighth order) in the system of ideas dominated by ninth-order marijuana. As long as you perceive her and marijuana at these high orders you will suffer huge errors and your behavioral system will be driven too hard to be effective. Your hard-driven, erratic, mostly punitive behaviors will contribute to the growing deterioration of your relationship with your child.

Following BCP, to correct this unhappy state of affairs, you might try to lower the order at which you perceive both marijuana and your child. You can't, however, simply change the way you perceive and say marijuana is just a smoke; you have to change your behaviors. You might start by arbitrarily setting aside some time on a Saturday afternoon when you and your daughter can go out for a bike ride, stop for a bite to eat, and maybe park the bikes and take a walk around a nearby lake. If she agrees to go with you, and she may, you should not criticize her at all. The subject of marijuana should be avoided. What you have forced yourself to do for a brief period is to accept your daughter as your child (sixth order) and run a seventh-order program with her in which there may be, for that short time, little or no error. If the afternoon goes well, you may be able, for the rest of the day or longer, to lower the order at which you perceive her because of that pleasant, error-free afternoon. Remember, it was the high-order world in your head that caused you the error, and even a short period of arbitrary, low-order, error-free time may allow you to lower it.

If you can do this, that is, find a behavior that allows you to see her for short periods at a lower order, and see that she may function well during these times, then, even though you know she is still smoking marijuana, the drug may be reduced from ninth order to sixth order. It's a sixth-order drug that many people, even effective people, smoke once in a while, but it will not cause her to "go to hell." This will cause you to criticize her less and yourself less, because criticism is almost always a behavior that is an attempt to correct the error of an unhappy eighth or ninth-order perception. Sixth-order and lower perceptions do not provoke much criticism from your redirection system. And the effect is circular; less criticism means less error, and less error less criticism.

Another way in which you might reduce your overall level of error and generally be less aggravated is to concentrate on seeing simple, unimportant, short-lived situations at the low order they deserve. You go into a restaurant and sit a long time with no service, getting hungrier by the moment. Finally a waiter comes over, perhaps apologizes, but in your state of hunger you perceive him as an incompetent fool out to starve you. Once you have this eighth-order perception of the situation you will suffer enough error to cause you to behave in a way that will almost guarantee an unhappy dinner and perhaps further poor service. Don't count on assertiveness here, you may get poisoned. If you can force yourself to accept the obvious fact that, no matter what the reason for the delay, he is finally here and see him as a waiter (third order), no more no less, and see yourself as a hungry diner (sixth order), your meal will go better. There are many everyday situations where we unnecessarily raise the order, increase our error, and suffer.

There are times when you may feel it necessary to perceive the world at a high order, but remember when you do, you need to have the behaviors to cope with that increase, because it will always cause more error. Too often we raise our order without realizing we don't have the behaviors to cope with what we have done. Also the higher the order the more we tend to see the world in S-R terms. When you see your boss as an S-R tyrant (ninth order) pushing you around, work is going to be harder than when you see him as demanding but also as a hard worker who insures the security of the company and your job (mostly sixth order). But it still gets back to having adequate behaviors. The more competent you are, the easier it is to see the world and your boss at lower orders. Less competent employees tend to perceive all parts of their job at very high orders. As they do so they drive their behavioral system harder and their incompetence increases.

While there are many specific applications of BCP to our lives that we cannot cover here, it seems important to discuss how BCP can be used to help us maintain the long-term sexual relationships that are fundamental to the way most of us choose to live. Partly to relieve the unrelenting sexual pressures of the old brain, the new brain has elaborated the need to belong and the need to love and coupled these with sex. Then to satisfy these intertwined needs the new brain has come up with the behavior of marriage, ostensibly a lifelong commitment common to most human cultures. Very recently in the Western World sexual restraint has become culturally less necessary for almost everyone, and as this has occurred the sexual need of the old brain can be satisfied independently of marriage. It is also less necessary that it be coupled with the new-brain needs of love and belonging. Because of this, people are having more difficulty maintaining marriage and even long-term sexual relationships short of marriage. They continue to marry or live together, perhaps more frequently than ever, and for a while sex is coupled satisfactorily to love and belonging. But if during the relationship it does not continue to be coupled they may divorce or separate and look for another, more compatible partner. When they find one they contemplate another marriage or its equivalent. These serial relationships do not prove that love and belonging are weaker needs than sex; they are just as strong, but they are much more difficult to share. Unlike sex, which is rather simple and, because it is derived from our old brain, much the same in all of us, our new-brain needs for love and belonging are much more complicated. To love and to belong we must share interests in family, work, play, and intellectual pursuits, a difficult process which takes up much of our waking lives. Sex, which is a powerful old-brain need that remains strong throughout our life, is much more easily shared than the more complex needs of love and belonging that are necessary to fulfill if we wish to stay with one sexual partner. Therefore, to live together for life, knowing that the elimination of a sexual error is now seemingly much more possible because our culture makes sex available, we must learn more than ever to develop loving and belonging behaviors. We must actively share these in our internal world; sex by itself will no longer hold us together. We should also mention that the economic security of marriage and children which used to keep many people together for life, even if they disliked each other, has now been almost reversed. Many people today are economically better off to live alone.

Many couples recognize this new real-world situation and live together before marriage trying to find out how much of their internal worlds, besides sex, they do share. If they are satisfied that they not only have many interests in common but also share need-fulfilling behaviors linked to these interests then they usually want to commit themselves to marriage. But if, later, things deteriorate there is nothing sacrosanct anymore about a "lifelong" relationship. It is no tragedy when people who are miserable with each other because their internal worlds are much different separate. The tragedy is when people try to force themselves to live together because of an external commitment like marriage. People who understand BCP will not depend on external commitments like marriage or a simple shared internal need like sex to keep them together. They will understand the tremendous importance of sharing their internal worlds and will work out ways to expand common interests and behaviors. And also very aware of the importance of keeping errors low, they will not criticize or attempt to control their partner in areas they do not share. They will understand that to work out the inevitable conflicts that arise from intimacy they must quickly be ready to compromise and negotiate because love and belonging cannot survive conflict.

Finally, as we begin to use BCP in our lives we will recognize that there are many times when we suffer an error, especially from a conflict, that some of the behaviors we consider will do little to correct; they may even make it worse. For example, we need a hated job desperately, but if we choose to depress we will lose it. In these times of chronic error, unrelieved even by symptoms like depressing and angering, we tend to suffer pain, disability, or sickness. As explained in Chapters 10 and 11, our disability is a behavior, our illness is caused by our old brain reorganizing. Understanding BCP may help us to choose a better behavior and even possibly help our own medical treatment if we recognize that we are suffering a psychosomatic illness.

First of all, if we understand BCP we at least know we hurt, are disabled or sick because we are suffering from a chronic error. We may not be aware of what the error is, but if we examine our lives carefully, by ourselves or with help, we will find that there is almost always a serious conflict that we cannot resolve. We are not suffering disabling headaches or arthritis or bleeding ulcers because of an external agent; it is something in our own internal world that is not satisfied. Facing this fact is hard for two reasons: (1) we don't want to change our internal world; it is even difficult for us to make ourselves aware of its existence. And (2) we have been taught all our lives that pain or sickness is our body's response to the stimulus of some outside agent or trauma; something has attacked us and made us sick.

This second point is especially hard to unlearn partly because this S-R explanation of disability and disease is reinforced continually by the popular media, but mostly *because we want to believe it*. Since the "fact" that sickness comes from an outside agent is standard teaching in medical schools, doctors also help us to believe that healing also must occur from the outside. Stimulus-response dominates here. Therefore, for most of us who don't understand BCP and for a lot of us who are trying to, it's easier to depend upon medical care to heal us than to take a look at our lives and see what the conflict is and how it can be dealt with better. As we said in Chapter 11, attempting to live by BCP places a burden on us that, when we are sick, seems almost too much too assume. "It's unfair to live in a BCP world where because I need my miserable job, I don't have the behaviors to be well. It's not my fault! The doctor should cure me."

Unfortunately, if we want to use BCP in our lives we must assume this burden. If your doctor practices medicine in a

BCP way he should be able to help you; many wholistic doctors are now doing this successfully. Still, with or without their help BCP teaches you to assume more responsibility for your internal world, and that is hard. But if you do assume this responsibility, you must be careful not to fall into the trap of thinking that the illness is your fault, that you should have done better. You must accept that all of your life, any behavior you choose, good or bad, is *your best choice at that particular time.* If you start searching for fault, you necessarily criticize yourself, increase your error and become more sick or disabled. What you must learn to say is "I have an error, probably from a conflict, and I must figure out something better than what I am doing now." If the sickness is resolving the conflict, as it may—many a person gets out of a bad work situation after a heart attack, or a back "injury"—it is not a good way.

At this seeming impasse, where we need behavior that we do not have, there is still something that we can do and that most of us are not aware of. Our brain would not have evolved this far without a way to tap the almost unlimited, but erratic, strength of our reorganization system, a way we will take up next and one that most of us can use.

14

Meditations

<del>&</del>

In my book *Positive Addiction* I told the story of a young monk who felt he was positively addicted to chanting. Early in his life, in fact in high school, he became addicted to alcohol and lived in an almost continuous alcoholic haze until age twenty-five. No stranger to the DTs, he felt that he was going to kill himself with drink. Then, as alcoholics rarely do, he took a look at himself on a sober day, said that there must be something better than this, and decided to chant. Each day for an hour he chanted the psalms; in six months he had stopped drinking, and in a year he had totally lost the desire to drink. In BCP terms he had removed alcohol from his personal world, something that few alcoholics, even long-term AA members, are able to do. He then studied, became a monk, and is very satisfied with his present position as chief monk in a small monastery near Irvine, California. What makes this story significant is that in response to my question, "What happens now if you don't chant?" he said with a laugh, "Don't ask." He claimed that when he failed to chant for several days, he experienced most of the symptoms of alcoholism—the shakes, the sweats, the upset stomach, and the feeling of impending doom. Now, as firmly hooked on chanting as he had been on drinking, he is an excellent example of those who enjoy a positive addiction. He believes his new addiction is highly beneficial, the down side minimal, because he enjoys chanting and enjoys the control of his life that he has gained through this process. He describes his satisfaction at being hooked into a behavior that positive addicts claim makes their life better in every way.

In *Positive Addiction* I describe how during each of the wide variety of activities that could be addicting, the person experienced a positive addiction (PA) or meditative state of mind. Using BCP I now believe that this meditative state of mind is a way to tap the potential strength of the reorganization system and in doing so markedly increase the ability of our behavioral system to function. It was, therefore, a meditation that enabled the monk to overcome alcoholism as it will help anyone who chooses symptoms or addictions in their effort to reduce large chronic errors. Even psychosomatic illness, which is an inadvertent result of chronic error that is not dealt with through symptoms or addictions, can sometimes be overcome if we can gain access to our reorganization system through meditation.

Meditations range from weak to strong. Among the weakest is the simple act of regularly taking a vitamin pill, a small, regularly scheduled beneficial act. The strongest are positive addictions such as running ten miles each day as an addicted runner. Any of them may allow us access to our reorganization system. The stronger they are, the longer this access will be and the more likely they will help us. *I would define a meditation as a way in which we can gain access to this system and tap its potential power.* We must remember that the reorganization system is a random system and that even if we gain access to it we don't necessarily receive help from it, but if we tap it in this way there is a good chance that we will. When the reorganization system acts through the process of meditation it is like a powerful healer who may or may not decide to help us but will not hurt us under any circumstance. It is the regular access that makes the difference; the more we become involved the more likely the help. Meditation will also help us gain more effective behaviors whether we suffer from a huge chronic error or are strong and healthy. It makes no distinction as to whether we need help or not, but if we do, the help will be more apparent and more dramatic.

In BCP terms, let us examine what happened that caused the young monk to stop drinking and to turn his whole life around when he began to chant. Let's assume he was experiencing a huge chronic error, perhaps from several conflicts, and that he had no behaviors to reduce the error. During this conflicted time he would tend to perceive himself as worthless, a sharp contrast to his inner world where he desperately desired to be somebody. Talking to him now, as an impeccably robed, successful monk, illustrates the contrast between the worthless alcoholic he was and the capable, fulfilled person he now is. When he decided to chant (as his meditation) he selected a specific behavior that he believed could be helpful to him; in his mind it would in some way fulfill one or more of his needs. It may be that he felt closer to God, it may be that he felt personably more worthwhile, it may be that it was fun, it may be that he felt chanting would give him freedom or that the discipline of chanting gave him more control over his life; whatever, he continued to chant because it was need-fulfilling behavior. In choosing to chant he selected a behavior that he could do easily and also a behavior that he would get better and more comfortable doing as he progressed. What is important about any meditation behavior, whether as difficult as chanting an hour a day, or as simple as taking vitamin C, is that (1) *you believe in the process,* (2) *you can do it easily,* and (3) *it is need fulfilling in some way.* (*Or if you take a medication it is not harmful.* Vitamin C, which is widely used as a weak meditation evidently can be tolerated in huge doses without harm; vitamin A or D in these quantities might be fatal). The more effort that the meditation requires and the more the meditation behavior is perceived as beneficial, the more powerful it will be in tapping the reorganization system. Therefore, running, chanting, yoga, zen, or swimming will be much more powerful meditations than taking vitamins, knitting, listening to music, or walking, all of which are effective but not nearly as strong, because they take so little effort.

What happens in BCP terms is that the more the meditation occupies our mind or predominates for that time in our inner world, the more powerful it will be. This is because the more it does, the more we will control for it alone and, in doing so, close down all of our comparing stations except the meditation station for this activity. Under these conditions, that is, when we have only *one station open and in that station we have little or no error,* I believe we gain access to our reorganization system. For example, if we perceive ourself chanting successfully for an hour daily, then during this period of time, when we are concentrating successfully on what we set out to do, we have no error and no error signal except the tiny signal that continues to drive the almost automatic chanting. Except for this activity our behavioral system is quiescent. We are not processing new information, we are not redirecting, and with no error we are not actively reorganizing.

The new-information system and the redirection system shut down with no difficulty; these systems are only activated by error. But the reorganization system is different; although it too is activated by error, we do not believe that it ever shuts down completely, perhaps because it is our fundamental behavioral system. It is the source of our creativity, from it most of our important behaviors were elaborated, and error or not we believe it continues in its random way to idle along because it must always be ready to be active. To shut it down would endanger our life. Even when we sleep, our dreams, which are reorganizing thought behaviors, seem to confirm that this system never shuts down.

With no error signal there is no active need for any part of our behavioral system to function beyond the simple, almost automatic, meditative behavior; therefore, what may happen is that in this low-error state we become aware of our own reorganization system. It becomes conscious to us in bits and pieces or in insightful random flashes. We even can experience long states of what we describe as altered consciousness, because for this low-error time we do not need our mind for its usual activities. As this altered state takes over we enter the meditative or positive-addiction state of mind. As it continues we may reach a total positive-addiction state of mind or, in zen terms, satori. When this occurs we have gained temporary but rather complete access to this powerful system. We become aware that something far different from our usual mental state is going on in our head. It is as if our brain is kind of spinning along on its own, or as one positively addicted runner described it, "It is as if my brain leaves my body and floats along on its own having a wonderful time. As it does it occasionally looks down and says, 'Look at that poor fool running his guts out when I'm having such a wonderful time.'" When the brain "spins out" or does its own thing, we get a feeling of relaxation, of power, a feeling that more and more we have control over our lives. This is accompanied by a variety of good feeling behaviors which usually accompany low-error activity, and our guess is that these good feelings occur because, aware of this powerful system, *we believe we are more in control of our lives.*

I admit that I am trying to infer what must go on from what happened. For example, the monk gained the strength to conquer alcoholism but became addicted to chanting, but this inference accurately fits the picture. Perhaps the reorganization system, as it idles along with no demands upon it, feeds or intimates to the quiescent redirection system that there are almost an unlimited number of potentially useful behaviors available. The redirection system, because it is inactive at the time except for the low-error meditation, is able to soak up these potential behaviors like a sponge. Remember, the redirection system is a learning system: it has learned from the reorganization system all of our lives but almost always under the pressure of an error signal from an uncontrollable error. Under this pressure it looks desperately for a behavior—almost any behavior—that will reduce the error, but in meditation with no error the redirection system accepts only behavior that seems sensible. As it does so it becomes augmented with behaviors that it did not have, and with these potentially usable behaviors it becomes stronger. When the meditation is over, when, for example, the monk stops chanting and returns to his ordinary life his redirection system, stronger because it has been augmented by input from his reorganization system, deals with error better than before. Of course, the reorganization system continues to idle along when we are not meditating and not suffering a large error, but it does not augment the redirection system at this time, because the redirection system is busy.

Reorganization becomes actively available to us only in very high-error or extremely low-error situations. But in high or really uncontrollable-error situations its use is restricted to reducing the particular error that activated it. As soon as the error is reduced we go back to redirection. If we can't reduce the error and we reorganize continually we are psychotic. Meditation, therefore, is the only way to tap the random creative resources of this system on a regular basis. With this added strength the young alcoholic was able to reject drinking and take better control of his life. If, to feel worthwhile, he wished to go to school and study it was now possible. Certainly the prime characteristic of a strong redirection system is to provide us with behaviors that give us the constant feedback that we have control over our life. And since this sense of control is a constant refrain of those who engage in good meditation this further supports our belief that this is where the strength comes from. There is no specific strength-building quality in chanting, running, zen, or yoga; it must come from the nonspecific involvement of the reorganization system independent of the variety of meditation practiced. The meditation is only the way to get there. The reorganization system is the heart of the strengthening process.

All of us have our own little irregular meditations, our own ways to relax, to pare our attention down to just one or perhaps a few stations. Almost any low-error activity will do this. It can be as simple as staring at a fire and watching it burn down, raking a garden, arranging a bowl of flowers, or baking a loaf of fragrant bread. It can be making love with a willing, noncritical partner. It is what all of us need but find so hard to do when chronic error drives us to the frantic symptomatic behaviors described in previous chapters. It can be literally anything as long as what we do is a low-error activity and we do it in such a way that we *accept* ourselves. If we *criticize* ourselves we create an error, an error signal, and drive our redirection system enough so that it becomes busy and meditation impossible. Therefore, the key to any low-error meditation activity is to do it in such a way that we accept ourselves. The activity per se is less important than the fact that we accept ourselves while we do it. Each culture seems to discover and rediscover continually a vast series of meditations, all of which serve the same purpose. When we find a way, like running, that works for us, even though this takes some time and effort, the feeling is so powerful and so pleasant that we can become positively addicted to the activity. This occurs because, when the reorganization system becomes temporarily dominant and we gain a sense of control, a natural, addicting pleasure chemical like enkephalin or endorphin may be produced in our brain. The monk suffers withdrawal symptoms when he fails to chant for a few days because when he stops he no longer produces the natural pleasure chemical that he has grown to depend on.

We can, of course, kick a positive addiction. We'll suffer for a while but not like a negative addict, because we are strong. Also we probably don't produce an amount of the natural chemical nearly as large as what heroin addicts inject. Generally there is no reason to stop a positively addicting activity. Even if a runner hurts an ankle or knee and cannot run, he may meditate mentally until it heals. For him it's not as good as running but it does prevent withdrawal.

Many people who engage in a meditative activity never reach a meditative state of mind. Some runners, for example, run for competition purposes, they run to gain a sense of self-worth, and when they run they are so demanding of their body that they never reduce their error to the point where they experience their reorganization system. When people talk of runners whose whole life is running they are talking of desperate, symptomatic, competitive runners, not relaxed, positively addicted runners. A meditation *cannot dominate* your life. It takes a short part of each day during which we try to achieve a low-error state. Runners or others who do nothing but their activity are frantically redirecting, they are not meditating. A meditation is a gentle, easy, low-error state, never desperate or frenetic.

Meditation, as we said, can occur in many forms; for example, bio-feedback, a popular new form of meditation, is an attempt to concentrate on consciously controlling physiology ordinarily well controlled by our old brain. For example, you might concentrate on lowering your own high blood pressure by thinking of a low figure like 120 as hard as you can. The bio-feedback machine provides an ongoing readout of your actual blood pressure, while you try to concentrate so hard on 120 that you lower the blood pressure. Since the new brain can set abnormal reference levels in the old brain, bio-feedback theory would hold that by concentrating the new brain on 120 it transmits this information to the old brain, which lowers the pressure. But this implies a much more direct informational process, new brain to old brain, than seems reasonable. It cannot be that specific; the old brain is not constructed to process conscious commands. Nevertheless, the blood pressure often goes down. Why? What we believe happens is that by concentrating on the blood pressure to the exclusion of all else you have begun to meditate. The feedback of watching the readout of your blood pressure is like the mantra or repeated phrase or sound in TM and other eastern meditations; it helps you to close off all other mental activity. The blood pressure returns to normal because the low-error meditation has tapped your reorganization system to give you the idea that now you have more control over your life. As the error of your life reduces and the new brain functions better the old brain is able to reset its reference levels to normal, and your blood pressure returns to normal.

This explanation is substantiated by an experiment reported by the TM people, in which a group with high blood pressure was taught TM, and a comparable group bio-feedback.* After several weeks TM seemed to be more effective in lowering the blood pressure. We believe it was more effective because it is easier to accept. Bio-feedback has too much potential for self-criticism built in; that is, if you don't succeed in reducing your blood pressure, you may criticize yourself for failing and not reach the state of meditation. TM, an old established meditation, has almost no possibility for self-criticism built into it.

Another interesting bio-feedback experiment used heart rate as the feedback.† People who were anxious when they spoke in public were told to concentrate on their heart rate and try to slow it down. When the readout showed them that they had succeeded they reported much less anxiety when making a speech. But the fact that this was a meditation and not true bio-feedback was shown when the experimenters gave the anxious public speakers false feedback. The readout told them that their heart rate was slowing when it wasn't. False or true they still reported much less anxiety when speaking in public. The false information worked as effectively as the true informa-

---

* TM is a trademark for Transcendental Meditation. This experiment was reported in a privately circulated book of TM experiments by David Wallace, Ph.D. who is the research director of the TM organization. He can be contacted through the Maharishi International University, Fairfield, Iowa.

† Gatchel, *Journal of Consulting and Clinical Psychology* 47:620–22.

tion; in fact, both test groups were identical in anxiety reduction. Obviously, it wasn't the slowing of the heart rate that reduced the anxiety, it was the fact that they were doing something they thought would help. They were involved in a meditation, the bio-feedback was incidental. What this also shows is that it's foolish to believe or to advocate that one meditation is better than another. What is better is the one that works for you. When they work, they all work in the same way. To argue that running is more effective than yoga is to argue the merits of your inner world over mine.

The same forces are operating when you take medicine *if you believe that the medicine is effective.* This placebo effect is real because it is a meditation. As long as you believe in the medicine, your new-brain will suffer less error, your old brain will then function better, and with it functioning at more normal levels any physical symptom or even a disease of reorganization will improve. This was graphically illustrated in a case reported by Carl Simonton in a booklet published in 1976.* One of the cases, reported by an investigator named Klopfer, is of a patient who had a far-advanced lymphosarcoma and begged to be treated with Krebiozin, a drug that about twenty-five years ago was highly touted as a cancer cure. Upon the initial administration of the drug, his tumor masses "melted like snowballs on a hot stove" and while he had previously required an oxygen mask to breathe at sea level, he became fully active and flew his own plane at 12,000 feet with no discomfort. When reports started appearing in the newspapers casting doubt on the effectiveness of the drug he returned to his bed, again riddled with lymphosarcoma. His physician, in a last attempt to offer him life, told him not to believe what he had read about Krebiozin, informed him that the preparation had deteriorated upon standing, and that it would be given to him again at double strength. All he injected was water,

---

* Carl Simonton, *Stress Psychological Factors and Cancer* (privately published, 1976).

but the man again showed rapid disease remission until it was announced conclusively in the news that both the AMA and FDA had found Krebiozin to be a worthless preparation. He died a few days after reading this announcement.

Here again, we see the powerful effect of error reduction; he believed in the drug, his new-brain reorganization system augmented his redirection system, he became more effective and more in control. When this happened his physiologic reference levels returned to normal, his old-brain reorganization (which we believe was hampering his immune system) stopped, and his normal immune system temporarily wiped out the lymphosarcoma. It all stemmed from the placebo or meditation effect of believing in the drug. When he stopped believing in the drug his new-brain error disrupted his old brain and his immune system, his cancer returned, and he died quickly. If we see placebos as powerful meditations they are easier to understand.

Besides placebos, bio-feedback, and the various positive addictions we've mentioned, there are many more, such as auto suggestion, guided imagery, self-hypnosis, Rolphing, relaxation responses, Transcendental Meditation, prayer, and a whole variety of oriental martial arts like Kung Fu. They all work if the follower believes enough to practice them diligently.

Perhaps the force of meditation as a cure in psychosomatic disease is best illustrated in the recent widely publicized case of the famous writer Norman Cousins, who "cured" himself of a crippling, sometimes fatal, spinal arthritic disease, ankylosing spondylitis. In his article, called "Anatomy of an Illness," in the May 28, 1977, *Saturday Review,* Cousins describes how he was in Russia in 1964 as chairman of an American delegation to consider the problems of cultural exchange. He worked hard and with increasing exasperation, caused by the difficulty of getting the Russians to cooperate. His last day was one of almost total frustration, and all the way home to New York the next day on a crowded, uncomfortable plane he fretted over what he had failed to accomplish. By the time he cleared customs he felt an uneasiness deep in his bones. A week later he was hospitalized with acute spinal arthritis. Even with the best medical treatment, he began rapidly to go downhill, and it looked as if he would suffer the full brunt of this ailment and be crippled and in pain for the rest of his life. When Cousins asked his doctor to give it to him straight he was told that he had one chance in five hundred of recovering. Facing these odds, he asked his doctor if he couldn't take over his own medical treatment, and to his surprise the doctor agreed. He tried the hospital for a while but found that the Chinese-water-torture treatment, typical of any large hospital, where there seemed to be little concern for the patients' comfort or convenience, was more than he could bear. With his doctor's cooperation he left the hospital and checked into the Plaza Hotel in New York City, where he engaged a deluxe room with superior service. He hired an extremely competent nurse to care for him and him alone, removed himself from all standard anti-arthritic medications, and discontinued all medical tests except the sedimentation rate, a simple test which reflects the activity of the disease. He did so because his doctor admitted that none of the tests or medicines were actually improving the 500–1 odds against him.

His own treatment was to call his friend Alan Funt and have him bring his funniest *Candid Camera* reels and show them regularly. Watching these unedited films, which Cousins said were far funnier than anything ever shown to the public, he laughed himself into a state of pleasant exhaustion several times a day. He was acting on the assumption that if stress and strain produce sadness and misery, laughter should be the opposite and what he needed was the opposite. In BCP terms, he was talking about producing on a regular basis an extremely low error state, because when we laugh we experience about the lowest error state possible.

He also put himself on an extremely high intravenous dosage

of vitamin C. As he watched the level in the bottle drop he could feel the strengthening effect of what he believed was a wonderful anti-arthritic and antistress vitamin. Sick as he was he began to enjoy the hotel comfort, the personal care of the nurse, and the sensible but extremely tasty diet. *And he believed in his treatment.* Of course, as any reader of this book would now suspect, when his "treatment" began to eliminate the many perceptual errors associated with his disease, his sedimentation rate started to drop, and he began to get better. Arthritis reverses slowly, but several years after the initial attack, except for some mild residual stiffening, he was judged completely recovered. He had beat the 500–1 odds against him.

His story, which he has expanded into a bestselling book,* has received so much publicity that it is almost common knowledge to most medical practitioners. He now lectures to medical students and faculties all over the world, telling over and over what he believes caused the "miracle." Cousins attributes a great deal of his recovery to vitamin C; my own interpretation would be that this fortunately nonharmful drug was the placebo portion of several powerful meditations that he cleverly arranged for himself. Without understanding BCP, Cousins recognized that in the hospital he was being treated much differently from how he would like to be treated. Somehow he knew he was in a high-error situation, and he did his best to remove himself totally from that bad scene. He recognized that he had no control, that his (redirection) system was being pushed just to cope with the "treatment" insults that he daily suffered at the hospital. When he got out *he took control* and laughed his perceptual error away. As he meditated with laughter and vitamin C his reorganization system augmented his redirection system to give him even greater control. With a lower error his physiologic reference levels returned to normal, his old

* Norman Cousins, *Anatomy of an Illness* (New York: W. W. Norton & Co., 1979).

brain functioned as it should, and his immune system stopped attacking his spine. His normal recuperative powers took over, and except for the slight scarring associated with healing he was cured.

It isn't necessary to say much more except to lament the fact that even with Cousins' lead it is unlikely that many of us could do this. Both we and our physicians would be too intimidated by the mandatory "treatment" system, giving us much less chance to beat the odds than Norman Cousins had. But if we understand BCP and use it in our lives, as I believe he inadvertently did, we will have a better chance than those who don't. To recover from diseases of reorganization we must correct the abnormal physiologic reference levels that are making us sick. We certainly can't all have the faith in vitamin C or the availability of Alan Funt, but there is still a great deal that we can do if we understand that with any meditation we have a better chance. And if we can find a physician who thinks this way our chances are even more improved.

A doctor and his wife who recognize the importance of meditation are Carl Simonton and his social-worker wife, Stephanie. They have pioneered a sensible meditation treatment for cancer that has prolonged the life and reduced the suffering of many people and seems to have produced a total remission in at least ten.* His treatment, simply stated, is to add a visualizing meditation to the traditional cancer treatment of radiation and chemotherapy. As a young doctor he had noticed that the mental attitude of the cancer patient seemed to be the crucial factor in determining the course of the disease. People who did not admit that they were doomed and mentally fought the cancer lived longer and with less suffering. And where they *believed* in the efficacy of the treatment they received they also seemed to do much better. What the Simontons do

* Simonton reported this in his paper entitled, "Belief Systems and Management of the Emotional Aspects of Malignancy," *Journal of Transpersonal Psychology* 7, no. 1 (1975).

is develop a regime for cancer patients to help them believe that they have much more control over their life and their disease than is ordinarily the case. The idea that we have control is fundamental to health because it is essential to living with low error. As soon as we lose control we begin to live with chronic and enlarging errors, and our physiologic system often becomes involved. To get this increase in control for cancer patients, who when they're told they have cancer undoubtedly suffer a huge error and lose control, they explain their concept of the disease. They also discuss the case of the man with the lymphosarcoma previously mentioned. When the patients ask how they can use these ideas in their treatment the Simontons tell them about a technique which they call relaxation and visualization training. Patients are taught to relax and while relaxing to visualize their disease. Then to treat it, they are to visualize their bodies' immune mechanisms attacking their cancer. They tell the patients to see this body defense system as made up of fierce white blood cells which attack and rip the cancer to shreds. Whether or not visualization of the immune system attacking the disease actually activates the real immune system we can't say, but what probably does help is the patients' new belief that they can do something specific to combat the disease. The Simontons recognize that what they are teaching is a meditation, and we agree: this is the core of the treatment.

In some cases Simonton reports complete recovery, but so far, cure is uncommon. Prolongation of life and more comfort is where they are, but they are working hard against a disease which strikes terror (high error) into those who suffer it. While this approach is a long way from the final cure for cancer it shows that to combat even this destructive disease we can enlist the powerful mechanism of the reorganization system with some good effect.

We live in a complicated world of chronic error, and while probably it was always that way, it seems harder and harder for most of us to believe that we have the control we would like to have over our own destiny. To get this belief will never be easy, but we should be aware that meditation allows us to enlist our reorganization system to help, and like Charley Brown we need all the help we can get. We would all benefit if we had more ways to spend part of each day without error. If we can find a meditation that does this it makes good sense to use it regularly.

15

*Helping Others: The Use of BCP with Reality Therapy**

☙ ❧

Recently, while I was lecturing on BCP psychology in St. Louis, a woman came up during a break and said, "I'm a headacher." I didn't know exactly how to respond to this abrupt confession, but trying to be helpful I said, "Well, maybe now that you understand that headaching is a behavior you will be able to choose a better behavior and get rid of your headaches." She said that she did understand that headaching was a behavior and that she had been thinking about my explanation for the past hour. It seemed obvious that she understood my BCP explanation perfectly, but when I repeated my suggestion she said with some finality, "I've thought it over and I think I'll just continue to headache."

This story sticks in my mind because I feel badly that this woman who understands BCP has such an unsatisfactory control system that she has decided that the price of headaching is evidently lower than any other behavior that she can think of. I believe that since she has such a quick ability to grasp

---

* For a much more complete discussion of Reality Therapy, see Naomi Glasser, ed., *What Are You Doing?: Case Histories in Reality Therapy* (New York: Harper & Row, 1980).

these ideas, if she would try psychotherapy with a good therapist, she could probably get the help she needs to choose a
much better behavior than headaching. I have no idea what
her situation is or what conflict she is attempting to reduce
with headaching, but I'm certain there is a conflict. My guess
is that it is in her marriage and that headaching, painful as it
is, seems to be the best way to deal with it at this time. It
may be that she has judged her situation correctly, but if she
were my patient, I have confidence that using the concepts
of Reality Therapy and BCP we could work out a much more
satisfactory behavior.

If you open the front cover of this book and again glance
at the chart, it becomes apparent that there are three places—
the behavioral system, the perceptual system, and the inner
world—where therapy can take effect. Of these the behavioral
system is where I would commonly attempt to help a person
who came to me with headaches or any other painful behavior.
We would work toward conflict-resolving behavior; it should
not be too hard to find a better one than headaching. I would
also keep in mind that working with the perceptual system
could help the client to perceive the external world at a lower
order. If, for example, the headaching woman is having marital
problems, perhaps in joint therapy her husband could be taught
to say when she serves him soup that is too cold for his taste,
"I'd like my soup a little warmer. I wonder if you could put
it back on the fire for a moment?" This comment would be
perceived by his wife at no more than the seventh order, which
is to engage *in a program* to warm the soup. It is unlikely
that this low-order perception would cause her to headache.
On the other hand, if, as usual, he said, "How come you always
serve cold soup?" a question of the eighth order, perhaps even
bordering on the ninth, she might start to headache before
he finished this error-causing remark. Obviously, in therapy
if we wish to apply BCP psychology, we would continually
try to help both husband and wife to perceive the world at

the lowest order possible, and to use this order when dealing with each other. This is not to say that high orders are always error-producing; they can be quite the opposite. For example, the man could have said to his wife, had the soup been delicious but just a bit too cool, "I just can't get over the fact that you consistently make such great soups. If this were just a little warmer it would be perfect." Here he could raise the order to confirm how good a cook she is and lower the headache risk to his wife. People who deal with the world at very high orders, that is, see everything in terms of good or bad or right and wrong are always going to cause and experience more perceptual error than necessary. In therapy this is grist for much good discussion.

Finally, there is almost no way to help someone improve the functioning of his or her control system without trying to get that person to take a hard look at the specific needs of the internal world. This seems simple, but just yesterday I was talking to a man whom I've helped toward quite a few better behaviors and also to perceive many previously high-order situations at lower orders. I asked him to focus for a while on his inner world, and together we looked at that part of the large BCP chart in my office. In response to my question "Is there anything important in your world that you're not satisfying right now?" he told me with some pain that he was chronically dissatisfied with his social life. He felt he was being rejected by a group that he desired to become a part of, and he didn't know how to get this acceptance. We discussed again how difficult it is to get others to be the way you want them to be, that is, how hard it is to behave in a way that causes others to alter their internal world. His approach was reasonable but it might not work. He then said, "Maybe I shouldn't really want these people, maybe I should find new friends, or what I ought to do is move away altogether." He found it hard, even in the accepting environment of my office, to come to grips with the high error in the social comparing station that he continued to keep open. As we talked of this perception that he could not control he said, "It's really difficult to tell you this, it seems so foolish for me to want this so much, yet I do." We all know how difficult it is to tell another person, even an accepting noncritical therapist, what it is that we really want. We don't like to admit to ourselves or anyone else that we can't get what we want. It's easier to say "I don't want it" when I do, than it is to say "I want it, but I'm not getting it." Among the most important qualities of a good therapist is to be someone to whom people can utter their most intimate wants and desires without fear they will be criticized, less accepted, or told that they have little chance of getting what they want. None of us likes to admit the painful perception that we don't have control over the situation. We have little behaviors of all kinds to help us to deal with the situation where we want something desperately but are fearful we won't get it. We say it's unimportant, or we tend to defuse the anticipated pain by saying we really don't want it, or we'll never get it, it's not possible, or we'll never be that lucky.

It is also important throughout therapy for the therapist to work to get the client to understand that her world is not the real world. This is difficult, but if Marie Antoinette were a client it would be vital. This goes on throughout therapy and probably is not learned until the end when many more satisfactory behaviors have been added to the client's output.

A good therapist recognizes that it takes time for a trusting relationship to build, of which *the essence is that it be without criticism*. If the woman with the headaches had come to me, eventually, when I felt that our relationship had reached the point of trust, I would have asked her flat out, "What is it that you want? Why are you using headaches to cope with what you want and are not getting?" If due to a large error the headaches are severe enough she may concentrate so hard on the idea, "I'd like to have less pain" that she can blot out what it is that she really wants. In this way her misery at least causes her error not to increase. But if she trusts me she will stop headaching while she tells me what she wants. Even as we set about trying to find a better behavior to control for what she wants she may remain headache free. If we can't find a good behavior she may choose to headache again, but more likely just our attempt to look for a better behavior will be help enough that she may not choose to headache again.

To help her I would use Reality Therapy, an approach I had developed into a series of eight steps, which, long before I knew about BCP, had worked extremely well to reduce error and, when possible, resolve conflicts. As I have just discussed, since BCP, I've decided to add to these steps the basic concepts of BCP, which I teach to my clients using the chart. I've believed for a long time that along with a warm, personal client-therapist relationship, much of therapy is teaching, but before BCP what I mostly tried to teach was better behaviors. Now I want to teach people how the control system works and use the concepts of Reality Therapy not only to teach better behaviors but also to evaluate and improve their perceptions and their internal world. Keeping this in mind, let's now take a look at the helping process that I use, Reality Therapy.

Make Friends—Step One

The first step of Reality Therapy is *Make friends,* and by that I mean that anyone who comes to see a Reality Therapist should feel that she is in the presence of a warm, concerned person who is desperately trying to help her in every way possible. Since I believe that there is a basic need for belonging and that we almost always control for this need, it is important that the therapy relationship do as much as it can to satisfy this need in those who come for help. It has been my experience that almost all the people who enter therapy believe that right now they don't belong as much as they would like to. The therapist can't fulfill this need totally—no one can fulfill this need totally for another human being—but he can give the client the very obvious perception that "while I'm seeing this therapist, I certainly do belong." Understanding BCP has reinforced the importance of this step. Many people have said to me when I've worked with them, "Why do I seem able to do things when I see you that I couldn't do without seeing you?" They look at me as some sort of magical person who has given them a capacity they didn't believe they had. I had never been comfortable with that statement, but I never knew exactly why. I recognized that when people felt that they belonged they grew stronger, but now, understanding BCP, it's obvious that when belonging reduces their total error they drive their behavioral system much less frantically. When they reduce their error signal they are able to come up with behaviors that were not possible when the system was being driven so hard. There's nothing magical about the process, and I no longer feel uncomfortable. When I believe they are ready we just look at the chart and talk about the fact that even a little increase in the sense of belonging reduces the total error, and the total error signal. We talk about the fact that the total error signal is the sum of all the errors in the open comparing stations, but when we reduce an important error like belonging, a substantial reduction is made in the total error. When this occurs, better behaviors immediately become possible. We may have to work them out, which we'll talk about shortly, but some are already there; they just weren't available because the system was being driven too hard. Remember that these steps are not a recipe to be used in cookbook fashion; step one goes on throughout the whole process.

Also, as therapy progresses and as a part of step one, I now ask what the client wants. I'll get more as time goes on, but I want to know as much as I can about the client's internal world as soon as possible. I don't expect to learn much immediately, and I certainly don't push, because I know that it is painful to face what we want without the behaviors to get it, but I also feel that there is a great reduction of error in just telling an accepting therapist what it is that you want. As soon as I judge there is a certain comfort, a certain level of trust, a certain sense that with me they *do* belong, and when they have tried a few better behaviors that we have worked out using steps two, three and four, then more and more I try to get to the areas that they don't want to face. Now I try to get clients to stop defending against what they want right now that they are not getting. This certainly was illustrated by the man who said how difficult this is to face, but because he had some good new behaviors which gave him more faith in his ability to control things, he was ready to face it. It was also illustrated by the headaching woman who for all practical purposes said, "I don't want to face what I want right now. I'd rather headache." As long as she headaches, all she will face that she wants is to get rid of the headaches. So now when I do therapy we will study the chart on the wall and take a hard look at the uncontrolled reference perceptions that are coming from the client's internal world.

What Are You Doing Now?—Step Two

This leads us to the second step of Reality Therapy, the question "What are you doing now?" Many therapeutic approaches ask people how they feel or try to find out a great deal about their past history. Reality Therapy concentrates on present behavior and mostly on the *doing component* of this behavior. By now we know that our behavior is comprised of doing, thinking, and feeling, but we concentrate on doing because it is the most tangible and most easily changed component. People tend to come for help complaining about the feeling component of their behavior because they are most aware of it. They say, "I feel depressed, I feel anxious, tense, I'm fearful that I can't leave the house," to cite a few common complaints. The thinking component is seen where they say, "I can't stop crazy thoughts from running through my mind, I can't study, I can't concentrate, my mind seems blank." Paining, a specific feeling component, is illustrated by the complaints of headaches, backaches, or a continually upset stomach. The angering, acting-out component is shown when someone says "I feel this overpowering anger seething within me, and I'm fearful I'm going to hurt someone." All of these are behaviors, all are unsatisfactory, and in most cases they are painful emotional behaviors clients want to overcome. But in order to change these behaviors, BCP points out that they need to recognize that what they are complaining about is not just a feeling, it is a feeling behavior.

Ordinarily this is not what people believe; they believe they are suffering from an emotional state like anxiety. To teach them that what they perceive is a feeling behavior we look at the chart together, and I explain that, no matter how complicated each of us may be, all we have is input and output and what they're complaining about is unsatisfactory output that arises from their behavioral system. As soon as they learn this— and it may take a while but it is possible to learn—then the second step, *What are you doing now?*, makes good sense. Remember, in step one we have begun to establish what they want, and this will continue as the relationship builds. So when we ask the question, "What are you doing now?" we're talking about the behavior that they're presently choosing to get what they want. Before they understand that what they are feeling is a behavior and that they are choosing it, clients will say, "I'm not doing anything; I'm so depressed I can't do a thing." But as they learn BCP they will begin to understand that what they are doing, depressing, is a behavior, and that because of the way our brain functions there is really no such entity as a state of depression. *Any ongoing feeling is a feeling behavior.* Since it is hard to help a person to get rid of what doesn't exist it is crucial that they learn that depressing is a tangible behavior which they must change if they wish to "feel" better.

If, however, they resist or the therapist believes that this concept can't be taught, then the therapist focuses on the doing component by saying "I accept that you feel depressed, but what are you doing?" If she is immobilizing herself in her house even the most resistant client will admit she is choosing to stay home. Ordinarily, this will lead to her understanding the whole process, but even if it doesn't, as long as the therapist understands, therapy can proceed. Therefore, we try to teach the output concept that long-term feelings are behaviors, but if we can't get a client to understand this basic BCP concept we can get her to accept that she must choose the doing component of her total behavior. We can work from this much although, as we said, as therapy proceeds we will usually get clients to understand the three component, doing, thinking, feeling, explanation of their behavior.

Is This Behavior Helping You?—Step Three

In this step we ask the client to evaluate all or any part of his behavior that he will admit to choosing. We ask, "Is sitting all day in the house working for you?" Or, if he understands BCP, "Is depressing working for you?" In the case of children we may ask if breaking the rules is helping them to get what they want. At this point the client must evaluate his behavior. We also must be aware that while we're asking him to criticize his own behavior, which will increase his error, the criticism is not destructive here because it will always be coupled with the next step of Reality Therapy, in which we help him to work out a better behavior. There's nothing wrong with criticizing yourself if you're going to use the criticism to drive your behavioral system toward a better behavior. If you criticize yourself and then increase your depressing, then the criticism is totally worthless. But the job of the therapist is to stop this from happening by quickly working toward a better behavior. If, as in the case of the headaching woman, she makes the decision (as she did) that headaching was helping her or at least that she can do no better, then she will continue to headache and therapy will fail. But, if she comes for help, from my experience this will be an unlikely outcome. Remember, the behavioral system is flexible and none of us has just one better behavior but probably ten better behaviors, if we can take the time and use the help to figure out a better way.

Make a Plan to Do Better—Step Four

In step four the therapist makes an active effort to help the person to figure out a better behavior. As you can see, steps two, three, and four, *What are you doing?*, *Is it helping?*, and *Let's make a plan to do better*, go together. Although in no instance is the behavior the client is choosing satisfactory, it will always be the best he or she can do at the time. That's how our control system works. We never choose to do anything that causes us pain and discomfort; we choose it because *right now* depressing or headaching reduces our error more effectively than any other available behavior. But in therapy we are a moment beyond right now; we are now a tiny step further down the road. The therapy relationship is a new time; the knowledge that we choose our behavior is new, and at this time a better behavior is possible.

A great deal of what goes on in Reality Therapy is talking about the possibility of a better behavior. Here the therapist has to be active, to offer behavioral choices, to teach, to let the client know that there are many behaviors which the client has not thought about. In some therapies it is considered poor practice for the therapist to suggest a behavior. To me, this is exactly the same as considering it poor practice to suggest to the ancient Chinese who were burning their houses down to roast pig (in Charles Lamb's famous essay) that an oven would work better. If the therapist suggests a behavior that is unacceptable or that won't work, it will be rejected by the client, either directly or by the fact that when they try to use it they can't make it work. As we have said from the first page of this book, we cannot get another person to do what does not fulfill that person's needs. If the client figures out a behavior and it works, that's fine, but quite often the client also comes up with a behavior that doesn't work. *Just because it is initiated by the client doesn't make it good.* Our behavioral system is a learning system and therapy is a teaching situation. If we don't direct teaching to this learning system that is always open to new behaviors, we are shirking what we should be doing. Our new-information system exists to learn new behaviors, and therapy should be a source of new information. What all of us need, as we can see from the chart, is a behavioral system filled with behaviors that will get us what we want.

Therefore, there is nothing mysterious about the core of the helping process, which is for the client to find new and better behaviors. But there will be times when no better behaviors are possible. We want Susan to marry us and she marries someone else. This happens often enough so that when we use step three to evaluate our behavior, we also must use it to evaluate what it is that we want and begin to modify our inner world if there is no reasonable behavior to satisfy what we want. We may have to come to the conclusion that we must get love from someone other than Susan. We use the same steps two, three, four to look at, evaluate, and perhaps change our internal world to make it more possible. To take another example, the client has been rejected over and over for the promotion that he desperately wants. He's been told by the boss that he will not get the promotion and that there is no sense applying for it again. The boss isn't lying; there's nothing the client can do to get what he wants. Is he doomed to suffer a huge perceptual error for the rest of his life? The answer is *it's up to him.* Certainly in a therapy situation I would talk to this client and discuss what other possibilities might fulfill the same need, perhaps the worthwhile feeling that he believes this promotion would give him. Perhaps he can find worth-whileness off the job in helping his children, going back to school, or getting involved in civic responsibilities. There are many different ways that one can gain worthwhileness besides a promotion. But to go in this direction, these specific possibilities have to be inserted by him into his internal world, and some of them must be discussed in therapy. There's no sense sympathizing too much over the fact that he is not going to get what he wants. That reduces his error, but it doesn't lead to better behavior. So looking at the chart, a good therapist might say, "Let's take a look at what is possible." There's no better way I've discovered since I've learned BCP to drive this point home than to look at the internal world on the chart and say, "What else could I help you to get into your world that would satisfy you? Let's take a look at the basic needs that are driving you. Right now one or more of them is not being satisfied. You think getting that promotion would satisfy everything? Maybe it would, maybe it wouldn't; we don't know. But we know that you're not going to get it. What else could possibly satisfy you now?" That's the therapist's task, to talk over what other specific needs would satisfy the client's general needs. To keep wanting something he can't get will lead anyone to misery.

Unlike the discussion of behaviors, with the internal world the therapist must be careful to draw the person into thoughtful evaluation and to suggest very little except the idea that right now the way the client's internal world is set up won't work. It is a much more sensitive area than behaviors; now we are dealing with the forces that drive us, and here the client must not feel we are pushing or we will increase his error. If one behavior doesn't work he can choose another with no resentment, but if he feels that his internal world is being manipulated he gets an immediate error and may lose the sense of belonging that he needs to keep therapy going. We can't tell another person what to want, but we can point out that what he now wants may be impossible to achieve.

We can also look at the chart and help people to lower the order at which they perceive certain situations. This may take some discussion and it's hard, but like talking about behaviors this is not a sensitive area. When the client begins to do this, even a little, she gets a marked reduction of error and is usually able to behave much better.

Get a Commitment—Step Five

The next step of Reality Therapy is to get the client to make a commitment to the therapist to try some new behaviors. Or perhaps, to try to perceive the world at a lower order or to change her internal world. Here we are mostly talking about behaviors and making a commitment to a plan to behave better. What should be worked out is a specific, understandable, and seemingly workable plan and then a commitment to try it. From a BCP standpoint what a request for a commitment does is to ask the client to include the therapist in her internal world, in essence, to help her to fulfill her needs. If the therapist gets a commitment then he is now tentatively accepted into the client's world. If the plan works out, the therapist is then more firmly accepted as someone the client believes has the ability to help fulfill her needs. In BCP terms, when the therapist is included in the client's internal world, the commitment is really to herself, not to the therapist.

The danger of commitment is that the plan may not be carried out. When this happens the client feels the failure of the plan and additional failure towards the therapist who has been accepted into her world. This means, of course, failure to herself, which would increase the error. This problem is avoided in Reality Therapy by making sure that no commitment is asked for that is not reasonable and possible. In the beginning, plans should be limited, very specific, and they should be increased slowly. Don't ask a person whose longest run is four miles to make a commitment to run a marathon next Saturday. He not only won't succeed in the marathon, but he'll be ashamed to come back and face you (and face himself). You might get a commitment from him to run five miles next Saturday if he had been running four, because it's likely he will succeed at five miles. When this happens the relationship will be increased, and he'll take you more into his world because you helped him with workable plans. As he experiences more success his internal world grows more possible.

No Excuses—Step Six

Step six is *Don't accept excuses,* and if the client offers excuses turn them down. Excuses are the client's way of saying, "Even though I don't have the behaviors, will you please accept me as an inadequate person?" Excuses are necessary because without them we would suffer too many perceptual errors. We have to get away with little inadequacies and not suffer too much, or we'll be so upset we won't function well. In therapy, however, with a definite, workable plan, the therapist should be tough enough not to take the excuses, to let the person suffer the error of the plan's not working, and then with the therapist's help, go back to steps four and five, negotiate a new plan, or rework the previous plan, get a new commitment, and keep trying. It's important that the therapist be dogged here. The therapist should transmit to the client the idea "I have faith in your behavioral system; I'm not going to accept excuses if you said you were going to do it, and I think you can. You have a functioning behavioral system; don't think you don't!" When we say that we have confidence in another person, what we're really saying is that we have confidence in her control system, especially that she will be able to change to a better behavior.

No Punishment—Step Seven

Step seven is *Don't punish;* in BCP terms this mostly means *Don't criticize.* Perhaps *Don't do anything to increase the error of the client* is another way to put it. People who come voluntarily for help or are sent for help—for example, a probation officer with an unwilling or recalcitrant probationer—have more error than they can cope with. Nevertheless, some people who need help may have to suffer *reasonable consequences* of their failure to follow the rules, as with an unruly class in school or parolees and probationers who don't follow the rules. Even if it does not fulfill their needs there has to be some sort of place where an out-of-order child or adult is restrained from continuing to do something which hurts others. At home, a screaming child should be walked to his room and, if needed, sat with quietly, or placed in his room until he quiets down. These restraints on the freedom to break rules or hurt others are reasonable consequences. When the child quiets down, then warmly offer to help him work out the problem. Continually point out to the child you are restraining that you are not trying to hurt him. Keep saying, while the child is restrained at home or school or even in custody like juvenile hall, that you are trying to teach a behavior that will not only work now but will work in the future. But you can't teach people while they misbehave. They must be restrained. For example, a small child spills the milk at the dinner table, and the parent goes berserk because in the parent's world milk should never be spilled. The parent's error causes the parent to scream, "Why did you spill the milk?" What the parent should do is to teach a behavior so the milk will be spilled less in the future. The best thing to say here is not the punitive, critical statement "why did *you* spill the milk?," but go back to step four and ask, "Okay, what's your plan now?" The child may be startled when you say that because instead of punishing him, which he may expect, what you're doing is asking him to learn a good behavior to handle the situation. Because you do not increase their error even surprisingly small children will be able to say, "Well, maybe I ought to clean it up." If they do then you should say, "That sounds like a good plan." When the child cleans it up his error is reduced, and he also has a tendency to be more careful the next time, because cleaning up his mess is not that pleasant. You have avoided the yelling that would increase the error to an eighth or even ninth-order, life-or-death situation. All that's been spilled is some milk. You've taught him better behavior by saying, "What's your plan?" He's doing it, and when you say, "Okay, how could we work out a way not to let this happen again?" he might say, "I'll be more careful," and that's far enough for now. If you use this system the child will be more careful, and there will be little milk spilled in the future. I can't stress too strongly that if you punish (or criticize) people who don't have adequate behaviors and are suffering from a large error, the punishment increases the error and makes the behavioral system less, not more adequate.

Don't Give Up—Step Eight

Most people whom you help place you in their internal world as a person they can count on to help them fulfill their needs. As we said, this decreases their error and leads to better behaviors. Some people take a great deal of time to develop more adequate behaviors, and if you give up while they still want you to help your giving up increases their error. A good therapist is stubborn and does not give up easily. He or she says, "I have confidence that we will figure out a way," and then hangs tight. Once the client develops the idea that you're not going to give up, this solidifies his feeling that here, at least, I belong. In many people the belonging station has a large, nobody-cares-about me error that takes a long time to reduce.

Because you don't give up, the client learns you care, and finally with a reduced error he learns to use more adequate behaviors.

This doesn't mean that you never give up no matter what the client does. There are times when you have to say, "If you want me to continue to see you, then you have to do something." What you're essentially saying is, "If you want to keep me as part of your world, then you've got to do some things on your own to fulfill your needs or I won't be a part of your world." This refusal to see certain clients is based on your knowledge that they do have adequate behaviors but are so comfortable "belonging" with you that they are not willing to use them. To do this properly takes good judgment on the part of the therapist, and the helping person should always be careful not to increase an error that the client can't handle. This book can't explain all the details of therapy. What I'm trying to do here is get the therapist to understand that there are times when a moderate increase in the person's perceptual error is worthwhile, providing—and this goes back to the axioms of Chapter 13—that you believe that the person has the behaviors to cope with this increase. If she doesn't then withdrawal by the therapist will be counterproductive.

Finally, this is just an introduction to the use of BCP in psychotherapy. As these ideas become better known more will be learned, but even this much has helped me to be a more effective therapist. It has given me a map, a way to go and a way to talk that both I and the client can follow, and it prevents therapy from getting bogged down in the helplessness of "I am not responsible for what I do, and because of the world I can't change." Here there are three definite places to change, and almost from the beginning some progress can be made in one or more of these three places: *our behavior, the way we look at the world, and the way we build our world.*

A Final Note

❦§❧

With BCP psychology we believe we can explain a great deal about why we behave (error and error signal) and how we behave (reorganization and redirection). We have proposed that we perceive the world in as many as ten orders to explain the process through which we build the world in our head. For example we cannot explain *why*, given similar conditions such as the same family and driven by the same general needs, we reorganize so differently that even in identical twins, reared together, one can be homosexual and the other heterosexual.

Most human problems stem from our inability to get along with each other. Because we find it so difficult to accept people with worlds different from ours, it seems to me that the next step in BCP should be to attempt to find out more about how our random reorganization system works. Maybe because it is random we can never do much more than postulate its existence, but it seems to me it is worth exploring. The mere fact that I have this relentless, random, creative system continually idling or churning inside fills me with wonder. Perhaps if we continue to probe for how it works it will reorganize and in some way reveal itself. If it does, it may also shed some light on the ancient philosophical question—which we have avoided in this book because so far it has no answer—who is it who builds my inner world?

INDEX

Index

Perry Hambright

WILLIAM GLASSER, M.D.

WILLIAM GLASSER, M.D., is an internationally known psychiatrist living in Los Angeles, originator with Dr. G. L. Harrington of Reality Therapy. Dr. Glasser's books include *Reality Therapy: A New Approach to Psychiatry, Positive Addiction, Schools Without Failure, The Identity Society,* and *Mental Health or Mental Illness?* Dr. Glasser is the founder of the Institute for Reality Therapy and has worked closely with the Educator Training Center.